*Also by the Authors*

JOYCE APPLEBY

Liberalism and Republicanism in the Historical Imagination
Capitalism and a New Social Order
Economic Thought and Ideology in Seventeenth-Century England

LYNN HUNT

The Invention of Pornography (editor)
The Family Romance of the French Revolution
The New Cultural History (editor)
Politics, Culture and Class in the French Revolution
Revolution and Urban Politics in Provincial France

MARGARET JACOB

The Politics of Western Science (editor)
Living the Enlightenment
The Cultural Meaning of the Scientific Revolution
The Radical Enlightenment
The Newtonians and the English Revolution

# Telling
# the Truth
## ABOUT
# HISTORY

Joyce Appleby

Lynn Hunt

Margaret Jacob

# Telling the Truth

## ABOUT

# HISTORY

W · W · NORTON & COMPANY

NEW YORK · LONDON

*The text of this book is composed in Galliard with the display type set in Garamond Oldstyle.
Composition and manufacturing by the Maple-Vail Book Manufacturing Group.
Book design by Marjorie J. Flock.*

First published as a Norton paperback 1995

Library of Congress Cataloging-in-Publication Data
Appleby, Joyce Oldham.
Telling the truth about history / Joyce Appleby, Lynn Hunt,
Margaret Jacob.
　　p.　cm.
Includes bibliographical references (p.) and index.
1. United States—Historiography. 2. History. I. Hunt, Lynn
Avery. II. Jacob, Margaret C., 1943–　III. Title.
E175.A67　1994
973´.072—dc20　　　　　　　　　　　　　　　　93-11536
ISBN 978-0-393-31286-7

W. W. Norton & Company, Inc.
500 Fifth Avenue, New York, N.Y. 10110
www.wwnorton.com

W. W. Norton & Company Ltd.
Castle House, 75/76 Wells Street, London W1T 3QT

*To our students and our teachers*

# Contents

# Contents

# Acknowledgments

THIS BOOK has been a real collaboration, and as a consequence all of the chapters express the views of all of the authors. Formal and informal conversations with colleagues and students have helped us to clarify our positions. None of them bears any responsibility for the positions we have taken—indeed, on occasion some have argued with us vigorously. We are especially grateful for detailed readings of an earlier version provided by Sheryl Kroen, Ruth Bloch, Drew Gilpin Faust, Phyllis Mack, Thomas Haskell, Frank Appleby, Martha Avery, Eric Hobsbawm, Donald Kalish, Joseph Rouse, Gabrielle Spiegel, Karen Orren, Bonnie Smith, Spencer Weart, James Miller, Virginia Yans, Carolyn Dewald, and Paula Scott.

# Telling
# the Truth
## ABOUT
# HISTORY

# *Introduction*

THIS BOOK confronts head-on the uncertainty about values and truth-seeking and addresses the controversies about objective knowledge, cultural diversity, and the political imperatives of a democratic education. It does so by focusing on the project of history, specifically by asking what people can know about the past that will help them elucidate the present. Our central argument is that skepticism and relativism about truth, not only in science but also in history and politics, have grown out of the insistent democratization of Western society. The opening of higher education to nearly all who seek it, the rewriting of American history from a variety of cultural perspectives, and the dethroning of science as the source and model for what may be deemed true, all are interrelated phenomena. It is no accident that they occurred almost simultaneously.

More people have now been to college or university than was the case at any time in the past. We should, and indeed do, know many things. Yet confidence in the value and truth of knowledge eludes just about everyone. This is especially true of historical knowledge. For example, once there was a single narrative of national history that most Americans accepted as part of their heritage. Now there is an increasing emphasis on the diversity of ethnic, racial, and gender experience and a deep skepticism about whether the narrative of America's achievements comprises anything more than a self-congratulatory story masking the power of elites. History has been shaken right down to its scientific and cultural foundations at the very time that those foundations themselves are being contested.

In the decades since World War II the old intellectual absolutisms have been dethroned: science, scientific history, and history in the service of nationalism. In their place—almost as an interim report—the postwar generation has constructed sociologies of knowledge, records of diverse peoples, and histories based upon group or gender identities. Women, minorities, and workers populate American and Western histories where formerly heroes, geniuses, statesmen—icons of order and the status quo—reigned unchallenged. The postwar generation has questioned fixed categories previously endorsed as rational by all thoughtful men, and has denaturalized social behavior once presumed to be encoded in the very structure of humanness. As members of that generation, we routinely, even angrily, ask: Whose history? Whose science? Whose interests are served by those ideas and those stories? The challenge is out to all claims to universality expressed in such phrases as "Men are . . . ," "Naturally science says . . . ;" and "As we all know . . ."

In contrast to the critics who have decried the impending death of Western civilization under the impact of the democratization of education, we endorse the insights and revisions made possible by that democratization. This book embraces a healthy skepticism, but it rejects the cynicism and nihilism that has accompanied contemporary relativism. It lays out a vision of the past and takes an intellectual stance for the present that seeks to promote an ever more democratic society. To achieve this aim, it is essential to confront the perennial controversies over national history, scientific integrity, and the possibility of truth and objectivity.

A host of questions present themselves. Do people need history, and if so, whose history and for what purposes? Is history a science or an art? Is history always in some sense propaganda? The answers to these questions might once have been obvious to educated people, but they are obvious no longer. At least one thing seems clear, however: rarely has history been such a subject of controversy. In the former communist world, aroused citizens toppled statues of Lenin and other discredited national heroes and threw out history professors and textbooks as hopelessly contaminated by Marxist ideology. When repressive governments fall from power, whether on the left or on the right, the citizens rush to find historical evidence of the government's previous misdeeds in order to fortify the will to reconstitute their nation. Because history and historical evidence are so crucial to a people's sense of identity, the evidence itself often becomes the focus of struggle. This is clear in the disturbing efforts of some groups to deny the reality of Hitler's final solution. Even in countries such as Japan where the state reserves the right to publish school textbooks, historians have fought in the courts for the ruling that the books must strive for truth and not for what will make people feel good about themselves.

In the United States, the effort to establish history standards for elementary, middle, and high schools set off a controversy that some interpreted as another round in the cultural wars begun in the 1960s. Critics of the older textbooks found them Eurocentric, racist, sexist, and homophobic, reinforcing the worst racial and sexual stereotypes rather than helping children and young people go beyond them. They celebrated the achievements, it was said, of dead white European males rather than showing the contributions of women, minorities, and the oppression of gays and other excluded groups. Whole new teams of writers have been hired to produce histories with perspectives thought to be more in tune with the values of a socially diverse society.

When new history standards were published in world and American history that sought to incorporate recent scholarship on women, African Americans, immigrants, and workers into the old story of male accomplishments, a new host of critics emerged to castigate the textbook reformers for negativity

toward Western accomplishments, casting them as bully propagandizers who valued politically motivated interpretations
more than the truth. They have been accused of deliberately
exaggerating the contributions of minority groups in order to
make those minorities feel good about themselves at the
expense of impartiality and a common sense of national identity. State commissions, professional conferences, and government officials have issued reports, with the result that the
public is alternately confused, irritated, and intrigued. Is history supposed to create ethnic pride and self-confidence? Or
should history convey some kind of objective truth about the
past? Must history be continually rewritten to undo the per-
petuation of racial and sexual stereotypes? Or should it stand
above the tumult of present-day political and social concerns?
Is the teaching of a coherent national history essential to
democracy?

The controversies could surprise many adults who remember their history courses, if they remember them at all, as drea-
ry catalogs of names, dates, and events rather than as
hothouses of debate about ethnic and national identity. The
great contemporary dilemma of relativism has drawn history
into the fray. Does every group or nation have its own version
of the truth? Is one history as good as another? What is the
role of the historian if truth is relative to the position of the
author? Because contesting visions of the past have failed to
create a comfortable consensus, and because change is the
essence of historical experience, some critics have argued there
can be no stable, knowable past. They have failed to understand that just because our definitions or descriptions change,
does not mean that the phenomenon being described does not
exist or cannot ultimately be known with some certainty. The
relativist argument about history is analogous to the claim that
because definitions of child abuse or schizophrenia have
altered over time, in that sense having been socially constructed, then neither can be said to exist in any meaningful way.

Let us be clear about what we, the authors, believe. We

view skepticism as an approach to learning as well as a philosophical stance. Since the Greeks, a certain amount of skepticism about truth claims has been essential to the search for truth; skepticism can encourage people to learn more and remain open to the possibility of their own errors. Complete skepticism, on the other hand, is debilitating because it casts doubt on the ability to make judgments or draw conclusions. It has only paradoxes to offer.

Yet skepticism is built into the very marrow of the West's cultural bones. By the time of the Enlightenment in the eighteenth century, some degree of skepticism had come to seem necessary for any true intellectual. Denis Diderot, one of the leaders of the Enlightenment, insisted, "All things must be examined, all must be winnowed and sifted without exception and without sparing anyone's sensibilities." In the new age announced by Diderot, thinkers would have to "trample mercilessly" upon all the old traditions and question every barrier to thought.[1] Nothing since that time has been taken as given or beyond questioning, not the classics, not the Bible, not the teachings of church or state.

Relativism, a modern corollary to skepticism, is the belief that truth is relative to the position of the person making a statement. It has generated a pervasive lack of confidence in the ability to find the truth or even to establish that there is such a thing as the truth. Relativism leads directly to a questioning of the ideal of objectivity, because it undermines the belief that people can get outside of themselves in order to get at the truth. If truth depends on the observer's standpoint, how can there be any transcendent, universal, or absolute truth, or at least truths that hold for all groups for many generations? We are arguing here that truths about the past are possible, even if they are not absolute, and hence are worth struggling for.

Reaction to the experience of World War II with its hor-

---

1. In his article "Encyclopedia," in the *Encyclopédie*, as translated in Keith Michael Baker, ed., *The Old Regime and the French Revolution* (Chicago, 1987),p. 84.

rendous new weaponry and the genocidal policies of the Nazi regime temporarily forestalled the progress of skepticism and relativism. The killing of Jews seemed to show that absolute moral standards were necessary, that cultural relativism had reached its limits in the death camps. But the lull was only temporary. Doubts spilled over the restraints of conscience and pressed against the maxims of Western philosophy. The inauguration of the atomic age in 1945 and the increasing interconnection between big science and big government impugned the disinterestedness of science itself. America's civil rights movement and the protests against the Vietnam War called into question the ability of scientists, policy makers, and professors to escape their own political prejudices. Ecologists complained that modern science in the name of progress had invented the engines of mass destruction and that industry was polluting the environment. In the twentieth century, Western civilization produced the most technologically sophisticated genocide ever seen in history. Progress, democracy, objective knowledge, and modernity itself no longer seemed to march in step towards the enrichment of humankind.

Skepticism and relativism are two-edged swords. They can be wielded to question the powers that be to promote a greater inclusiveness, but they can also be employed to question any kind of knowledge whatsoever. They can be used to say that knowledge about the past is simply an ideological construction intended to serve particular interests, making history a series of myths establishing or reinforcing group identities. Skeptics and relativists—sometimes known as postmodernists—often talk about the social construction of scientific knowledge, leaving the impression that the linguistic conventions of science have less to do with nature and more to do with the sociology of the scientists. The conclusion seems inevitable: because science is an elaborate power game coded mathematically, it ensures the dominance of those who possess it. In this way they have confused the social nature of all knowledge construction with the self-interest of the constructors, forgetting that all social beings participate in the search for knowledge and sometimes do so successfully. Success comes when the found knowledge can be understood, verified, or appreciated by people who in no sense share the same self-interest.

We believe that these difficult questions can be understood by anyone willing to read a book about them. If the public is perplexed about the meaning of history and how it is interpreted, then historians are at least partly to blame. It is time historians took responsibility for explaining what we do, how we do it, and why it is worth doing. Most people have little sense of the historian's vocation or how history teachers learned what they write and lecture about. History courses, at all levels, convey a specific subject matter—the American Revolution, late imperial China, Russia under the czars—but they too rarely foster an understanding of what historians do when they research and write history.

This book tackles in a general way the underpinnings of our history writing, the assumptions and values that lead to the search for historical truth. It examines critically the relevance of scientific models to the craft of history. It confronts the role that history plays in shaping national and group identity, and it offers some theories of our own about how objectivity may be possible and what sorts of political circumstances foster critical inquiry. Thus it takes up questions about relativism, truth, and objectivity that have in the past been left to philosophers. The aims of this book are simple and straightforward but also ambitious: to provide readers with some sense of history's relationship to scientific truth, objectivity, postmodernism, and the politics of identity within a democratic framework. Despite these ambitions, the book nevertheless argues that what historians do best is to make connections with the past in order to illuminate the problems of the present and the potential of the future.

In the pages that follow we show how historians have conceptualized their task in the past, particularly how history has gone from telling a simple story to answering a complex array of questions about the human experience. The ambitions of history have changed over time, expanding to include general questions of historical development—itself a new idea in the eighteenth and nineteenth centuries. Yet even as the ambitions of history have grown, so too have questions about history's ability to tell a story with any certainty.

A democratic practice of history encourages skepticism about dominant views. At the same time, belief in the reality of the past and its knowability is essential to a practice of history. To collapse this tension in favor of one side or the other is to give up the struggle for enlightenment. An openness to the interplay between certainty and doubt keeps faith with the expansive quality of democracy. This openness depends in turn on a version of the scientific model of knowledge, based on a belief in the reality of the past and the human ability to make contact with it. Such faith helps discipline the understanding by requiring constant reference to something outside of the human mind. In a democracy, history thrives on a passion for knowing the truth.

Even in a democracy, history involves power and exclusion, for any history is always someone's history, told by that someone from their partial point of view. Yet external reality also has the power to impose itself on the mind; past realities remain in records that historians are trained to interpret. The effort to establish historical truths itself fosters civility. Since no one can be certain that his or her explanations are definitively right, everyone must listen to others. All human histories are provisional; none will have the last word.

Such a democratic practice of history—one in which an ever-growing chorus of voices is heard—will depend upon objectivity, defined anew as a commitment to honest investigation, open processes of research, and engaged public discussions of the meaning of historical facts. These offer the best chance of making sense of the world. There is every reason for democratic citizens to expand their commitment to pluralistic education and continue their appraisal of the accounts that define them as a nation. National histories will still be necessary; so too will be faith in the ultimate goal of an education: the rigorous search for truth usable by all peoples.

# PART ONE

---◇---

# Intellectual
# Absolutisms

# ◇ 1 ◇

# *The Heroic Model of Science*

I N THE EIGHTEENTH CENTURY a small group of determined
reformers established science as the new foundation for
truth, a granite-like platform upon which all knowledge
could rest. The absolute character of their truth mimicked
the older Christian truth upon which Westerners since late
Roman times had come to rely. They transferred a habit of
mind associated with religiosity—the conviction that transcendent and absolute truth could be known—to the new mechanical understanding of the natural world. Eventually they grafted
this conviction onto all other inquiries. The study of history
became the search for the laws of human development. Understanding the challenge to truth in an age in full revolt against
inherited certainties means going back in time to discover how
and when science became an absolute model for all knowledge
in the West.

Pure, elegant, simple, and clear when summarized by its
laws, natural science with its experimental method came in the
eighteenth century to be seen as the measure of all human truth.
Imitate mechanical science, follow its methods, seek laws for
everything from human biology to the art of governing—that
was the advice bequeathed to the Western world by the Enlightenment. We call this model of science heroic, because it
made scientific geniuses into cultural heroes. Until quite recently, heroic science reigned supreme. The heroic model equated
science with reason: disinterested, impartial, and, if followed
closely, a guarantee of progress in this world. Science took its

character from nature itself, which was presumed to be composed solely of matter in motion and hence to be "neutral." In the words of a true believer, a sociologist of the 1940s, "The stars have no sentiments, the atoms no anxieties which have to be taken into account. Observation is objective with little effort on the part of the scientist to make it so."[1] Now it is possible to put heroic science in a historical context and assess the way it has molded Western thinking. Its hubris, its accomplishments, its absolutist claims are all part of our story.

The neutral, value-free, objective image of science inherited from the Enlightenment had wide influence in every discipline until well into the postwar era. Right up until then, the rationality presumed to be the sole force at work within science acted as the magnetic needle guiding other forms of modern knowledge, including historical knowledge. It also anchored the truth ascribed to Western political and economic systems. As one recent believer in the model puts it, "At the heart of modernity is the trust or faith in scientific reason, understood as the source not only of vast powers but of authoritative guidance as to how to use those powers."[2] Faith in the guidance as well as the power provided by heroic science consoles traditionalist critics who dogmatically assert not only the truth but also the superiority of Western values.

Contemporary disillusionment frames our examination of heroic science. Compromised by two world wars and a long Cold War in which science and technology played critically important roles, the heroic model of science looks deeply flawed today, no longer workable as the foundation of all truth-seeking in this or any other culture. Science has lost its innocence. Rather than being perceived as value-free, it is seen as encoded with values, a transmitter of culture as well as physical laws.

1. From *Bulletin of the American Association of University Professors* (1948), quoted in Robert N. Proctor, *Value-Free Science? Purity and Power in Modern Knowledge* (Cambridge, Mass., 1991), p. 176.

2. Thomas L. Pangle, *The Ennobling of Democracy: The Challenge of the Postmodern Age* (Baltimore, 1992), p. 3.

Even the truth still found in science seems different in character—more provisional, less absolute—than it did to the enlightened eighteenth-century forebears who first gloried in it. True to their age, late-twentieth-century historians of Western science have become skeptical in ways that the true believers of the eighteenth-century Enlightenment and beyond would have found unimaginable, as well as irreverent. In this skeptical and iconoclastic vein, they examine the history of Western science in order to discover how Western culture acquired its distinctively absolutist image of science.

The philosophes of the eighteenth century, aided by political reformers and industrialists, invented the heroic model of science. They led an international movement for reform described as enlightened, and science functioned as the most powerful weapon in their arsenal against traditional institutions of church and state. With a bias against religious authority, the philosophes looked back at the discoveries of the previous hundred years and marveled at the trials through which science had been forced to pass. As they angrily surveyed the constraints set by the religious and political authorities, they concluded that only genius, uninhibited by superstition and prejudice, could account for the wondrous discoveries that began with Copernicus and ended with Newton. The laws of science seemed so absolutely true and so different from the medieval view of nature that only the godlike rationality of the seventeenth-century architects of the new heliocentric and mechanical science could explain the West's liberation from ignorance. As eighteenth-century polemicists triumphed in the cultural war against the clergy and churches, their secular vision amplified the heroic stature awarded to the great scientists. Ideas of progress and methods of reasoning became viable alternatives to the older intellectual absolutisms inherited from the Christianization of the West.

Newton's *Principia* consolidated and made accessible the new scientific understanding of nature as mathematical and mechanical. As a separate, autonomous, and supposedly value-free realm of knowledge, Newton's science, the philosophes claimed, could be attributed solely to the progressive insights of earlier geniuses: Copernicus, Kepler, Galileo, Descartes, and Boyle. To borrow a phrase made famous by Isaac Newton, each scientist in his turn saw further because he was standing on the shoulders of giants. Even so, the creation and survival of the new mechanical science had seemed a difficult and precarious process. According to the enlightened commentators, the seventeenth-century giants of science, on whose shoulders the philosophes themselves stood, penetrated a fog spread by centuries of ignorance. They battled with clergy and churches and at moments risked martyrdom. From the accounts of censorship and arrests in the lives of scientists, it seemed clear that the new natural knowledge fought its way through a battlefield strewn with the corpses of theologians, philosophers, censors, and metaphysicians, not to mention magicians, astrologers, and alchemists.

One of the earliest histories of science survives from the 1750s in a set of scientific lectures given to aristocratic gentlemen and ladies in The Hague. It told the story of science from Copernicus onward, as one of genius following upon genius, and the tale unwound while the lecturer taught the fundamentals of the new science: heliocentricity, Boyle's law of gases, Newton's law of universal gravitation.[3] The truth of the laws only seemed to confirm the truth of the history. The lecturer also explained how the universe was an ordered and harmonious place to be mastered by science, to be improved by simple machines and mathematical rigor applied to earthly as well as celestial phenomena. This eighteenth-century history of science did not differ substantially from what was taught right up to the 1950s.

For the philosophes of the Enlightenment the victory of science had been revolutionary. It meant the victory of reason

3. The history was woven into the physics lectures of Prof. S. Koenig, given in The Hague, 1751–52 (University Library, Amsterdam, MS X.B.1).

over superstition, or as they put it, of light a
of darkness. "Let Newton be and all was ligh
Pope. Predictably, given the force of Christ
West, science also had its prophets, saints
preached not dogma for new heavens but the men...
venting a new earth.

## The Origins of Scientific Neutrality

Coming out of the Scientific Revolution, the heroic model
of science solidified in the early eighteenth century under the
impact of Newton's *Principia*. Using geometrical demonstrations, Newton established that the laws of motion and inertia
which work on bodies here in this world also apply to the
heavens. With a simple mathematical equation, it became possible to predict the rotation of the planets at any given moment.
Postulating universal gravitation as a force acting at a distance
and using crude but serviceable measurements of the earth's
diameter, Newton was able to offer a single, elegant explanation for the positioning of the planets, the sun, and the earth.
Building upon the mechanical laws of local motion bequeathed
by Galileo and using a method of analysis and synthesis that
proceeded from experiment and mathematical demonstration
to generalization and then back again to systematic investigation, Newton moved from the laws of local motion illustrated
experimentally to celestial phenomena explicated mathematically. He offered in one book more replicable laws about physical nature than had ever been assembled in any work in the
history of human thought. Contemporaries and subsequent
generations saw the publication of the *Principia* in 1687 as the
single most important event in the early modern history of
printing.

Earlier seventeenth-century scientists and philosophers had
laid the groundwork for the *Principia*. Scientists such as Galileo,
who had approached nature as a mechanism, as bodies moved
only because impelled or repelled by other bodies, prefigured

ewton's ideas. Galileo and his contemporaries experimented with everything from wooden balls to the movement of water in relation to its weight, and they discovered, for example, that a body in free fall accelerates in such a way that the distance it travels is proportional to the square of the time taken to travel. Imagine a vacuum, Galileo said, drop within it bodies of various weights, and all of them would increase by the same speed and left to their own, meeting no resistance, would fall unimpeded forever. Rather than imagining a universe at rest unless put in motion by the Prime Mover, the God of scholastic theologians, Galileo's experiments permitted those who could follow his logic to imagine nature as a self-regulating mechanism.

The most farsighted of the men who came to be seen as giants with broad shoulders were the seventeenth-century prophets of science who provided a vision of what science could mean both for habits of thought and for the material order. A full century and a half before the Industrial Revolution, Galileo's contemporaries and admirers, Francis Bacon and René Descartes, appealed for practical, ordinary men to take up the new science. Bacon and Descartes fashioned new values for an age they could only dimly imagine. They exhorted their contemporaries to leave theology to the clergy and war-making to the aristocracy and embrace a new form of disciplined learning. Bacon urged thoughtful men to go out into nature not to hunt but to observe. Baconian empiricism tied the experience of nature to the search for applications, and in its emphasis on utility, Baconianism was farsightedly industrial. Bacon even invented a utopian kingdom of science, the lost island of Atlantis, where science would solve all the problems of everyday life: disease would be conquered, food plentiful, and lives unimaginably long.

Unlike Bacon, the French philosopher Descartes allowed himself few explicitly utopian moments. While as a good English Protestant Bacon could live his life at home, in the 1630s Descartes stayed out of France and found freedom abroad. In the safe haven of the Dutch city Leiden, he published his *Discourse on Method* as an alternative to the medieval philosophies taught by the clergy who controlled the French universities. Illustrated on its title page by a peasant digging his field, it insisted in clear and simple language that every movement or change in nature had to be explained mechanically, that is, by the pulling and pushing of bodies against one another. No spirits or magical agents, no inherent tendencies, belonged in a philosophy of nature that encompassed everything from the movement of the planets to the action of the nerve endings in the human hand. In the Cartesian universe, pain results not from an affliction of the soul, but from impulses traveling to the brain. In the place of speculations by medieval philosophers and theologians, Descartes proclaimed that "a practical philosophy can be found by which . . . we thereby make ourselves, as it were, masters and possessors of nature."[4]

Safe from the Inquisition that in 1633 had condemned Galileo, Descartes lived and wrote in the Dutch and largely Protestant cities because, as he explained, in them men got on with their business and left others to their speculations. He even thought that the old medieval cities of France were ugly and he adored the geometrical neatness he found in the Dutch commercial towns. He preferred cities built by a single architect, as he put it. Without fully realizing the implications of their message about individualism, commerce, and applied science, both Bacon and Descartes helped tie the success of science to a commercial and eventually industrial capitalist order. The linkage was reinforced throughout the economically expansive eighteenth century when new manufacturing technologies seemed only to confirm the wisdom of seeing the universe as an interlocking series of pushing and pulling mechanisms.

From the time of Descartes onward, the practice of the new

4. René Descartes, *Discourse on Method* [1637] (London, 1968), p. 78. For the title page of the original French edition we have used the copy in the Van Pelt Library, University of Pennsylvania. The engraving with its radiating sun also suggests divine illumination.

science was remote from the luxurious life at the courts of Europe, as well as unrelated to the religious practices of the Christian churches. Science pointed away from the medieval, away from rote learning controlled by clerical schoolmen in the service of bishops and nobles, and away from a leisured culture devoted more to the hunt than to the collection of natural artifacts. Not surprisingly, science fared better in Protestant and northern countries than in Catholic and southern Europe. Despite their differences, scientists and Protestants shared a common Roman enemy. Descartes's life illustrates that it helped to have Protestant censors who were less efficient and internationally organized than those employed by the Inquisition. Descartes got into bitter quarrels with Calvinist clergy in the Dutch Republic, but unlike Galileo, he was not threatened with arrest.

When the *Principia* first appeared, it seems that only about a dozen Europeans could get through the mathematical language in that dense Latin tome. Even the political philosopher John Locke, Newton's contemporary and a trained physician, could not master the proofs without assistance. But when the first twelve or so mathematically gifted readers picked up Newton's *Principia* and struggled to its final chapter, the Baconian vision had prepared them for what they found there. These early Newtonians quickly took their discoveries to a wider audience. With the assistance of journals, handbooks, demonstration lectures, and even sermons, the Newtonian message spread throughout literate Europe and the American colonies. A generation later, its contents had been opened up to anyone who could afford to attend a scientific lecture. Quite ordinary men, and even an aristocratic woman, Madame du Châtelet, became teachers of mechanics.

As proclaimed by Bacon and Descartes, and later fulfilled by Newton's laws, science seemed to be not only neutral and universal, but also solely the work of genius. This focus meant, however, that other key elements in the origins of modern science were obliterated. In fact, science depended upon the relatively open communication of ideas and countless experimental demonstrations done before select members of the new scientific societies. The institutionalization of science through learned societies and pulpit oratory created an essential context for its survival. Even Newton relied upon a network of communication that crisscrossed London, Oxford, and his own university at Cambridge. Some of his earliest followers were English clergymen who from their pulpits used the new science to support order and stability in church and state.

Through all of these efforts, Newtonian science became a key element in both the Enlightenment and the Industrial Revolution. By the late eighteenth century, both transformed the mental and more slowly the material universe of western Europe, which in turn made the progressive, heroic model of science seem infallible to successive generations. Through science, educated elites acquired a skeptical stance toward theology and revealed religion, which in turn easily encouraged hostility toward entrenched, unresponsive institutions in both church and state. As we will argue, the new, reforming mentality inspired a cultural war with orthodox Christianity that began in Western Europe and continued right up to the French Revolution.

The importance of science in Western modernity can be traced to far more than the anticlerical polemics of Voltaire and his friends. Newtonian science, as embodied in applied mechanics, became the essential intellectual ingredient, the mental capital, of the Industrial Revolution. By the last quarter of the eighteenth century in Britain the same people who thought of themselves as enlightened, as teachers and appliers of Newtonian mechanics, were often the profit-seeking promoters of steam engines, canal companies, or factory-style manufacturing. In the pursuit of their interests they had spread the message of applied science more deeply and widely in Britain than in any other Western country.

The reputation of science was vastly enhanced when it was credited with the most fundamental social transformation ever wrought in human history: the mechanization of human labor through the application of power technology to manufacturing and transportation. The first industrial entrepreneurs believed that if properly applied, science would enhance material wealth, and for them science generally meant applied mechanics. When they installed a steam engine, or devised a machine for spinning cotton, or brought in an engineer to improve the available supply of water power, they acted as true Baconians using the sophisticated mechanical knowledge available to their age to produce unprecedented progress. The veneer of science overlay the ruthless pursuit of advantage.

Once it was rendered simpler and its laws were memorized, the *Principia* made the universe accessible and its interrelated principles of weight and motion became applicable to the movement of everyday heavy objects. When new levers and pulleys lifted, or steam engines pumped, or canal waters were raised to greater heights, the same principles operated because Newtonianism explicated simple mechanical operations while relating them to the movements of the planets. The new science from Copernicus through to Galileo and Boyle had been tied into a package of mechanical laws, which could be grasped as the science of mechanics by engineers, merchants, entrepreneurs, and country gentry. For those who possessed them, science and education became the twin engines of progress. Late in the century Thomas Jefferson expressed his faith in the link between science and progress by ordering a composite portrait of the life-sized busts of Bacon, Locke, and Newton.[5] Miniature planetary systems with movable globes circling the sun in elliptical orbits, made by skilled workers in copper and wood, adorned the elegant homes of entrepreneurs and merchants as well as aristocrats.

In England by the middle of the eighteenth century the civil engineer emerged as the harbinger of innovation, the slayer of

5. Noted in Joyce Appleby, *Liberalism and Republicanism in the Historical Imagination* (Cambridge, Mass., 1992), p. 300, citing *Papers of Thomas Jefferson*, ed. Boyd et al., vol. 15, pp. 384–98; vol. 14, p. 561.

tradition and the status quo. Late in the century a traveler to the coal-rich hills of Derbyshire or to the workshops of Birmingham could marvel at the enclaves of mechanization, at the longer canals, deeper mines, and stronger engines made possible by applied mechanics. Few wrote at length about the consequences for the laboring classes. The eighteenth-century British civil engineers became the new priests, and the salvation they offered was dramatically visible. When James Watt perfected the steam engine, he could congratulate himself as an experimenter and a theorist,[6] fulfilling the promise made by Bacon and Descartes.

Like Josiah Wedgwood (of porcelain fame), Watt and his Birmingham entrepreneurial friends believed in the power of machines the way pilgrims had once believed in relics. They found it hard to believe that anyone would resist their progress. British engineers spread the new techniques from Bohemia to western Pennsylvania. When French spies came to investigate English workshops they marveled at the machinery, but also at the division of labor imposed among workers that left only the mechanizer and industrialist with full knowledge of the entire manufacturing process. The rationalizing encouraged by science brought many new forms of power. In the course of the eighteenth century, science made its way from the giants to the capitalists and the appliers; its universality was further guaranteed by its accessibility to lesser, if diligent, mortals. Heroic science fostered the age of machines.

From the eighteenth century onward, Westerners would also judge other cultures by their science and technology. By the 1740s, European travelers concluded that the absence of Western techniques and mechanical thinking signaled cultural inferiority.[7] The belief in science's ability to dominate and sub-

6. Birmingham Reference Library, Birmingham, U.K., M. Boulton to J. Smeaton, 14 March 1778, on their "experiments" and "theories." Supplied through the kindness of Eric Robinson. Cf. A. E. Musson and Eric Robinson, *Science and Technology in the Industrial Revolution* (1969; reprint New York, 1989).

7. Michael Adas, *Machines as the Measure of Men: Science, Technology, and Ideologies of Western Dominance* (Ithaca, N.Y., 1989), ch. 2.

jugate nature was also invariably expressed in gendered language. Science became a truly masculine activity; nature (although not the atoms that composed it) was described by feminine metaphors, and she could be tamed and dominated. Excluded from scientific societies, their needs ignored in the agendas of mainstream scientific research, Western women like the laboring classes in general joined much of the rest of the world on the periphery of modern science.[8] Yet as Westerners women and workers eventually shared in the actual economic improvement as well as the intellectual transformation derived from science and technology.

The power attributed to Newtonian mechanics is not a gloss that subsequent generations put on the Industrial Revolution. The link between science and industry had been made by contemporaries. At the moment when all the elites of Europe looked with wonder at British manufacturing, a French minister in charge of trying to catch up put the challenge succinctly: British power lies in "mechanics. In that secret resides its industrial power." In a confidential report, Napoleon's envious and worried minister said that the absolute necessity to transform and mechanize industry had already been resolved by England in a most decisive manner. The lever of its industry lay in applied mechanics, and "the overwhelming gravitation of the mass [of England's production] makes everything conform to its orbit."[9] The Newtonian metaphor could not have been more appropriate. Back in the 1620s and 1630s, Bacon and Descartes promised the wonders of science applied; British engineers and mechanists of the eighteenth century made good on the promise, at least for themselves.

From this distance the progress of science and technology after the death of Isaac Newton in 1727 seems neither accidental nor the work of a few great minds working in isolation from

8. This research on the gendering of science and its implications is examined in Sandra Harding, *Whose Science? Whose Knowledge?* (Ithaca, N.Y., 1991), ch. 1 and 2.

9. Archives nationales, Paris, F12 502.

their environment. Even giants, never mind their imitators, have a social context. The greater freedom of printing and the relative absence of clerical authority in northern and Protestant Europe meant that by the middle of the eighteenth century, southern Europe fell comparatively into scientific and technological stagnation. The French schools and colleges, especially the ones controlled by the Jesuits, resisted teaching Newtonian science until the 1750s. As one historian has put it, "If Newton finally triumphed in France it was probably over the corpse of the Jesuit order."[10] Given the repressive circumstances found throughout much of eighteenth-century Europe, it is easy to understand why science gradually became a symbol of unfettered truth. During and after the democratic revolutions in Western Europe, their initiators and supporters would cite the progress of British industry and the backwardness of Catholic and southern Europe to argue for the freedom of market and press and for educational reform that included the teaching of science at every level.

The new science with its experimental method depended upon open inquiry among communities of scientists free from clerical control and tied into international networks of communication. In the West, science became one of the major beneficiaries of what contemporaries described as the new Republic of Letters. Republics in the Western imagination stood for freedom and citizen participation, harking back to the glory of Rome before its imperial decadence. To summon the idealism associated with freedom and independence, the enlightened opponents of censors invented a literary republic of the mind, a semi-clandestine international zone of universally accessible intellectual neutrality. In this imaginary public sphere of the literate, science would reside, regardless of how much the censors wanted to control it. The invisible republic worked, and Western science flourished in the nascent civil society of the

10. L.W.B. Brockliss, *French Higher Education in the Seventeenth and Eighteenth Centuries: A Cultural History* (Oxford, England, 1987), p. 366; also p. 455.

voluntary societies, academies, reading clubs, and coffee houses that emerged in the European and colonial cities of the eighteenth century. You could find out more about Newtonian science in a London coffee house that sponsored weekly demonstrations and lectures than you could in most French colleges before 1750.

In the experimental method of the new science developed during the Scientific Revolution—and in its fundamentals practiced to this day—true knowledge about nature occurs only after careful and replicable investigations performed by a distinctive method of experimentation that requires both evidence and theories that seek to find patterns, or what are called laws, at work in nature. Most important, the method must proceed and be recorded in such a way that any experimenter can repeat the procedure and in the process validate or refute its findings. But in the original, heroic version of why science works, the method also gave a new and distinctive identity to the researcher. He must become like Newton was imagined to have been: a giant of reason who peers at nature with eyes that are value-free, neutral, and objective. Newton's famous dictum that he did not "feign" hypotheses came in the course of the eighteenth century to symbolize the belief that science had carved out a space within the human mind where an unprecedented neutrality reigned unchallenged.

In consequence of the heroic understanding of scientific method, the study of nature should be, as it was believed to be with Newton, motivated and guided solely by the search for truth, which, as it turned out, came to consist only in what could be proclaimed as general laws, universally applicable. Once embracing this posture, the researcher sought above all to be objective, and in this model objectivity was equated with neutrality. The value-free knowledge that he discovered (from the seventeenth century until quite recently, the literature of science generally assumed that its doers and readers would be men), if verified repeatedly by other experimenters, would correspond to what is really in nature.

The heroic model of science presumed a tight, and relatively uncomplicated, fit between nature and human knowledge of it. After all, the law of universal gravitation works in every language and every cultural setting. Bodies in free fall accelerate in measurable units proportional to the time they have traveled. The logic of heroic science anchored itself on Newton's achievement and capitalized upon its truth. Absolute truth all of the time rather than lesser falsity, or provisional truths, became the nature of science. Realism, the belief that things can be known in ways that correspond with their actual objective existence, acquired an extraordinarily bold justification. Scientific knowledge got credited with a degree of verisimilitude only possible if mirrors resided within the heads of the scientists. The mind was imagined to be a blank slate upon which sense impressions wove their messages. The clear scientific eye became transparent as it faced nature, made so by the method and rigor only experiment and mathematics could impart to its gaze. As the mirror image of nature—itself now rendered into value-free matter possessing only weight and measure—heroic science was eternally true. Not just true in certain controlled circumstances, nor true enough for the time being, but true always and absolutely.

Properly and openly pursued, heroic science offered transcendence, the reward given to those especially smart people whose rationality rendered them transparent toward nature. The laws of science enabled rational human beings to escape time and hence history, or even to imagine that they could end history, by mirroring nature in their minds and finding a body of knowledge that survived from epoch to epoch and remained true despite repression, censorship, brutality, war, plague, and famine. In this account the intellectual self-confidence of the scientist was matched only by his heroism, a selfless courage to stand up against censors and ideologues. The rationality of science derived from the disinterested posture of its practitioners, their openness to all criticism (if based upon experimentation), and from their refusal to countenance belief, opinion, self-interest, or passion in the search for truth about nature. Eventually the rhetoric of heroic science made science so collective an enterprise, so much the result of selfless international discussion, that the person of the scientist, his allegiances, prejudices, and interests, bore no relation to what could be attributed solely to abstract science.

Sometime in the late 1940s after the Manhattan Project, haunted by the fear of nuclear power, Westerners in large numbers began to see the need to understand the values and motives of the scientists who ushered in the nuclear age. In effect they rediscovered the scientist as an agent, rather than simply a servant, of historical change. Those who now held such power had to be probed, their backgrounds and values questioned. For the first time it became necessary to get away from the eighteenth-century portrait of the scientist as a selfless participant in the new Republic of Letters. Ironically, the heroic image of science had obliterated the human agency at work in any scientific enterprise.[11] It came as something of a shock to discover the scientist as partisan and policymaker, caught between the ideals of scientific openness and progress and the military necessity of mass destruction. Nothing in the previous history of science, as it had been told from the Enlightenment onward, had prepared Westerners for science in the context of nuclear power and the Cold War.

### Science Becomes the Guarantor of Progress and Power

During the Enlightenment, elite Westerners constructed first an image of nature, then an industrial reality, directly expressive of the power of Western science. Like early industrialization, the scientific image of nature emerged first in Britain; eventually it would become distinctively Western. So impressive was Newton's science that liberal clergymen in England

---

11. We have been helped in this discussion by Lorraine Daston, "The Ideal and Reality of the Republic of Letters in the Enlightenment," *Science in Context*, 4 (1991): 367–86.

actually used the Newtonian universe to illustrate the order and design imposed by the providential hand of the Deity, imitated by the institutions of church and state. Theirs was a new, cerebral religiosity they liked to call rational religion. It had very little in common with a miraculous version of Christianity, with relics or miracles, or with expectations of an imminent millennium. It replaced the fear and anxiety that nature once evoked with hope inspired by an ordered, harmonious, knowable world. The English garden of the period spoke volumes: gone were the clipped hedges and geometrical pathways imitative of Versailles. In their place came thickets, artificial lakes and streams amid carefully manicured forests. Now confident of nature tamed, the English gentry could invent the illusion of wildness. A similar religiosity permitted Thomas Jefferson to write his own version of the New Testament shorn of what he believed were its contradictions. So sure was he that he could distinguish the words of Jesus from Gospel chroniclers—"they stood out like diamonds in a dunghill"—that he took scissors to the sacred text.[12]

The new religiosity and sensibility that imagined nature as free and yet ordered had a political analogue in the eighteenth-century English and American systems of constitutional and parliamentary government. The Newtonian universe acted as an imaginary backdrop on which to project prescriptions for order, stability, harmony, and freedom. Running as it were on its own mathematically knowable forces, the universe of the *Principia* became a model for balanced governments and self-regulated economies, for elections, constitutions, and free markets. The imitation of these British and American forms in other parts of Western Europe after the French Revolution only further validated the cosmic imagery. The democratic revolutions late in the century enhanced the myth of heroic science.

The myth and the imagery of self-regulation did conform

12. For a copy of it, see Thomas Jefferson, *The Jefferson Bible: The Life and Morals of Jesus of Nazareth,* introduction by F. Forrester Church (Boston, 1989).

to a certain historical reality. Constitutional governments could be distinguished from political systems run by absolute monarchs and court-appointed bureaucrats who up to the spring of 1789 still walked the gardens at Versailles. Representative governments also nurtured very different forms of commercial life. Absolutist monarchs encouraged commerce and industry, but only by controlling them through licenses, privileges, and state-sponsored inventiveness and monopolies. By contrast, the steam engines of the British industrialists with their self-regulating condensers and feedback devices went hand in hand with the self-regulation of relatively free enterprise, assisted by wider though hardly universal access to elections, political parties, lobbying, and parliamentary committees. When in 1776 Adam Smith wrote about the invisible hand that guaranteed the stability of an apparently chaotic market, he could do so because he relied upon the hand of the Great Mathematician, the God of Newtonian science.

Smith's imagery was accompanied by a new reality. The Industrial Revolution—to this day the model of what science and technology can offer to agricultural societies seeking to escape poverty—occurred in part because more than any other place in Western Europe, eighteenth-century Britain witnessed the application of mechanical science to the manufacturing and transportation systems. In continental Europe that application was delayed and industrialization only accelerated after the French Revolution.

Throughout the West, constitutional, republican, and democratic forms of government proved to be more compatible with the needs and interests of industrialists. In every country where they achieved political power, they revised the curriculum of the schools and universities to reflect the importance of scientific education and to enshrine the heroic model of science. The Enlightenment and the Industrial Revolution paved the way for the importation of science and its methods into all the other branches of disciplined learning.

In the West the compelling progress attributed to science

and technology arose in tandem with a distinctive political culture now almost exclusively associated with representative government. It is not clear if the Industrial Revolution can be
imitated or reinvented in other essentially agricultural societies,
but it is clear that the penetration of scientific and technological
knowledge deep into society hastened industrialization. Historians can affirm that in the eighteenth century a new scientific
culture worked to greatest advantage in conjunction with representative and relatively free capitalist, as opposed to absolutist, systems of government. Because historically their success
was tied to intellectual freedom and representative institutions,
science and technological innovation belong on the side of the
long and continuing struggle for democracy. Western science's
originating moment coincided with, as well as it reinforced,
commercial expansion, enlightened reform, and revolution. In
gratitude for escaping medieval restraints—and forgetting or
ignoring the miseries caused by early industrialization—Westerners gave science an aura of absolute validity.

## The Cultural Wars of the Enlightenment

A century before the beginning of the Industrial Revolution, the opponents of absolutism had already seized upon science as a weapon in their arsenal. What better than to take up a
new body of knowledge that rested upon a new standard of
truth—human reason, experiment, observation, mathematics—and new forms of social communication—scientific societies, academies, public lectures and printed texts, freely
circulated. As a cultural war, the Enlightenment began in the
1690s. In the ensuing fray, critics attacked established churches,
religious dogmas, kings, even devils and witches, as either deluded or the upholders of backward-looking tyrannies, ignorance, prejudice, and superstition. John Toland's *Christianity
Not Mysterious* (1696) lashed out at Christian dogmas and mysteries as irrational. In the anonymous *Treatise on the Three Im-
postors* (1719), Jesus, Moses, and Mohammed were condemned

as the three, while Voltaire's famous *Candide* (1759), castigated slavery, most religions, and the pomposity of the aristocracy. In the last decade of the seventeenth century, ideas were put into print that were unimaginable twenty years earlier, but that, much to the horror of the clergy, became commonplace twenty years later. These ideas remain to this day feared and hated, and where tyrannical political power still exists, great harm can befall their believers. In late 1992 the Saudi Arabian government beheaded a twenty-three-year-old man because, it said, he had "insulted God, the holy Koran, and Muhammad the prophet."[13]

In Western Europe the decades prior to the 1690s were typically a time of bitter religious warfare and political upheaval. But in the final decade of the century, the established pattern of intolerance clashed with a new cultural force. Newly empowered English and exiled French Protestants pitted science and liberal political theory against the Catholic Church and divinely sanctioned monarchs. The exiled Huguenots were the highly motivated gadflies and propagandists for religious toleration, citizen participation, and government by contract rather than fiat. In 1685, Louis XIV had given them an ultimatum: convert or leave. He wanted one king and one faith. The French monarch's effort to eliminate the Protestant minority had been underway for some decades, but only in the 1680s did Louis and his ministers think they could achieve the final consolidation of the absolutist state. Go into the jail records still surviving in Paris and there listed below the name of the inmate read the crime against "king and faith": "Protestant."

A pure, Catholic state would more loyally obey the glorious Sun King—at least so went the theory behind absolutism. Louis XIV got his way against the French Protestants, but not without first creating within France and much of the rest of Western Europe a new dissident counterculture. Its strength derived, however, from events far outside the borders of France. In

---

13. Others have also been imprisoned there without trial for blasphemy. See *Human Rights Watch World Report 1993: Events of 1992* (New York, 1992). p. 336; also *Washington Post*, October 1, 1992, pp. A18–19.

England in 1688–89, Anglicans and other political dissenters from the effort to impose absolutism and Catholicism effected a successful coup d'état. They exiled King James II, brought in a new king and queen, and insisted on government by parliament, a bill of rights, and legal religious toleration for all Protestants. The Revolution of 1688–89—sometimes called "Glorious"—gave unprecedented constitutional life to parliamentary government in England and ushered in an era of legally protected freedom of the press and religious toleration. Suddenly the persecution across the Channel in France began to look like more than simply another example of state-enforced orthodoxy. Reformers opened a cultural war against absolutist monarchy and in favor of representative government, one that also ranged the secular against the religious, and religious toleration against what was labeled ignorance and prejudice.

By the 1690s in France, Protestants had been either rebaptized or locked up in the Bastille along with counterfeiters, thieves, and even alchemists. Among the exiled were many Protestant intellectuals who took their journalistic skills with them to England, to the American colonies, or to Protestant cities like Amsterdam or Geneva. With their pens they created an idealized portrait of English government. Into the same enlightened story they wrote a newly triumphant parliament, Newtonian science, a restrained but established Protestant church, and legal toleration for all Protestants. The chorus of protest against absolutism soon included new voices like the philosophe Voltaire, who claimed that England was superior because of the absence there of legally protected social estates in which rights were largely a matter of birth or royally granted privileges. Anglophilia became the trademark of the emergent Enlightenment, and the philosophe—ranging from Pierre Bayle through to Benjamin Franklin and Mary Wollstonecraft—became a new cultural type who could be a pundit, prophet, fighter against tyranny and oppression, original thinker, elegant writer, sometime pornographer, reader of science, host of salons, or occasional freemason.

Relying on their reading of Locke and Newton, French exiles and philosophes rushed into print with any idea that looked dangerous to entrenched or repressive authority. "There is a mighty light which spreads itself over the world, especially in those two free Nations of England and Holland. . . . it is impossible but Letters and knowledge must advance in greater proportion than ever."[14] So wrote an English republican of the early eighteenth century to his friends, a circle of French exiles living in the Dutch Republic. The metaphor of light would survive throughout the century because it conjured up religious toleration and relative intellectual freedom and progress.

The Enlightenment—the era when modernity begins—got its name, as Kant explained later in the eighteenth century, from the enterprise of spreading light into the dark corners of the human mind. From the 1690s onward, science led the way. The philosophes grabbed learning out of the hands of the clergy and argued that all knowledge, whether about morality, or politics, or history, could be scientific. The goal in every area of inquiry became the objective search for general principles; all knowledge could be systematized. Even the acts of reading and speaking, the interaction of the human mind with language, whether ancient and Biblical or modern and non-Western, could be understood scientifically. As a consequence, the philosophes began to search for the roots of all languages while also inventing the first encyclopedias. In other words, the philosophes only started with the *Principia*. They reconstituted every branch of the existing knowledge tree and even invented new branches. To drive home the point, the French philosophe Diderot adorned his 1751 encyclopedia with the first graphical representation of the newly cultivated tree.

As part of their polemic, the philosophes pruned and cut as well as cultivated. They denigrated certain subjects and elevated others. In the process, history emerged as a discipline, not in its

---

14. Rex A. Barrell, ed., *Anthony Ashley Cooper, Earl of Shaftesbury* (1671–1713), *and 'le Refuge Français' Correspondence* (Lewiston, N.Y., 1989), p.92.

professional and scientific garb as it is now practiced, but in far more secular form than what Louis XIV's chroniclers were writing. His admirers had written to show the hand of God at work in history, particularly at the French court. The philosophes discarded such pieties along with the Biblical account of human origins and destiny. They emulated English writers like Lord Clarendon, who wrote the first history of the English civil wars, and especially the Whig apologists, who wrote to justify the Revolution of 1688. By the late eighteenth century, historians initiated a practice now familiar to anyone who has read a history book. They read old documents and chronicles for what they could reveal about the people who wrote them. They began to examine what professional historians subsequently called primary or original sources.

Along with a secularized approach to history, the European philosophes also developed new approaches toward old languages and texts. Reading old documents, indeed reading any document, is never as simple as it looks. Even picking up the local newspaper you ask, well, why did they run that story? Or, I wonder what party that journalist has joined? In effect, the practitioners of secularized history began to ask those sorts of questions of every text, including, most outrageously, the Bible. The criticism of texts, how they are read and interpreted, was known in the eighteenth century as it is today as "hermeneutics" or by the older term "philology." Once it had been the preserve of pious monks poring over ancient fragments or of Protestants eager to disprove the Catholic Church's interpretation of a Scriptural text. All that changed during the eighteenth-century Enlightenment.

Beginning with the new dictionaries and encyclopedias, enlightened literary criticism, the hermeneutical art, subjected myths and stories to rigorous scrutiny. Ruled out of court were the Biblical stories and the fables of the ancients. While the contents of any museum illustrate that eighteenth-century artists adored the ancient gods, secularized intellectuals did not. Most of the philosophes thought gods and their myths to be barbarous, the imaginative handiwork of deceitful storytellers and priests. The philosophes also cast a cold eye on church history; just writing about churches served in their view to elevate them. The language in a text, the words on the page, became too important to be left to clerical interpreters. The words had to be enlisted in the enterprise of creating wholly secular and scientific learning, but with consequences for learning only recently apparent. In the cultural wars of the present generation, language, with the many uses and abuses that can be attributed to it, has figured prominently in the arsenal of weapons.

To make hermeneutics over into their service, the philosophes had to combat over fifteen centuries of Christian tradition. In those centuries Biblical scholars laid claim to the Word of God as their province. They invented hermeneutics. They classified words, found their origin, assessed their meaning by reference to other texts written at the time, all for the purpose of assisting with the meaning of Scriptural passages. In their understanding of Genesis, Moses was the first historian, and the creation and deluge were actual and decisive events in the past. The beginning of the world could be dated with precision; some said so too could its end. Seventeenth-century Biblical hermeneuticists, most of them clergymen, pieced together all the ancient textual evidence they could find and concluded that God created the world around 4000 B.C. Then human history began, and its continuing enactment occurs in the shadow of the supernatural. Protestant clergymen went even further. They also sought evidence about the end of history, about the second coming of Christ and the millennium, and they subjected the words of the Bible to intense scrutiny to find it. They believed that if they could pin down the chronology of the ancient kingdoms, close textual reading combined with mathematical computation might predict the end of the world.

In their cultural warfare against the clergy and the Biblical version of hermeneutics, the philosophes of the Enlightenment contemptuously dismissed church history and the millennium. They labeled people who go around predicting the end of the

world enthusiasts or madmen. They satirized pious interpretations of texts which seemed to contradict everyday experience
or flew in the face of the new science. The Bible may say that
the sun moves, they argued, but that is just a pious metaphor
analogous to the tall stories found in the Greek legends. Using
fossil evidence, the French philosophe Buffon, one of the founders of geology, rejected the starting date 4000 B.C. as an irrelevant piety.

If the Biblical account of history could be disproved, then
history became an entirely human and secular domain, an infini-
tude of time with no one in charge. But philosophes did not
stop with fossils. Being almost to a man graduates of religious
schooling, they simply expropriated the techniques of hermeneutics for their own uses. Why confine close textual analysis to
the fables of the Bible and thus by default leave the clergy in
charge? The Enlightenment elevated hermeneutics into a tool
for critical inquiry in every branch of learning. With so many
assaults being waged on traditional learning, with so many
battles being engaged in the cultural war, Diderot described
the follower of the Enlightenment as an eclectic, a skeptic and
investigator who "trampling underfoot prejudice, tradition,
venerability, universal assent, authority—in a word, everything
that overawes the crowd—dares to think for himself, to ascend
to the clearest general principles, to examine them, to discuss
them, to admit nothing save on the testimony of his own reason
and experience."[15]

Created by eclectics, skeptics, anticlericals, scientists, religious exiles, and journalists, the Enlightenment set the terms of
the modern cultural project: the individual's attempt to understand nature and humankind through scientific as well as linguistic means, methods that have now been brought into every
branch of learning. In the midst of so many repressive societies
and governments, "the majority of them despotic," the reform-

15. From his article on eclecticism in the *Encyclopédie* (1751), see Denis Diderot, *Encyclopédie ou Dictionnaire raisonné des sciences, des arts et des métiers,* Nouvelle impression
en facsimilé de la première édition de 1751–1780 (Stuttgart, 1966), vol. 5, p. 270.

ers of the eighteenth century proclaimed in their books and journals the existence of "a certain empire, which holds sway over only the mind." That empire "we honor with the name Republic, because it preserves a measure of independence, and because it is almost its essence to be free. It is the empire of talent and of thought."[16] Its members "form a species by their merit, and fain a reputation as brilliant as that of the great powers of the earth." In this far from modest vision, a new kind of person emerged in the eighteenth century: hard to govern, suspicious of authority, more interested in personal authenticity and material progress than in the preservation of traditions, a reader of new literature, novels, newspapers, clandestine manuscripts, even pornography, all especially produced for an urban market that grew decade by decade.

Since the Enlightenment defined the modern idea of the individual, philosophers and political movements hostile to the Western cultural enterprise have focused on the Enlightenment. They attack one of its primary tenets: the autonomous individual as a cultural ideal. Where Immanuel Kant celebrated the emancipation of the individual mind from the fetters of prejudice and superstition, others have seen a more dangerous product. Critics on the right have seen this individual autonomy as subversive of church, state, or community, and more recently, critics claiming a place on the left have seen the glorification of reason as a dangerous illusion or as an excuse for repression and greed, or as simply and singularly a mask for colonial aggression and male domination. Both sides, then and now, sense that Kant's motto for the Enlightenment, "Dare to know," was never an idle threat.

From the vantage point of the West in the twentieth century, cultural wars can sometimes look like the pastimes of intellectuals with too much time on their hands. But the Enlightenment acquired a distinct political meaning. From the French Revolution onward its opponents blamed the Enlight-

16. *Histoire de la République des Lettres en France* (1780), pp. 4–5.

enment for having caused revolution. In the present, cynics who say Western democratic ideology sanctioned racism and sexism condemn the Enlightenment for its smugness, elitism, and myopia about Western imperialism. Most philosophes are, after all, dead white European males.

However arrogant and myopic, the philosophes of the Enlightenment had sought truth with a purpose: the reform of existing institutions. Their passion had been ignited by the late-seventeenth-century revulsion against absolutism, against the French government's persecution of Protestants. But the philosophes wanted to move beyond religious intolerance and get to the heart of the problem. First they attacked the clergy, then religious dogmatism, and finally, after the movement had become international, their heirs went after the very structure of the old-regime governments. The late-eighteenth-century revolutions—the American included—cannot be understood without first understanding the power of enlightened ideals and the social setting which nourished them.

Under the banner of spreading science and toleration, the philosophes used the printing press to great effect. Literacy and reading focused by current affairs created a new public, and within the public sphere emerged what can be identified as civil society. Affluent urban readers with some leisure time created for themselves social lives outside of church and family in voluntary associations, political parties, reading clubs, scientific societies, salons, Masonic lodges, and literary and philosophical clubs, where educated men and some women met, read, and discussed separately from family, church, or state. This social milieu responded to enlightened ideals which were attractive to self-motivated, literate, comfortable individuals, hence to the individualism of commercial society at its very origins. Built into the needs of the commercially free and affluent was the desire for freedom to publish and to assemble as well as to buy and to sell. The commerce in Enlightenment, both as knowledge purchased in books and journals and as the lived experience of free associations, wedded the Enlightenment enterprise to Western market society, to a commerce that could include everything from cotton to slaves, and to the liberal conception of the autonomous individual. None of these mores or institutions were compatible with the traditional society and institutions of the West, with guilds, monasteries, convents, separate courts for clergy, monopolies controlled by state officials or censors, folk beliefs, and customary practices. Things were lost with the advent of modernity that had once given great consolation, even protection.

When faced with restrictive regimes, protective of traditional interests and intent upon controlling access to knowledge as well as to commerce, enlightened ideals could inspire revolution. First in 1776 and then in the 1780s, democratic revolutions broke out on both sides of the Atlantic, in the American colonies, then in the Dutch Republic, Belgium, and France. Drawing upon republican political ideals, some as old as the Renaissance, but adding to them a new faith in science and progress, late-eighteenth-century radicals and revolutionaries thought they were fulfilling the Enlightenment's mandate. The cultural war waged by the intellectuals of the Enlightenment had revolutionary implications.

Out of the crucible of the eighteenth-century revolt against tradition came the human sciences, first history, then psychology, sociology, and anthropology. As professional disciplines they were created in the decades after the French Revolution and in response to it. The late-eighteenth-century revolutions suddenly made history and the human sciences in general vitally important. Assessing the meaning of the Enlightenment and the French Revolution became one of the important tasks of history. But that process of assessment was never a tame exercise in curriculum development. Because of the French Revolution, nineteenth-century advocates of the new social sciences were split ideologically as to the role the new disciplines should play in society. Liberal historians agreed with the Enlightenment enterprise of reform. Other social scientists and historians spurned the Enlightenment as the cause of the French Revolution and regarded both as aberrations that tragically departed from the long centuries of Western stability once ensured by monarchs, aristocracies, and churches.

But so well had the Enlightenment vision of science succeeded that neither side wanted to go back to the methods and practices used in the era before the Enlightenment. Both opponents and supporters of the French Revolution enlisted secularized history as their guide and weapon; and neither would give up the mantle of science. Conservative nineteenth-century historians such as the German Leopold von Ranke repudiated the Enlightenment's program for reform. Liberal historians, often allied with the bourgeoisie of city and industry, built upon it and the legacy of the French Revolution and advocated radical change. Yet neither side went back to history as it had been in the hands of chroniclers, church apologists, or millenarians. In that sense the cultural wars of the eighteenth century were won by the philosophes. The discipline of history, as discussed in the next chapter, depended upon their achievements.

## Protestant Science and
## the American University

The bold contrast between philosophe and cleric was always clearer in Catholic than in Protestant Europe. Louis XIV's persecution of Protestants structured the polemics of secular culture for nearly a century. By the late eighteenth century the Enlightenment project looked very different in both Britain and America than it did in continental Europe. Differences also existed between the British and American responses to the irreligion and anticlericalism of the French philosophes. Schematically speaking, the Enlightenment began in Britain, crossed the Channel to the continent, where, particularly in France, its dissident counterculture took a violent turn against the clergy. In the last decades of the century, enlightened principles then traversed the Atlantic and were generally more cherished in the American colonies than in the Old World of their origin. The

American enthusiasm for the Enlightenment, perhaps best exemplified in the life of Benjamin Franklin, took a practical direction toward scientific experimentation and political activism and largely bypassed the radical atheism of the French encyclopedists. By contrast, in the last decades of the eighteenth century all but the most radical British intellectuals had become suspicious of the Enlightenment. They associated it with atheism, then with rebellious colonists and finally with the excesses of the French Revolution. Running through the complex responses of the English-speaking world on both sides of the Atlantic is the thread of Protestantism.

Early-modern Protestants were heretics of the Word. They had made the Bible their weapon against the dogmas of the Roman Church. In addition, seventeenth-century English Protestants forged a distinctive alliance which would last in high culture well into the nineteenth century: science properly understood could support religion. The English Puritans of the mid-seventeenth century championed both Parliament and the Bible, and they were prepared to wage war against their king—beheading him in 1649. In the process they gave Anglo-American culture a distinctive understanding of science and religion. As a result, the American version of the Enlightenment was less angry, less anticlerical, and more confident of progress. The Protestant version of Enlightenment put Americans on a path that still influences cultural life. In other words, history matters: whatever their background, participants in American culture never entirely escape the colonial Protestant past and the Founding Fathers' receptivity to the Enlightenment.

In striking contrast to the continental Catholic clergy, seventeenth-century English Protestants and the Puritans who went to the American colonies thought that they could have their Bible along with their science. Both would be sticks they could use to beat the Roman Catholic or even the Anglican clergy. Baconianism helped to infuse their faith in science with Protestant piety. From Bacon they got explanations that thrilled the Protestant heart: "When it pleased God to call the Church of

Rome to account for their degenerate manners and ceremonies
. . . it was ordained by the Divine Providence, that there should
attend withal a renovation and new spring of all other knowledge."[17] Bacon's emphasis on collecting data and on painstak-
ing, laborious experience as the key to knowledge in effect tied
the Protestant work ethic to the empirical study of nature.

The nineteenth century Anglo-American view of science
never entirely escaped its seventeenth-century Puritan and revolutionary context. The Puritans bequeathed to modern thought,
and particularly to the nineteenth-century university, a union
between God's word and his work, between the study of the
Bible and the study of natural science. This tradition established
an important, distinctively Anglo-American variation on the
heroic model of science: the scientist need not be at odds with
the clergyman. He could be pious yet enterprising in the pursuit
of natural knowledge. His religiosity might be more cerebral
than emotional, but it could also be vaguely, even deeply Christian.

Had the continental and atheistic version of the Enlightenment triumphed over the Anglo-American Protestant version
of science, both British and American universities of the nineteenth century would have been far more secular institutions
than in fact they were. But until well into the nineteenth century
the heroic understanding of science and the Bible coexisted in
American and British universities. The demise of the Bible in
English-speaking universities occurred only slowly, and then
after a midcentury struggle in which scientists enlisted every
intellectual ally they could muster. Now mature disciplines,
history, hermeneutics, geology, coupled with the all-important
new Darwinian evolutionary science, contributed decisively to
the dethroning of the Bible. It was as if Anglo-Americans waited
until the mid-nineteenth century to fight (and win) the last
battle of the Enlightenment.

17. Francis Bacon, *The Advancement of Learning*, ed. Arthur Johnson (Oxford, England, 1974), p. 42.

Until then, Anglo-American universities rejected the materialism, atheism, and anticlericalism associated with science by the continental philosophes. In effect, they sheltered themselves under a compromise between what Protestants liked to call God's work, i.e., science, and God's word, the Bible. In the 1880s, the head of a leading American state university prescribed that "in choosing members of the faculty the greatest care should be taken to secure gifted, earnest, reverent men, whose mental and moral qualities will fit them to prepare their pupils for manly and womanly work in promoting our Christian civilization."[18] In 1915, it was still "customary in state universities, no less than in denominational colleges, to question a candidate for appointment concerning his church connections. Any church connection will do," claimed an article in *The Nation*.[19]

Yet the compromise between work and word had always been fragile. Gradually after the 1850s it collapsed as historians and scientists forged an alliance aided by the new hermeneutics. This controversy can be seen as a repeat performance of the way eighteenth-century continental philosophes had structured their cultural war with the clergy. A small group of English and American geologists first challenged the original Baconian compromise when they sought to research and lecture about geology as if the Bible had nothing of importance to say geologically. "The physical part of geological inquiry ought to be conducted as if the Scriptures were not in existence," Lyell had asserted in 1832.[20] The separation of geology from Biblical history required nonetheless an attack on the scientific validity

18. Quote from the inaugural address of James B. Angel given in the 1880s, in Bradley J. Longfield, "From Evangelicalism to Liberalism: Public Midwestern Universities in Nineteenth-Century America," in George M. Marsden and Bradley J. Longfield, eds., *The Secularization of the Academy* (New York, 1992), p. 55.

19. Ibid., p. 56.

20. As quoted in James R. Moore, "Geologists and Interpreters of Genesis in the Nineteenth Century," in David C. Lindberg and Ronald L. Numbers, eds., *God and Nature: Historical Essays on the Encounter Between Christianity and Science* (Berkeley, Calif., of 1986), pp. 322–50, quote p. 337.

of Biblical stories. Victorian geologists such as Adam Sedgwick and William Whewell, both Anglican clergymen teaching at Cambridge University, labored to expose the contradictions and inconsistencies in the Biblical stories by the use of philology, ancient history, and fossil remains. The holy text could now be read like every other text and be submitted to the scrutiny of scientific hermeneutics.

Just as the philosophes had prescribed, nineteenth-century scientific hermeneutics turned the scientific method on the Bible itself, anchored it historically and linguistically, and asked that its words be related to other words in other historical texts. Put bluntly, the Bible was relativized. Once opened to hermeneutical scrutiny the words about the seven days of creation became merely linguistic puzzles to be unraveled by reference to ancient cosmologies as revealed in other texts from related times and places. In taking on the Bible within a Protestant context, scientific history armed with hermeneutics met the last challenge to its dominance over the story of the past and emerged triumphant. Interpreting the Bible literally became the province of religious fundamentalists, not something that educated people could bring themselves any longer to do.

Leveling the status of the Bible also cleared a space wherein a mature history of science emerged. Emboldened by the victory of history and hermeneutics, secular intellectuals looked for new objects of inquiry. If history and hermeneutics could ally with science in order to establish the autonomy of all three from religion, then history and hermeneutics could be joined together triumphantly in writing the history of science itself. Such an enterprise would give further stature to science, and it would therefore also defeat those who thought that only Christian gentlemen should be allowed to teach in the universities. Self-consciously polemical, scientific and secularized historians began to write the first histories of science, of science triumphant. These first Anglo-American histories of science sought to show the truth of science and to affirm its heroic nature as value-free, separate from social influences, true and objective.

Andrew Dickson White, a founder of Cornell University, was the greatest nineteenth-century historian of science. In his *A History of the Warfare of Science with Theology in Christendom* (1896), White described the authority of Scripture as "the tyranny of sacred books imperfectly transcribed, viewed through distorting superstitions, and frequently interpreted by party spirit."[21] White devoted nearly half of his two-volume history of science to the rise and importance of hermeneutics (what he called philology or higher criticism). It had shown that the Biblical stories were based upon myths and legends, interesting in themselves, but meaningless as either history or geology. The scientific study of the Biblical texts, in White's view, was "a service rendered to humanity . . . in substituting a new and correct rendering for the old reading of the famous text . . . which had for ages done so much to make our sacred books a fetish."[22]

Together, history and hermeneutics would liberate both themselves and science from clerical influence. White also praised the Morrell Act of 1862 which set aside public lands in every state for the establishment of universities where science and technical education could be taught along with the humanities and social sciences.[23] It marked a great step forward in placing science and technical education on an equal footing with classical literature while also democratizing American higher education, and assisting in breaking the clergy's hold over higher education.

For White, science, history, and hermeneutics together formed a liberal and progressive bulwark against backward-looking historical forces. Laymen like White and his liberal and secular allies, such as the historian Herbert Baxter Adams, wanted the education of young gentlemen to be taken away from the clergy with their Bibles and placed in the hands of a laity with

---

21. Quoted in David C. Lindberg, "Science and the Early Church," in Lindberg and Numbers, *God and Nature*, p. 19.

22. Andrew D. White, *A History of the Warfare of Science with Theology in Christendom*, vol. 2 (New York, 1960), p. 387.

23. Ibid., vol. 1, pp. 413–14. Many state universities owe their existence to this act.

scientific training. Celebrating the eventual triumph of this secular vision, White concluded that "on both sides of the Atlantic the great majority of the leading institutions of learning are under the sway of enlightened public opinion as voiced mainly by laymen [and thus] the physical and natural sciences are henceforth likely to be developed normally, and without fear of being sterilized by theology, or oppressed by ecclesiastism."[24] In other words, White believed that the heroic model of science had taken over the curriculum of American universities. In the long run he proved to be right.

The educational and intellectual reforms of the late nineteenth century did indeed create a professionally trained class of gentlemen leaders as well as historians who could teach and write about the triumph of their values: science; liberty as conceived by the English gentry and enshrined in the American constitution; reason; republican virtue.[25] In the final triumph of the American Enlightenment, White and his allies firmly attached a triumphant history of heroic science to the ideals of the secular republic.

What such men had not foreseen was the arrival into the American republic of thousands of immigrants, few of them middle-class Protestants and many of them Catholics and Jews. White and his liberal allies had envisioned the new state universities as places that would educate enlightened white men of Protestant background in applied science. Although they specifically linked this education to industrialization, they did not imagine it as education for the workers. The liberal and secular reformers of the late nineteenth century sought no change in the class or racial origins of the men who would govern the country. They simply wanted them to have a more secular and hence more scientific orientation. Women never even figured in their plans.

White's view of the warfare between science and theology (he carefully tried to say that it was not between science and

24. Ibid., p. 414.

25. Dorothy Ross, *The Origins of American Social Science* (Cambridge, England, 1991), pp. 70–75, and ch. 4 on the threat of socialism.

religion per se) was widely held by Anglo-American historians until very recently. Even those who claimed that Western religious doctrines encouraged the birth of modern science have embraced the fundamental doctrine bequeathed by the Victorians: science is a separate body of knowledge, immune from the subjectivity of all other branches of knowledge, which should wherever possible follow its example. In the Anglo-American tradition, the history of science allied science with liberalism and elevated both to the altar of reason and the secular republic. The followers of science worshipped in a temple where ignorance, censorship, bigotry, and superstition—sometimes equated with religion—had no pew.

The twentieth-century followers of White's vision of the history of science wrote about such exemplars of seventeenth-century English science as Robert Boyle and Isaac Newton in ways that left out their extraordinary religiosity. Historians of science taught right up to the 1960s that the greatest tension these heroes had to reconcile was between their science and their religion.[26] It never occurred to anyone that the two might have been so merged as to be for them inseparable. The borders between heroic science, religion, and, of course, magic were reinforced smugly and assuredly, by a history of heroic science emanating from American and British universities.

The American university was the creation of a distinct and inherited version of Western high culture: secular because of late-nineteenth-century reformers like White, deeply confident in the power of heroic science, and committed to excellence in every branch of science and technology, regardless of how or to what purpose it might be applied. In the field of history, students were meant to learn the political narrative of Western development with particular attention to American and British

26. For examples see R. S. Westfall, *Science and Religion in Seventeenth Century England* (New Haven, Conn., 1958); G. R. Cragg, *From Puritanism to the Age of Reason* (Cambridge, England, 1950). For a meditation on where the subject of science and religion is now, see James R. Moore, "Speaking on 'Science and Religion'—Then and Now," *History of Science*, 30 (1992): 311–23.

institutions. English, American, and foreign-language literature departments utilized and taught hermeneutic techniques based on the close readings of great texts. Such works were deemed suitable as the replacement for what had once been the centerpiece of all Anglo-American literary education, the Bible.

American universities transmitted a legacy of essentially eighteenth-century origin: the Enlightenment as understood in the Protestant and republican culture of the original colonies and as modified in the late-nineteenth-century process that enshrined science and hermeneutics. This was a powerful legacy, embraced with an absolute confidence once accorded only to churches and kings. The teaching of history, whether about parliaments or science—from Plato to NATO—seemed only to reinforce the wisdom of the turn taken in the eighteenth century, the success of the Enlightenment enterprise. The heroic model of science ensured the truth-seeking of the other disciplines against charges of being nothing but the self-serving artifice of old elites. In this self-confident atmosphere the discipline of history flourished until well into the 1960s. Anchored by well-enrolled surveys of Western civilization and American democracy, history was one of the major beneficiaries of the confidence in progress that science, heroically conceived, had built.

# ◇ 2 ◇

# Scientific History and
# the Idea of Modernity

IN THE NINETEENTH CENTURY, historians had championed an explicitly scientific history, and in so doing they had embarked upon a new and challenging kind of enterprise. Until then, historians chronicled, narrated, and assessed historical events, but they did not cast their methods and their goals in the mold of heroic science. Indeed, the heroic model of science itself made science seem eternally true, while history remained contingent. Science developed grand, overarching, and invariable laws; history more modestly dealt with what changed in human affairs.

Once science and history got linked together, dramatically new forms of historical knowledge became possible. Explanatory history—the search for the laws of historical development—was born in the nineteenth century: it bequeathed a powerful analytical tool useful to all peoples trying to make sense of where they had been and what they were becoming. Every history book available today—including those about the "end of history"—reflects the enduring power of that nineteenth-century vision of scientific history.

In the mid-nineteenth century, history became a profession. It began to take on its modern form as an organized, disciplined inquiry into the meaning of the past. Certified professional historians with university training in scientific methods of archival research and documented writing began to claim rights to the past. These new historians developed the model of explanatory history that enabled the West to understand itself and the rest of the world within one universal, secular framework compatible with the universality of Newtonian laws. Building upon the Enlightenment belief that society itself was a human artifact and could be known by humans, scientific historians helped lay the foundations for the modern social sciences.

The nineteenth-century modernization of history rested on a new conception of time drawn from Newtonian science. Western historians made time universal and evolutionary and arrayed all the peoples, structures, and institutions in every epoch along its line, labeling each people and era in terms of its level of development. Time became real and sequential, and historians became those who could measure development by progress toward modern, Western time. This scientific history with its companion idea of modernity eventually erected an intellectual absolutism of its own, but it began, as did the heroic model of science itself, as a challenge to the earlier absolutisms of throne and altar and to histories that were meant to show the hand of God at work among saints and rulers. When the process of creating modern history was completed, Biblical time lay in ruins and the dreams of millenarians came to be seen as grand self-delusions.

It is not easy to grasp the significance of the new scientific conception of time because Westerners take it so for granted. They assume that everyone's time is the same, that it is a universal continuum experienced by all people in the same fashion. The hour may be different in Tokyo or Tehran, but the concept of time is the same, or so common sense seems to insist. That commonsensical notion is, however, relatively recent and derives most directly from the Newtonian conception of time as an absolute, real, and universal entity. Newtonian laws can predict where a planet will be at any given moment in the year because time is imagined as independent and everywhere the same.

New ways of measuring time foreshadowed and then reinforced the scientific notion of universal time. Western Europeans invented mechanical clocks, as an improvement on sundials and water clocks, in the fourteenth century. Christianity, at least as practiced by monks, seemed to require more punctuality than the other religions of the world. The first of the mechanical clocks were giant show clocks designed for public display on churches or city halls, and they had minimal effect on the lives of ordinary people. In the second half of the fifteenth century, miniaturization made mechanical clocks available to wealthy individuals, and time thus passed, as it were, from the rulers and clergymen to the upper classes. Not until the 1860s did reliable cheap Swiss watches become available to the general population.[1] Not surprisingly, many of them were made by Protestant workers to whom historians may now credit not only the modern work ethic but also ways of measuring how long you have been at it. In the early nineteenth century, employers began to force industrial workers to regulate their work habits by the factory clock, bringing to ordinary people the experience of time as an ever-present, standardized sequence of units disciplining the cadences of work and daily life.

The experience of time did not depend entirely or perhaps even primarily on timepieces themselves. In the seventeenth and eighteenth centuries, two new forms of imagining the social world appeared—the novel and the newspaper.[2] Both made people think of themselves as living lives simultaneous with other lives in a homogenous time measured by clocks and calendars (and not by relationship to salvation or the hereafter). The readers of novels or newspapers follow the lives of people they will never meet but can readily imagine as acting in time and over time like themselves, because they are contemporaries. In any one novel, many of the characters do not meet each other, but they are all depicted as part of one social world, living

1. David S. Landes, *Revolution in Time: Clocks and the Making of the Modern World* (Cambridge, Mass., 1983).

2. Benedict Anderson, *Imagined Communities: Reflections on the Origins and Spread of Nationalism*, rev. ed. (London, 1991), especially pp. 9–36.

simultaneous lives that bring them into unexpected connections with each other. Whether reading alone or in groups (as with early newspapers), readers of novels and newspapers knew that they were reading what many other people were also reading at the same time and reading about people acting in their time frame (unlike the prophetic time frame of the Bible). Thus the very act of reading novels and newspapers established a new kind of mental community based on a version of Newtonian time. It also reinforced expectations that human actions in society, like motion in nature, could be explained in terms of scientific cause and effect.

Crucial transformations in the categories of historical time paralleled the homogenization and standardization of the ordinary person's experience of present time. But historical time was not neutral or empty. The modern idea of historical time was linear as opposed to cyclical, secular as opposed to religious, universal rather than particular to any epoch, nation, or faith. Most important, it had a direction—that is, it was cumulative in some fashion. The new historical sense of time reproduced the universalizing, standardizing time of the scientists, but for human rather than natural history. Being linear, historical time promised to reveal a higher meaning, but being secular, that meaning could be found only in human affairs, not in divine providence. The new characteristics of time did not appear all at once, and many historians continued to espouse one or more elements of previous time schemas. But by the last decades of the nineteenth century, most educated Westerners possessed a universal and universalizing sense of time that was, moreover, ideally suited to the new age of European imperialism. It gave the West a civilizing mission based on modernization—a process that came to mean making everyone else like the West.

Those who promoted the new notion of time passionately believed that they were inaugurating an age that would surpass in achievement—in progress—all that had come before. To be scientific and modern was not dry and academic; it promised a decisive break with the past, a daring leap into the future, and the prospect of continual progress. Progress and modernity thus marched hand in hand. Belief in modernity meant faith that accumulated knowledge, when diffused and applied, could only lead to improvement, to better living standards. Humans were not simply condemned to repeat their past mistakes, enslaved to tradition. They could instead create a better future through an analysis of human experience. The heroic model of science directly inspired this modern perspective inherited from the Enlightenment. In modernity, improvements could now be imagined in this world, not in some distant pie-in-the-sky paradise.

A new relationship to the facts of history followed from the new conception of time. The disciplining of history, its metamorphosis into a scientific discipline, became possible only once a new notion of time had emerged. If time was imagined as universally the same and history construed as a secular story of its unfolding, then it made sense to train historians in universities according to secular, standardized, scientific methods. The development of new techniques of teaching and research guaranteed the mastery of facts. The master historian would teach students how to distinguish fact from legend by the rigorous examination of documents. History would henceforth depend on research in archives and original sources as tests of the facts. University training would teach an attitude of impartiality toward those facts. This mastery of the facts with its emphasis on patient accumulation of information and relentless curiosity about sources provided the second crucial element in scientific history in the West.

## Mastering Time and Inventing Modernity

Before there could be moderns, there had to be ancients, men and women who did not think of history as a body of knowledge revealing a pattern or having a meaning. For the Greeks and Romans, history concerned persons, things, or events

but did not exhibit overarching meanings or p
showed only the inexorable effects of human
nesses, and ambitions. Because it was not a sep.
itself, it did not depend on any particular idea of time.
could be repetitive or not, cyclical or something else; no one
was sure.[3]

Building upon Hebrew antecedents, Christianity introduced a new linear notion of time into the Greco-Roman world.
The Judeo-Christian line of time literally began at one moment
and would end at another, and it revealed God's purposes. In
the Christian schema, the turning points of sacred history—the
Creation, Jesus's life and death, and the prospect of the Last
Judgment—set the framework for all historical time. If you
carefully opened the pages of the New York Public Library's
well-preserved copy of Werner Rolewinck's *Bundle of Chronol-
ogies* from 1474, for instance, you would see two lines running
in parallel through the text. One line measures time since the
beginning of the world and the other measures time before and
after the birth of Jesus. The year 2907 after the moment of
Creation, for example, corresponded to the year 8622 before
Christ's birth. Rolewinck incorporated the histories of ancient
peoples and even legends about such imagined peoples as the
Amazons into his account of Biblical history. Sacred history
gave all of time its meaning.

The Christian time schema occupied scholars right into the
seventeenth century. Archbishop James Ussher, a seventeenth-
century Irish-born cleric of the Church of England, insisted
that the world began precisely in 4004 B.C. (and probably in
the morning), and Isaac Newton cautiously expected that it
might end around 2000 A.D. (we hope he was wrong).[4] Such

3. Gerald A. Press, *The Development of the Idea of History in Antiquity* (Kingston and
Montreal, 1982).

4. On the general question, see Martin J. S. Rudwick, "The Shape and Meaning of
Earth History," in David C. Lindberg and Ronald L. Numbers, eds., *God and Nature:
Historical Essays on the Encounter Between Christianity and Science* (Berkeley, Calif.,
1986), pp. 296–321.

views linked the study of history to the highest religious purposes and gave the historical process a teleology in which every event in history connected in some way to a central divine story. The influence of the Christian time schema remains in the Western calendar, which marks all time according to the benchmark of the birth of Jesus; time is either B.C. ("Before Christ") or A.D. ("*anno Domini*," Latin for "in the year of the Lord"). Alternative forms such as B.C.E. for "Before the Common Era" do not really challenge the Christian dating system.

Christian historians wished to link all previous history to one universal story, informed by their faith. They explained events by reference to God's direct divine intervention. Late-sixteenth-century Spanish chroniclers, for example, attributed the Spanish victory over the Muslims at the Battle of Lepanto in 1571 to the appearance of the Virgin Mary in the heavens. Only a few years later, Elizabeth I of England celebrated the defeat of the Spanish Armada, dashed by storms along the English coast, by issuing a medal that read: "God blew, and they were scattered." Colonial American historians believed that God had delayed the discovery of North America so that Protestants could settle their part of the New World. These are not the sort of explanations of historical events that a student would now give to questions on the Graduate Record Examination.

Between the fifteenth and eighteenth centuries, the Christian scheme of history steadily lost credibility. Certainty and conviction about God's purposes in human affairs gave way to growing doubts, made more subversive by the attacks of Enlightenment propagandizers. Under the accumulated weight of new knowledge about the ancient Greeks and Romans and peoples in distant lands, the historical facade of the Christians cracked. A new sense of historical time emerged, thanks in part to the promise and example of breakthroughs in science. By the 1740s, when one of Newton's once close associates went about the philosophical societies talking up the end of the world, people thought him to be a bit dotty.

Europeans in the seventeenth and eighteenth centuries began to develop what is now called a historical consciousness—that is, an appreciation of how the passage of time changes institutions and renders past societies strikingly different from contemporary ones. The study of classical models helped initiate this breakthrough in thinking about the past. As Renaissance scholars learned more and more about the ancient world in their quest to model themselves on ancient examples of politics, law, and literature, they discovered that there were actually enormous and unbridgeable differences between classical institutions and their own.

In England during the seventeenth century the scholarly interest in antiquity acquired a practical urgency when the open hostility between king and Parliament ended with King Charles I's execution. Witnesses record that a long, anguished moan rose up from the crowd when the severed head of the king was displayed. No longer obedient subjects, the regicides had to find another basis for public order than that of the divine right of kings. They looked to the histories of Athenian democracy and the Roman republic to supply a new model for political action. An avid interest in classical republicanism fostered a deepening awareness of how social institutions accommodated the specific needs of people at a particular time and place. Having put themselves beyond the comfort of habitual obedience and customary usages, members of England's upper class also encouraged the study of Parliament and the common law, creating a new body of historical knowledge about England's ancient constitution.[5]

Under the pressure of these various changes, the turning points of sacred history eventually gave way to a secular, linear periodization of ancient, medieval, and modern, which still dominates history writing today. Progress in this world replaced salvation in the next as the goal of human participation in time. The movement toward the modern, rather than the fall

5. J.G.A. Pocock, *The Ancient Constitution and the Feudal Law* (Cambridge, England, 1957).

from God's grace now defined the direction of history. It is hard to imagine a more fundamental reorientation of the human place within time.

Language itself reflected these monumental changes. The English adjective "modern" first came into usage at the end of the sixteenth century. Derived from the Latin word *modo* for "just now," it referred to the present or recent time as opposed to the remote past, but soon came to mean as well new-fashioned, not antiquated or obsolete. In other words, in the seventeenth and especially in the eighteenth century, "modern" came to mean better. Historians began to call their age modern so as to distinguish it from what came before. The Middle Ages, a term which first came into use at the end of the seventeenth century, pointed, as the term suggests, to the period between the ancients and the moderns. By implication, the Middle Ages were less advanced than the modern period; they were, as the French Enlightenment philosophe Condorcet said, a period of "the grossest ignorance extending over all nations and all occupations."[6] With the spread of the idea of progress, the modern period became the standard by which the past was judged. Even the ancients, who had long served as models in almost every field of learning, now seemed surpassable if not actually inferior. The new science, in particular, had shown this to be true. If the laws of human history could be understood, time would bring progress, not decline.

The transformation of Christian into secular time was not just a mental exercise. Better material conditions affected how people felt about the future (though they did not yet have opinion surveys about consumer confidence!). As chronic food shortages and periodic famines gave way late in the seventeenth century to agricultural improvements and then to a new industrial order, prosperity and growth seemed not only possible but permanent, even if they depended on the misery of slaves or

6. As quoted in Ernst Breisach, *Historiography: Ancient, Medieval, and Modern* (Chicago, 1983), p. 207. Breisach offers a useful overview of concepts of history.

workers. The fixed material limits of the medieval period had been conspicuously vaulted, and contemporaries asked themselves how this had happened. Sustained innovations shattered that old sense of social life endlessly repeating itself with little variation—at least for those men and women who benefited from the changes.

In a mood of newly aggressive confidence, eighteenth-century historians began to write a story of improvement and then of progress. In their story of progress, a major reversal occurred. Optimism about the prospect of steady amelioration of the human lot in this world displaced pessimism about the inexorable decline in the human condition since the Garden of Eden. For elites, the Christian framework of time no longer seemed relevant to natural or human history. The moderns had come to seem smarter than the ancients while simultaneously the old could now be "classified." In the same spirit, British elites developed the notion of "classics" in music which could be enjoyed because of their distance from the modern and the contemporary.[7]

In eighteenth-century Scotland, a remarkable group of philosophers and scholars, numbering among others Adam Smith and David Hume, took upon themselves the task of analyzing how these changes had come about—how, for example, one could explain the wealth of nations, to echo the title of Smith's famous work. Answers to questions about the transformative material changes in eighteenth-century Europe took the form of conjectural or philosophical history—a reasoning from what was true of the present back to the conditions that must have prevailed at the dawn of history.[8]

The writers of the Scottish Enlightenment came up with a four-stage theory of social development. In their view, human society passed in succession from domination by hunters and

7. William Weber, *The Rise of Musical Classics in Eighteenth-Century England: A Study in Canon, Ritual, and Ideology* (Oxford, England, 1992).

8. See, for example, Richard Olson, *The Emergence of the Social Sciences, 1642–1792* (New York, 1993).

gatherers to shepherds to farmers to merchants. A number of important conceptual breakthroughs accompanied this historical sociology. The Scottish writers observed that human beings, acting within these different moral and material contexts, like those limiting the food supply of hunters and gatherers or the mobility of farmers, produced patterns of social interaction best described as developments rather than mere changes. Probing for the causes of these processes, they further elaborated the notion of unintended consequences, the most famous being that of Smith's invisible hand of the market, in which men and women bought and sold in pursuit of their own profit, but, constrained by competition, unintentionally enhanced the productivity of the whole society. As the term "conjectural history" implies, these historical schemes were conjectures based more upon deductions from a few known facts than on evidence from an abundance of empirical findings, but they undergirded historical consciousness in important ways.

The philosophes of the Enlightenment confidently argued that if human beings could develop science and comprehend the laws of nature, then they could also remake society, politics, and every other realm of human life. Progress was possible, they insisted, because humans were basically good, not fundamentally evil as Christianity had taught. John Locke's depiction of the human mind as a blank slate waiting to be written on made it possible to believe that education could transform any human being and hence any society. His widely influential views encouraged the belief that social engineering could mold a new kind of individual. Not coincidentally, the modern idea of revolution took shape at this time.[9] Revolution no longer meant a cyclical return to a point of departure, as in a revolution of a planet around the sun, but rather came to mean a jump forward into the previously unknown, an experiment in Lockean social

9. Christopher Hill, "The Word 'Revolution,'" in *A Nation of Change and Novelty: Radical Politics, Religion and Literature in Seventeenth-Century England* (London, 1990), pp. 82–101.

engineering. Revolution in this sense depended on an idea of the modern. Arguably, modernity first took shape in late-seventeenth-century England where the institutions of monarchy and church were irrevocably weakened. Modernity and the origins of democracy in the West are thus implicated one in the other.

The kind of schematic history that we are telling here raises an important issue that is worth lingering on for a moment or two. Because in this book we use the language of development deployed in the eighteenth and nineteenth centuries, we run the serious danger of giving our own story a very teleological cast: the history of history could only move forward, we seem to imply, when the supposed defects and deficiencies of past conceptions were recognized and corrected. By definition, the defects and deficiencies are those characteristics that dropped out of history as it became a modern, academic discipline. Such an account is bound to appear teleological in retrospect, if only because we are trying to tell a long story in a very short space. So we want to emphasize as strongly as possible that the story only seems to be so purposeful from our perspective of hindsight. Along the way, the direction was far from obvious to contemporaries (and even now, it is not clear how history will develop in the future). In this short space, we also necessarily omit most of the bitter conflicts that swirled around the men (and few women) who invented the academic discipline of history. Every step forward was contested and negotiated; we tell of outcomes more often than of those processes of contestation and competition.

The development of the new idea of progress did not leave much room for appreciation of the past on its own terms. In the heat of the cultural wars of the Enlightenment, many philosophes denounced history, especially of the Middle Ages, as the repository of all that was cruel, barbaric, and backward. One school primer from the time of the French Revolution, for example, labeled history "the registers of the unhappiness of humanity."[10] The English feminist Mary Wollstonecraft believed that "brutal force has hitherto governed the world," and in her view, the science of politics was still in its "infancy."[11] History was the nightmare of past superstitions that science and social engineering might transform. Progress aided by science and technology meant leaving the past behind like outgrowing an unhappy childhood.

Every decisive cultural movement produces its own reaction, and the Enlightenment was no exception. Already in the midst of its triumph, some scholars, artists, and poets began to champ at the bit of a reason that seemed arrogant and impervious to the darker, more exciting, emotional, and creative sides of life. The Romantics, as they were soon known, valued emotion over reason, an almost religious response to the wonders of nature over scientific detachment, and the mysteries of history over the brash efforts to escape from it. Some Romantics even sought refuge in an idealized medieval world, seeking out old castles, the more ruined the better, and in the process inventing a modern sensibility known as the gothic.

Among the most influential of the Romantic scholars of history was Johann Gottfried Herder. Arguing that each culture and every historical epoch had to be understood on its own terms, Herder urged historians to adopt a posture of respectful deference toward the past. "Each age is different, and each has the center of its happiness within itself," he insisted. Even the Middle Ages possessed "something solid, cohesive and majestic." This insistence on the integrity of the past, on its right to be taken on its own terms, eventually enhanced the confidence of historians. Ironically, despite Herder's insistence on the difference between cultures and epochs, his position also made time itself into an even more universal continuum in which each epoch had its own role to play, a role that remained to be discovered by the historian.

10. Louis Trenard, "Manuels scolaires au XVIIIe siècle et sous la Révolution," *Revue du Nord* (1973): 107.

11. Miriam Brody, ed., *A Vindication of the Rights of Woman* (New York, 1992), p. 122.

History, Herder said, revealed the soaring spirit of ever-youthful nations and their irrepressible cultural differences. Herder coined the term "nationalism" and made the nation the unit in which time marches forward. In a vision that was both Romantic and deeply nationalist, Herder underlined the need for a national folk identity: "Let us follow our own path . . . let men speak well or ill of our nation, our literature, our language: they are ours, they are ourselves, and let that be enough."[12] A sense of one's history, Herder maintained, should be celebrated because it shaped national and ethnic identity.

From the end of the eighteenth century onward, personal identity was consequently linked to nationalism and required an elaborate ethnic heritage, even where none had existed before. All at once, seemingly, nations began to discover—or rediscover—themselves. The first official grammar for Russian, for example, appeared in 1802, the first Ukrainian one in 1819. Slovene, Serbo-Croatian, and Bulgarian all took shape as separate languages in the first decades of the nineteenth century. Everywhere, scholars rushed to discover literary and historical forebears who would give the nation a long lineage. Not surprisingly, history books, along with grammars, dictionaries, and the study of folklore, stood at the forefront of struggles for national identity and independence throughout the nineteenth and twentieth centuries. The invented community of the nation called out for historical grounding, even if it had to be essentially created for the occasion.[13]

The history of nations got its sanctification in Georg W. F. Hegel's doctrine of historicism, which held that truth is rooted in history itself. History revealed truth, and nations were its carriers. The German philosopher lectured and wrote decades before Germany achieved national unity. His lectures were avidly followed by nationalistic students, even though his prose

12. As quoted in Isaiah Berlin, *Vico and Herder: Two Studies in the History of Ideas* (New York, 1976), pp. 191, 182.

13. On the rapid proliferation of lexicographical endeavors to found nations, see Anderson, *Imagined Communities*, especially pp. 67–82.

was difficult, even impenetrable. In Hegel's inimitable prose, "History . . . has constituted the rational necessary course of the World-Spirit—that Spirit whose nature is always one and the same, but which unfolds this its one nature in the phenomena of the World's existence."[14] In historicism, the truths of reason (Hegel's "rational necessary course of the World-Spirit") could not be discovered outside of history.

Hegel's historicism reversed the usual relationship between philosophy and history. Until Hegel, all great thinkers worshiped at the altar of philosophy because it asked the important, eternal questions. Hegel insisted that philosophical truth itself was only revealed in history, and especially in the struggle of nations to define themselves. Time now enveloped thought. Only as history advanced, he claimed, could humans encounter truth. No one could escape history; progress depended on recognizing the direction of history and moving with it. Today many of Hegel's ideas are considered quaint, anachronistic, biased, and even racist; he thought that Protestants were more evolved than Catholics in spiritual values, that the blacks of Africa had no moral sentiments or self-control, and that the state of Prussia alone had developed a real moral framework. Yet even the ability to judge Hegel himself depends on his sense of history as a developmental process. Critics think of themselves as seeing more and better than Hegel did because they have the benefit of more historical hindsight. In Hegelian terms, as history marches forward, it reveals more and more of the meaning implicit in it and moral judgments improve accordingly.

Even though nothing could have been further from his intention, Hegel opened the way to relativism, that is, the idea that truth depends on historical circumstances. If truth is revealed over time, then any truth, moral, scientific, or political, also changes over time and is never permanent. What seems to

14. Georg Wilhelm Friedrich Hegel, *The Philosophy of History*, tr. J. Sibree (New York, 1956), p. 10.

be true today may not be true in the conditions of tomorrow; what is true for some people is not true for others. Thus, even as Hegel's views lent great prestige to history, now conceived as an essential framework for philosophy, they also created potential problems for the idea of historical truth itself. Were there no absolute moral standards that transcended the particularities of time and place? Was the role of historians simply limited to explaining how previous people had thought and acted without passing judgment on those thoughts and actions?

Although historicism prepared the way for relativism, none of the leading figures of nineteenth-century European intellectual life embraced either moral or epistemological relativism before the 1880s. Arguably the most influential thinkers of the nineteenth century, Auguste Comte, Charles Darwin, and Karl Marx all believed in the absolute truths of science. History revealed scientific laws that could be discovered once and for all. Each of them in a very different way helped to take history down from its Hegelian spiritual shelf by making it entirely secular, scientific, and explicitly evolutionary. Comte insisted that history revealed scientific laws. Darwin offered the most compelling scientific model of such a law in his theory of natural selection. Marx proclaimed himself the discoverer of the equivalent laws in human history. Contemporary Westerners still live under the influence of—or in revolt from—their ideas.

The French sociologist Comte coined the term "positivism" in the 1830s to capture his view of the scientific status of historical laws. Inspired by heroic science, Comte maintained that progress in all knowledge as in science depends on developing general laws out of direct observations of phenomena. He believed that human history had passed through a theological stage (childhood) and a metaphysical stage (youth) and was now entering the "positive" stage (adulthood) when events would be explained by scientific laws. "It is time," Comte insisted, "to complete the vast operation begun by Bacon, Descartes, and Galileo, by reconstructing the system of general ideas which must henceforth prevail amongst the human race."

Comte was not excessively modest about his aims. He provided all the details of administration for a new Western society, including a new calendar, festivals, worship of new positive saints, and new churches. He predicted that he would one day preach the gospel of positivism in Notre Dame Cathedral.[15]

Comte himself was not much interested in history as practiced by historians, and his own writings were very speculative and theoretical, but his theories had a great impact on historians. Positivist historians, as they came to call themselves in the nineteenth century, left out the speculative parts of Comte's own philosophy and concentrated instead on his prescriptions for method. They insisted that historians must begin with the documents and the facts they revealed and then develop their generalizations on a scientific model. Careful collection of documents, patient study and comparison, and the gradual accumulation of information would itself reveal the laws that determined historical development. Positivism, in one form or another, dominated the social sciences until well into the 1950s.

Darwin based his law of natural selection on the patient amassing and comparison of facts so beloved of the positivists, but when it came to public attention in 1859 it had the shattering impact of a bombshell. The full title of Darwin's book suggests its potential for controversy: *On the Origin of Species by Means of Natural Selection, or the Preservation of Favoured Races in the Struggle for Life*. Constant bloody, desperate struggles for the survival of each species marked the passage of time in Darwin's model of natural history. In the midst of all this strife, operating almost on another plane, biology randomly produced continual mutations. The species that prevailed in this situation were the ones lucky enough to have developed in ways that assisted their survival. The order and harmony of Newton's universe did not hold in biology.

Darwin insisted on the accidental nature of the developmental process. Species survived because they proved to be the

15. Karl Löwith, *Meaning in History* (Chicago, 1949), pp. 72, 90.

fittest, but they had no control over the process of mutation that made them fit in the first place. Unfortunately, Darwin was immediately misunderstood on this crucial point, and the idea of the survival of the fittest was soon taken up by racists, imperialists, and what became known more generally as social Darwinists. Although Darwin referred to pigeons and not people when he used the word "race" in his title, others used his work to explain why Europeans colonized other parts of the world (they were the superior race), why war was good (the death of the loser was "natural"), and why Anglo-Saxons should form their own organizations to rule the world. Eighty years later, Nazi racial ideologists would construct a rationale for genocide out of the same themes. Sometimes no matter what the intention of the author, books are like seeds thrown in the wind, settling in unexpected places and sometimes sprouting in stunted or misshapen form as a result.

The law of natural selection of the fittest ignited a cultural war in Darwin's time (one which continues today in the United States) between the promoters of secular science and the defenders of traditional religious values. Many hailed Darwin as the Newton of biology, and supporters viewed the evolutionary debate as nothing short of a new Reformation. By substituting natural selection for Providence, Darwin undermined the Christian belief in a divine plan and the special place of human beings in the universe. Cold, random chance ruled nature, according to Darwin, not a beneficent design. Even human beings, he argued, had not always been the same; as a species, they had probably evolved from primates. Humans, like apes, bees, and lizards, were subject to the pressures of evolution. Outraged critics protested that Darwin had reduced all humanity to the level of beasts, and opponents shouted "monkey, monkey" at speakers who defended Darwin's principles.

Where Hegel saw history as revealing the truth of the human spirit and Darwin detected the operation of the laws of nature, Marx found truth in the material laws governing human society. Marx aimed to understand the changes wrought by the

Industrial Revolution. At the base of every society lay its economic mode of production, he believed, and that in turn shaped everything in human history, including politics and culture. The mode of production determined in particular the nature of social relations and class struggles within each society. The transformation of one mode of production into another—from feudalism to industrial capitalism, for example—propelled history's forward movement. With the passion of a revolutionary, Marx propagated his discoveries. He proclaimed material forces, often expressed as a class struggle between the haves and the have-nots, to be the engine of historical change—the equivalent, in other words, of Darwin's principle of natural selection.

Exiled from continental Europe for his revolutionary activities, Marx sought his historical laws not in the laboratory of nature but rather in the archives available in the British Museum in London. There, under its magnificent rotunda, he burrowed his way through mounds of documentation about the workings of industry and capitalism. Never modest, he aimed to change the course of history by understanding its laws, unifying the Enlightenment, the French Revolution, and the Industrial Revolution into the first complete theory of history as a secular and materially based human process. Inspired by Hegel, but substituting matter for the World Spirit, Marx believed that human reason could penetrate the material meaning of history, and in particular the laws of the development of capitalism. These laws would lay the foundation for the revolutionary transformation of capitalism into communism. As Engels put it, "Just as Darwin discovered the law of development of organic nature, so Marx discovered the laws of development of human history."[16] Marx was convinced that if the victims of history understood the laws of historical development, and especially the laws of capitalism, they would learn how and when to seize control over the present and the future. There had been

16. Breisach, *Historiography*, p. 298.

revolutions before Marx, but with his theories revolutionaries could imagine themselves to be scientists.

Marxism captured the imagination of intellectuals and ordinary people too because it made sense of the brutal transformations wrought in economic and social life by the process of industrialization. Marxism also offered a theoretical explanation for the whole of human history as well as for each particular epoch within it. The idea of progress, historicism, and a scientific history seemed to come together in Marxism. Here was a vision of history informed by heroic science that offered a concrete social and economic model of the meaning of progress (the triumph of one mode of production over another), that sought the laws of change within the process of history itself (and thus was historicist), and that claimed a scientific status for the inexorable workings of social laws (and thus was determinist). Marxism also seemed to make revolutions inevitable and endorsed their benefits.

You do not have to be Hegelian, Comtian, Darwinian, or Marxist in your views in order to appreciate this series of breakthroughs in the conceptualization of human time made by the last third of the nineteenth century. Ever since then, most educated people in the West have been in some sense historicists, for they believe that their lives, both individual and collective, take shape in time, now conceived as a universal, secular continuum. Westerners cannot imagine their societies without this secular history of themselves. The schools teach it from the early years, and one of the first things children learn from their parents is their own place in this history. Colonized people learned it from Western colonizers; they then proceeded to rewrite their parts in the scripts.

The current debates about history simultaneously depend upon and challenge the Western mastery of time. Multiculturalism as a movement, for example, depends very much on historicism, for it rests on the belief that every epoch (and by extension every people) creates its own form of historical truth.

It is in many respects very Herderian, even Hegelian. Yet multiculturalists and other critics of modernity also question whether the Western universalizing, standardizing sense of time is adequate for the present age. They object to the effacement of alternative versions of time found in other cultures or in oral traditions. They are suggesting, in effect, that international and national units of time be displaced by something more specific to each group's identity.

## The Mastery of Facts

The theorists of modern history like Hegel and Comte provided an intellectual rationale for history's importance. But writing history involved more than this intellectual rationale; it required as well a mastery of the facts, that is, a knowledge of the standards by which historians sifted facts from legend. This process of sifting had often been haphazard or at best an individual affair. Historians became professionals and greatly extended their influence when history became an academic discipline in the nineteenth century with commonly accepted standards of inquiry and verification. Using archives and libraries as their laboratories, the new professionals embraced the scientific model to legitimize their standards.

In the wake of Hegel's revalidation of history in the 1820s, historians in the many German states began to develop professional standards for historical work. They were not the first to insist that history should be truthful. Thucydides, for example, had criticized his Greek predecessors for failing to distinguish between fact and legend, and the humanist historians of the Renaissance took special delight in unearthing historical forgeries perpetrated by church authorities for their own purposes. However, from the point of view of the self-proclaimed scientific historians of the nineteenth-century German universities, none of these previous efforts had done more than scratch the surface of the scientific model.

If Newton could hold a mirror up to nature and explain its

workings, then historians ought to be able to do the same for the past. To be scientific, consequently, history needed something like a laboratory and something like physical evidence. The seminar rooms and archives where university scholars taught and did research became the laboratories of history; historians sought their evidence amid the dust of actual documents and other traces left by the past. Through the seminar, invented in the 1830s by a German professor of history, Leopold von Ranke, the master teacher taught the techniques of reading and dissecting historical documents. Students learned to compare the documents rigorously; newly opened state and church archives became places where truth might be found through an interrogation of document after document. Ranke's students (all men) saw themselves as "intimate disciples" of the beloved master. "He would break into joyous laughter," one of them reported, "when he succeeded in destroying a false tradition or in reconstructing events as they occurred."[17] It is hard to imagine that quality of enthusiasm in most history classrooms today.

When professional historians wrote according to the scientific model, they employed the distant (not laughing) voice of the omniscient narrator, familiar from the realist novels of the nineteenth century and modeled on the voice of the scientists in their laboratory reports. The omniscient narrator stood above superstition and prejudice to survey calmly and dispassionately the scenes of the past and tell a truth that would be acceptable to any other researcher who had seen the same evidence and applied the same rules. In this way, with science as their model both in terms of research and writing, the German universities trained the first professional historians and soon exported them to the United States. They transformed American classrooms into seminars where every student became a seeker, an imagined re-creator of the past.

In his very first book, published in 1824, Ranke insisted that

17. G. P. Gooch, *History and Historians in the Nineteenth Century* (Boston, 1959), quote p. 107.

historians should give up the still-dominant view of history as a collection of moral instances teaching lessons through example (as in the current practice of citing the examples of appeasement at Munich or the failures of the war in Vietnam). "To history has been attributed the office to judge the past and to instruct the present to make its future useful. . . . at such high functions this present work does not aim—it merely wants to show how things really were."[18] "How things really were," that search for a scientific mirror of the historical past, soon became the motto for a scientific and objective history. Historians had to learn to overcome their prejudices and present-day interests in order to get at the truth of events in the past. Each historical epoch had to be taken on its own terms, as Herder had insisted.

Ranke's own histories were hardly disinterested. He wrote history in support of German nationalism—becoming official historiographer for the Prussian state in 1841—and believed that history revealed the hidden hand of God. Yet his techniques for training historians were eagerly taken up by professors of history in other countries who had quite different views of the meaning of the past. Ranke started his seminar in his study at home and trained two generations of men (one of his students was the crown prince of Bavaria) in the need to approach documents in a critical or hermeneutical spirit. The emphasis on professional training remained even when Ranke's own interpretations of history fell out of fashion. In recognition of his international influence, the American Historical Association named him its first honorary member when it was founded in 1884.[19] He was the international model for the master historian, and his name long seemed synonymous with the goal of objectivity.

18. As quoted in George H. Nadel, "Philosophy of History Before Historicism," *History and Theory*, 3 (1964): 291–315, quote p. 315.

19. For a good discussion of Ranke, see Lionel Gossman, *Towards a Rational Historiography*, in *Transactions of the American Philosophical Society*, vol. 79, part 3, 1989, p. 32; and Peter Novick, *That Noble Dream: The "Objectivity Question" and the American Historical Profession* (Cambridge, England, 1988), pp. 28–29.

By the 1880s, historians had taken several steps toward forming an organized professional discipline in Europe and the United States. Although amateurs still wrote history and even dominated the early years of the American Historical Association, regular forms of training in the classroom and official organizations to oversee standards had both been established. Professionalization went hand in hand with the project for a scientific history; professionalization was supposed to guarantee a scientific attitude of detachment. To be a professional meant being certified (through a higher degree) as having learned the self-discipline necessary to go beyond self-interest, bias, prejudice, and present-day concerns. This scientific professionalism was graphically demonstrated by the founding issue in 1876 of *La Revue historique,* which explained that the new journal would demand from its contributors "procedures of exposition that were strictly scientific, where every statement must be accompanied by proofs, by references to sources and by citations."[20] If one failed to use such methods, one could (then and now) both publish and perish.

Historians of the end of the nineteenth century conceived scientific history as objective because it was not concerned with philosophy or theory. The facts got priority. In words that seem to come out of the mouth of Mr. Gradgrind in Charles Dickens's *Hard Times,* a French historian exhorted his colleagues at the opening session of the First International Congress of Historians in 1900 (the meeting itself being another sign of professionalization):

We want nothing more to do with the approximations of hypotheses, useless systems, theories as brilliant as they are deceptive, superfluous moralities. Facts, facts, facts—which carry within themselves their lesson and their philosophy. The truth, all the truth, nothing but the truth.[21]

20. Gabriel Monod, *La Revue historique,* 1876, as quoted in Guy Bourdé and Hervé Martin, *Les Ecoles historiques* (Paris, 1983), p. 141.

21. As quoted in Novick, *That Noble Dream,* pp. 37–38.

Where Gradgrind's facts signaled a cold and oppressive view of a world without emotion, the historian's facts stood in the speaker's mind for a kind of liberation. An amazing turnabout had taken place. History had long been considered the servant of philosophy; now historians aimed to sever their discipline from philosophy in the interest of attaining scientific results. Facts came before philosophy; theory was a "useless system." History had to be autonomous as a discipline if it was to be objective and scientific. To this day, blood pressure rises among some historians at the very mention of the word "theory." Chapter 6 will explore some of the reasons why this might be so.

By the beginning of the twentieth century, the new professional historians had developed a scientific model of their craft that set it apart from philosophy or theory. They had been influenced by the insights of philosophers and theorists such as Hegel and Comte, but they had no desire to follow the same philosophical and theoretical veins in their own work. They believed that history could contribute to progress only if historians behaved like scientists. Just as Newton's law of gravitation applied in every country and culture, so too good history should be able to transcend national differences. As Lord Acton explained to his collaborators on the *Cambridge Modern History*, "our Waterloo must be one that satisfies French and English, Germans and Dutch alike."[22] Although historians differed about just how scientific history could be and about the role of generalization or general laws, history went its way henceforth as a discipline almost wholly separated from philosophy. The philosophy of history was and still is a branch of philosophy, not history.

### Imperialist, Scientific History in the West

Historians founded an independent, autonomous discipline by developing new notions of time and new professional

22. Breisach, *Historiography*, p. 284.

codes of conduct. These developments took place in the context of intense intellectual and political struggles, pitting secularizers against Christian clergymen and then professional academics against popularizers, amateurs, and various forms of true believers. The very idea of a historian transcending his or her prejudices to write a scientific history of the march toward modernity depended as a political project on the Enlightenment sense of the modern and of progress. Once established, however, those political origins were often forgotten. Over time, professional historians set up their own kinds of absolutism in the name of universal (synonymous with Western) science and progress, and they set out to incorporate the whole world into their schemas of interpretation. We call this ambition imperialist in recognition of its universalizing and globalizing impulse. We do not imply that individual historians always, or even most of the time, wrote in support of imperialist policies.

Despite its many varieties, professional history in the twentieth century has been usually written under the sign of "modernization," the general process by which the West, defined as the paradigmatic model, and then the rest of the world became modern. This can hardly be surprising, given that the idea of modernity has shaped the development of Western history ever since the eighteenth century. And history is far from alone in this emphasis. In the early decades of the twentieth century, as economics, sociology, political science, psychology, and anthropology each established their own autonomous spheres of inquiry, one main question guided research in all of them, as well as in history: how did the modern world come about, and what lessons does the Western trajectory toward the modern offer to the rest of the world? The operating principles of industrial markets or technology transfers, the forms of modern social and political interaction, the psychological effects of growth and differentiation, and the impact of rapid change on Third World peoples—all these can be seen as derivatives of the main question about modernization.

Two great social theorists of the early twentieth century, Max Weber and Emile Durkheim, both wrestled with these questions and gave answers that are influential to this day. They sought alternatives to Marx's analysis of modernization, but they started from the same Enlightenment standpoint as Marx: we are modern, and our task is to understand what that entails. In contrast to Marx's insistence on modes of production, social struggle, and revolution, the German social theorist Weber underlined the synergistic effects of markets, states, and bureaucracies in integrating ever larger groups of people, while the French sociologist Durkheim emphasized the corrosive impact of increasing differentiation of functions, growing isolation of individuals, and the breakdown of community and guild structures. Whatever their differences of emphasis and interpretation, Weber and Durkheim were both much less optimistic than Marx about the long-term results of this process. Yet along with Marx, they helped give birth to the long-dominant modernization perspective, in which history is mustered to explain the origin of the forces that make the modern world modern.

Marx, Durkheim, and Weber inspired the three main schools of Western historical interpretation in the twentieth century: Marxism, the French Annales school, and American modernization theory. As the label suggests, Marxist history owes its origins to Marx's own trenchant diagnoses of modernity. Durkheim's emphasis on the effects of long-term social processes can be seen in the French Annales (so named after its flagship journal) school's interest in broad demographic and economic trends rather than in traditional political, diplomatic, or biographical accounts. American social-scientific models that developed in the 1950s and 1960s under the rubric of "modernization theory" (a special case of what we are calling more generally the modernization perspective) showed the impact of Weber's comparative studies on the origins of modernity. Needless to say, all history writing in this century does not fit neatly into one of these three categories, and Annales school history and modernization models cannot be very easily divided between the legacies of Durkheim and Weber. Yet as general models for the goals and methods of history, these three lines of interpretation have been primary, especially since World War II.

Lumping Marxism, the Annales school, and American modernization theory together does run the risk of mixing apples and oranges, or perhaps even apples, walnuts, and broccoli, so different are the three in some respects. Marxism has influenced history writing since the 1870s, and in some places it has been directly associated with a ruling party. Only Marxism, moreover, ever achieved the dubious status of a recognized national and international orthodoxy. The Annales school took shape as a branch of French history just before World War II and then extended its impact internationally, but it—like Marxism—has remained relatively uninfluential in the United States. American modernization theory was the specifically American answer to Marxism, but it came directly out of American sociology and political science in the post–World War II period and never had much influence outside the United States.

What the three have in common, however, is at least as important as their considerable differences: all three were imagined by their adherents as universally applicable and scientific in method and thus all three helped foster a Western history that aimed to homogenize the study of all other places and times into general Western models of historical development. Whether historians emphasized class struggle (Marxists), broad demographic changes (Annales school), or the development of new networks of investment and communication (modernization theory), they expected their explanations to apply to the whole world, and they confidently set out to show that their models could work everywhere. Nobody escapes the modernizing process.

Marx offered the boldest, most provocative account of modernization with his analysis of changing modes of production and class conflict leading to revolution. In British and French universities in the 1930s and 1940s, some of the brightest young historians were attracted to Marxism and in some cases joined the Communist Party. In the postwar era, the best of them—Christopher Hill, Eric Hobsbawm, E. P. Thompson, and Albert Soboul—wrote books that shaped a generation or more of historical thinking. Their emphasis on "history from below" inspired the rejection of the traditional histories of political leaders, ideas, and institutions in favor of the social history of workers, servants, and the poor. History graduate students still learned the methods of Ranke in their seminars, but debates about Marxism and its relevance often fueled their passion for the subject.

Marxism had the most direct influence in Eastern Europe, because it was the official ideology of ruling parties in the Soviet Union and its satellites after World War II. In the Soviet-bloc countries, historians had to declare their allegiance to Marxism if they wanted to publish books and hold professional positions. The situation was much more complicated in Western Europe. There, Marxism might have remained a dry academic question (in the absence of successful revolutionary movements) had it not been for Hitler and the rise of fascism in the 1930s. For many Western intellectuals, only Marxism seemed to have enough ethical, political, and social clout to combat fascism, and they did not or would not see the dangers of the Marxism being put into practice in the new Soviet Union. Thus Marxist history found very different outlooks in Eastern and Western Europe. In the east, Marxism not only dominated but excluded all other options, at least on paper, while in the west, Marxism reemerged in the 1930s as an oppositional ideology.

In the United States, the impact of Marxism has been more diffuse and general than in either Western or Eastern Europe. Few American historians have written explicitly as Marxists, but Marxism has nonetheless forced historians in the United States to consider systematically the effects of capitalism on social and political conflict and to pay more attention to the historical fate of the lower orders. Many historians who reject the main lines of Marxism—the emphasis on inevitable revolution or the ubiquity of class struggle, for instance—still believe that history is fundamentally a material process in which economics shapes social, cultural, and political life. Even anti-Marxists were shaped by their interactions with the Marxism they encountered in their general education. The Annales school and modernization theory gained adherents in the West, after all, precisely because they were non-Marxist modes of historical explanation that still took the question of modernization seriously.

Marxists considered their history just as scientific as that of their competitors, if not more so. Western Marxists, in particular, maintained that Marxist history could be impartial even when it was motivated by a passion for change. One of the greatest socialist historians in the English-speaking world, R. H. Tawney, insisted in 1912, "If a man wants to do serious scientific work in any sphere, he must become impersonal, suppress his own fancies and predilections, and try and listen to reason speaking in him."[23] This was still very similar to the Rankean vision, and it is this impartiality that supports the ambition to subsume all history under the Marxist framework.

Many historians nonetheless rejected Marxism because they associated it with determinism and reductionism, i.e., with efforts to reduce all of history to material causes, thus overlooking the influence of ideas, emotions, personalities, and accidents. The association of Marxism with communism after the Bolshevik revolution of 1917 in Russia further tainted Marxism for many historians and even made some of them suspicious of any effort to explain history in terms of general laws or theories. The search for the correct historical laws seemed hopelessly mired in revolutionary politics. The ideological thrust of Marxist-Leninist history-writing in Eastern Europe can be seen in a speech of 1931 given by the Russian historian M. N. Pokrovsky, who described the tasks of the Society of Marxist Historians as "the unmasking of the bourgeois historians" (the historians of

23. J. M. Winter and D. M. Joslin, eds., *R. H. Tawney's Commonplace Book, Economic History Review*, Supplement 5 (Cambridge, England, 1972), pp. 41–42.

the West still influenced by capitalist ideology) and coming to grips "with its fundamental enemy in the period ahead—the deviationists" (i.e., those who deviated from the true Leninist line within Marxism). For him, this meant that history "must reveal and submit to a merciless Marxist-Leninist analysis."[24] It was precisely this image of submission to an ideology that troubled many historians in the West.

The French Annales school offered an alternative to Marxism in the postwar period, yet it relied on an equally and perhaps even more ambitious vision of history. French historians of the school tried to solve the enduring problem of history's relation to the other disciplines by developing a concept of "total history," the none-too-modest notion whose very name conveys the design to comprehend everyone's history in one general model. In total history, historians would incorporate the methods of all the other social sciences in one great project of synthesis. History would be the queen of the social sciences by virtue of its ability to assimilate everyone else's methods and topics. Lucien Febvre explained the need for total history: "Man cannot be carved into slices. He is a whole. One must not divide all of history—here the events, there the beliefs."[25] Annales history had to be "total" if it was to respond adequately to the challenge of Marxism by developing an alternative model of a universalizing history.

The great systematizer of the Annales school was Fernand Braudel, who in the 1940s wrote his first great work while interned in a German camp for prisoners of war. Braudel developed an influential three-tiered model of historical explanation. Climate, biology, and geography in the bottom tier ruled over

24. As quoted in Fritz Stern, *The Varieties of History: From Volatire to the Present* (Cleveland and New York, 1956), pp. 336–38.

25. As quoted in Breisach, *Historiography*, p. 371. For the history of the Annales school, see Traian Stoianovich, *French Historical Method: The Annales Paradigm* (Ithaca, N.Y., 1976); and Bourdé and Martin, *Les Ecoles historiques*. The Annales school got its name from the journal *Annales d'histoire économique et sociale*, founded in 1929 by Marc Bloch and Lucien Febvre. The journal moved to Paris in the 1930s and took its current name, *Annales: Economies, Sociétés, Civilisations*, in 1946.

long-term population movements and economic trends. Social structures and patterns, more clearly subject to the fluctuations of the medium term (defined usually in units of ten, twenty, or even fifty years), constituted a second order of historical reality. Politics, culture, and intellectual life were viewed as a third, largely dependent level of historical experience. In a famous passage, Braudel likened the events of history so prominent in traditional accounts to "surface disturbances, crests of foam that the tides of history carry on their strong backs."[26] What mattered was not the quickly disappearing foam but the enduring factors of material life that made up the tides pulling the waves themselves. All of world history could be explained in terms of those historical tides.

The Annales model of total history resembled the Marxist paradigm, especially in the dominance ascribed to long-term economic developments over political and intellectual ones. But the Annales school deemphasized class struggle and modes of production and underlined the importance instead of underlying demographic processes. Annales historians insisted particularly on what Durkheim had called "social facts"—long-term processes such as population growth or contraction, price curves, harvest yields, tax receipts, and the like. These indicators could be studied through serial records and quantifiable methods that measured the ebb and flow of societies.

Under the leadership of Braudel, the Annales school developed a wide following in the 1960s, especially in Europe and Latin America. By the 1970s, the prestige of the school was worldwide; the *International Handbook of Historical Studies* published in 1979, for instance, included more index entries for the Annales school than for any other subject except Marx and Marxism.[27] The Annales school's emphasis on economic and

26. Fernand Braudel, *The Mediterranean and the Mediterranean World in the Age of Philip II*, 2 vols., tr. Siân Reynolds (New York, 1972; French edition 1949), quote vol. 1, p. 21.

27. Georg G. Iggers and Harold T. Parker, eds., *International Handbook of Historical Studies* (Westport, Conn., 1979).

social history soon spread even to the more traditional historical journals. By the early 1970s, economic and social history had
replaced biography and religious history as the largest categories after political history in many conventional journals.[28]

The Annales school—along with Marxism—fostered the
growth of social history in the twentieth century. Whereas
nineteenth-century historians had made vague references to "the
people," social historians in the twentieth century sought to
uncover the lives of ordinary people in all their richness. Ordinary people—peasants, workers, immigrants, for example—had
been left out of traditional historical accounts because they did
not make the political and military decisions for a whole society.
By questioning the lasting importance of those political and
military decisions and emphasizing instead the enduring demographic patterns—of marriage, childbearing, and death, for
example—which shaped societies over a much longer term, the
Annales school helped establish social history as a field of research.

American modernization theory, the third of the major
schools of historical interpretation in the twentieth century,
aimed to unify the increasing diversity of historical research in
its own non-Marxist model of historical development. As defined by one of its early proponents,

there is a single process of modernization which operates in all developing societies—regardless of their colour, creed, or climate and regardless of their history, geography, or culture. This is the process of
economic development, and . . . development cannot be sustained
without modernization.[29]

28. Alain Corbin, "*La Revue historique:* Analyse du contenu d'une publication rivale
des *Annales*," in Charles-Olivier Carbonell and Georges Livet, eds., *Au Berceau des
Annales: Le milieu strasbourgeois, L'histoirie en France au début du XXe siècle* (Toulouse,
1979), p. 136. For other journals, see Lynn Hunt, "French History in the Last Twenty
Years: The Rise and Fall of the *Annales* Paradigm," *Journal of Contemporary History,* 21
(1986): 209–24.

29. Daniel Lerner, as quoted in Charles Tilly, *Big Structures, Large Processes, Huge
Comparisons* (New York, 1984), p. 46.

In this characteristically circular definition, modernization and economic development were intimately linked; economic development was the key process in modernization but economic development could not take place without modernization, which was defined to include a shift from agriculture to industry, the rise of cities, the expansion of education, particularly in science and technology, and a host of concomitant intellectual and psychological changes. Many modernization theorists, following Weber's lead, emphasized the role of intellectual and psychological changes in producing a rational and autonomous self that was essential to modernization more generally. What is most striking in the definition of modernization, however, is not so much its circularity as its aim to be all-encompassing. According to modernization theory, all developing societies, whatever their differences, were bound to go through a similar set of changes. This was universal history with a vengeance, with all of its imperialistic implications for non-Western societies.

Modernization theorists studied how the process came about in the past in order, in part, to develop models for understanding the Third World in the present. One of the most influential modernization models was W. W. Rostow's takeoff theory of industrialization. Rostow developed a model of what he termed "industrial takeoff" based on the Western experience in the eighteenth and nineteenth centuries with the hope of applying it to non-Western societies. Focusing on Britain in the last quarter of the eighteenth century, he used mechanical notions of acceleration and force to describe the self-sustaining process of industrial growth that had itself been assisted by applied mechanics.

Modernization theorists generally emphasized the destabilizing impact of rapid economic and urban growth and its tendency to promote political violence in a variety of forms (actually their Durkheimian side, one example of the dangers of schematic categorization). One theorist explained, "The very fact that modernization entails continual changes in all spheres of a

society means of necessity that it involves processes of disorga-
nization and dislocation." Social problems, group conflicts, and
protest movements (the very things that were increasingly apparent in the 1960s) could all be explained as the strains of
modernization.[30]

American historians did not need modernization theory to
point them toward social history. In the first decades of the
twentieth century—before the French Annales school had even
taken shape—a group of American historians called the New
Historians urged their colleagues to escape "from the limitations formerly imposed upon the study of the past" and include
the widest possible range of sources in their analysis.[31] The
experience of democracy and diversity inevitably put "the social" on the agenda of historians. But without a theoretical
model like Marxism or totalizing methods like those proposed
by the Annales school, the new history in America ran the risk
of increasing fragmentation. Modernization theory promised
to subsume all this new research under one coherent model.
For a time, it gained many adherents. In a general review of
contemporary historical writing in the United States published
in 1980, for example, modernization theory ranked in importance right alongside the Annales school, Marxism, interdisci-
plinary developments, specialization, quantitative methods, and
social science and social theory.[32]

This list is suggestive, for it links the three dominant models
of history in the twentieth century with the professionalization
of history as a discipline, with its relationship to the other social
sciences, and with quantitative methods. Like the Annales school,

30. S. N. Eisenstadt as quoted in Tilly, *Big Structures,* p. 54. For Rostow's theory of
industrial takeoff see, W. W. Rostow, *The Stages of Economic Growth* (Cambridge,
England, 1960).

31. James Harvey Robinson defined the new history as including "every trace and
vestige of everything that man has done or thought since first he appeared on earth. . . .
Its sources of information extend from the rude flint hatchets of Chelles to this morning's newspaper." As quoted in Stern, *Varieties of History,* pp. 265, 258.

32. This ranking is based on the index to Michael Kammen, ed., *The Past Before Us:
Contemporary Historical Writing in the United States* (Ithaca, N.Y., 1980), pp. 511–24.

modernization theory offered the prospect of making history more like a social science, and it was often linked, like the Annales school, to the use of quantitative methods in historical research.

For their proponents, the systematic collection of quantifiable documents and the application of quantitative measures guaranteed the scientific status of history and held out the promise of a true universalization of method. Quantitative methods could be applied to any culture, any epoch, and virtually any historical question. They were thus ideally suited to the study of modernization across the world. Historians used statistics to prove the efficiency or inefficiency of slave economies, to develop models of family life in preindustrial and industrial times, and to trace the impact of European diseases on native populations in the New World. The more historians used statistical techniques, it was hoped, the more their discipline would resemble science itself. Quantitative methods seemed ideal for ensuring detachment and impartiality, for letting the facts speak for themselves, in short, for mathematizing history. Thus the use of quantitative methods enabled Western historians to make even bigger claims for the purview of their discipline.

Despite its initial promise and its association with quantitative methods, modernization theory's direct influence proved to be short-lived. Just as it had risen on the wave of Third World tumult in the aftermath of decolonization in the 1950s and 1960s, so too it then fell into disrepute in the wake of the Vietnam War. In the United States modernization theory came under attack for a variety of reasons. Some historians found it inherently ahistorical because it was based on sociological theorizing. Others criticized it as ethnocentric because it used development in the West as a standard for judging non-Western societies and cultures. In addition, modernization theory came under fire because it was prominent in strategic studies undertaken during the Vietnam War. As a concept it was tarred by the brush of American efforts to intervene in Third World politics.

For all these reasons, modernization theory receded into the background and now claims few dedicated adherents in historical circles. Yet despite the decline of modernization theory as a model, the questions that it posed remain as vital as ever and continue to exert a profound influence on historical study. The mere existence of journals such as *World Development* and *Comparative Studies in Society and History* shows that many scholars continue to seek lessons in the modernization of the West for current-day economic and political development. In the 1990s historians and social scientists emphasize the differences between the West and other areas of the globe, rather than assuming the operation of a universal model, but they still take Western development as a fundamental starting point for comparison.

Although modernization theory declined in influence, the belief in a scientific history and the idea of a total history remained powerful until very recently. The appearance of computers made quantitative methods even more attractive and held out the prospect of a rapidly accumulating store of knowledge. Moreover, knowledge of the world seemed crucial to success in the continuing Cold War, and the American government consequently funded new area studies programs (Southeast Asia, South Asia, Soviet Union and Eastern Europe, Latin America, etc.), study in foreign languages, and research in history about every corner of the globe.

All of this work rested on the principles that had evolved since the mid-nineteenth century: a modern, scientific history could incorporate every place on earth into one secular universal story with the aim of understanding the patterns of development. Even though most individual historians no longer aimed to tell the whole universal story themselves in the manner of Hegel or Marx, history as a discipline depended on the belief that professional historians were writing pieces of that story. Getting the story right would help push forward the process of modernization (and progress) itself. As subsequent chapters will make clear, in the United States every element of this vision has now come under attack, raising questions about the future of history itself.

Before turning to that story of challenge, however, it is important to recognize the remarkable power of the notions of impartial science and scientific history in the service of modernization. The heroic image of an unprejudiced, dispassionate, all-seeing scientific investigator seemed to promise not only unparalleled material improvements through science and industry but also the end of superstition, fanaticism, and all other forms of intellectual and political absolutism. By developing the modern concepts of historical time as standardized and universal and of the role of the historian as master of the facts of everyone's history, historians were able to set themselves new tasks. They told the story of progress toward the modern, of history as emancipation from the darkness of the past. Their history now had a meaning deeply implicated in the modern world. Despite the horrors wrought by modern warfare and technology, most historians continue to embrace modernity as the only alternative to the ignorance and relative poverty of most "traditional" societies.

In telling history "as it really was," unencumbered by interpretations of divine will or recourse to the Bible, historians believed themselves to be facilitating progress toward the modern. Historians thus helped establish a distinctly Western mastery, not only of time and facts as universal entities, susceptible to study by any impartial investigator, but also, eventually, of everyone else's history. The social history of workers, slaves, and immigrants and the histories of Third World peoples could all be incorporated into the dominant Western models of historical development, whether in the form of Marxism, the Annales school, or modernization theory. These models were all imperialist in their aim to encompass everyone. At times, they served the purposes of Eastern-bloc or Western-bloc political imperialism—and thus the Cold War—as well. Some Marxist history helped bolster Soviet-style communism; some modernization theory directly served U.S. interests abroad; and the

Annales school seemed to offer a third path with the same general result, Western (but in this case Western European) mastery. The next chapter will show how these new notions of history worked themselves out in the American national saga, a saga informed by the belief in a people's unique suitability for progress and for modernity.

° 3 °

# *History Makes a Nation*

B Y THE TIME the United States became a nation in 1776, history had been wrenched from the hands of balladeers and chroniclers and entrusted to the philosophes, who were busy sinking the firm footings of rational inquiry under all forms of knowledge. Still dazzled by the ability of Newton to explain the solar system, many Western thinkers came to believe that the movements of human beings, like those of celestial bodies, could be comprehended through scientific laws. This intellectual shift made the past more than a repository of facts, because it now seemed to contain clues about the direction of the future.

In this transit from poetry and chronicles to social science, historians took on the responsibility of sifting through the facts about past events in search of the underlying logic shaping the course of social development. Influenced by Herder and Hegel, they asserted that a new political entity, the nation, embodied human purposes and hence should be studied for its clues about the meaning in unfolding events. Thus history and science, which had recently been converted into sources of information about the human enterprise, became intimately associated with a third modern force, the nation.

Nations themselves had become prominent parts of the European landscape, because in the early nineteenth century the wars of the French Revolution had carried radical reform to France's neighbors, toppling assorted European monarchs from their thrones. Where the word "kingdom" indicated a territory belonging to a single ruler and "country" suggested a land where people had lived long together as subjects, "nation" evoked the very modern concept of men and women self-consciously banded together into a political union. With nationalism as an engine of political and social reform, people looked to national history to illuminate the course of human progress that had brought modern nations into being.

Nations figure as places on the map or as sovereign states resplendently personified at international gatherings. Their definition as collections of people is much more elusive despite the fact that nations only exist because of the will of their citizens to accept themselves as a unified body. Watching the fierce loyalties of ethnicity dissolve national states in Eastern Europe, one cannot help but wonder what are the invisible ties that weld a people into a nation. For Americans at the time of independence, that question was highly pertinent, because they had to create the sentiments of nationhood which other countries took for granted. There was no uniform ethnic stock, no binding rituals from an established church, no common fund of stories, only a shared act of rebellion. Americans had to invent what Europeans inherited: a sense of solidarity, a repertoire of national symbols, a quickening of political passions.

The superior resources for fixing a national identity which Americans lacked and other countries enjoyed were well depicted in a French schoolboy's geography text of the 1960s. The book's centerfold featured a line of French men and boys, visually paired by their clothing, stretching across two pages like a string of paper dolls. At the far left, the man and boy, obviously father and son, were dressed in contemporary clothes, the man holding the hand of the next boy, who wore knickers and knee-high boots with his father in a double-breasted suit and fedora. The next pair were dressed in the fashion of the turn of the century, and so on across the two pages, ending with a Carolingian father in doublet and hose. No viewer could miss the essence of French nationhood; it sprang from an unbroken chain of French fathers who had lived long in the land and propagated. This imaginative drawing graphically captured that fact while underscoring the masculine underpinnings of modern nationalism.

With the ratification of a new American Constitution in 1789, a structure of central authority came into being in the United States (a noun used with a plural verb at the time), but only a handful of Americans—most of them revolutionary leaders—felt the national sentiments necessary for the survival of the new political creation. As one contemporary metaphorically noted, the new Constitution had raised a federal roof without federal walls. Twenty years later, the problem was less acute, but still a subject of concern. In 1809, during the last month he spent in the White House, Thomas Jefferson received a letter from the Westward Mill Library Society of New Brunswick County, Virginia, inviting his patronage. "Our society," the secretary wrote the president, "is composed of farmers, mechanics, Justices of the Peace, ministers of the Gospel—Military Officers, Lawyers, School masters—merchants—postmasters, one member of the Assembly & one member of Congress." He then gave the names of the six directors for the year: "Hubbard Hobbs—John Harrison (both planters) Joseph Percivall (a naturalized citisen), Jesse Coe (an Elder in the Methodist Church) Joseph Saunders (a Deacon in the Baptist church) and Mark Green (a Major in the Militia of Virginia)." In closing his letter the secretary posed an arresting question: "Query will such an heterogeneous body ever firmly . . . . coalesce?"[1] Here in microcosm was the macrocosmic problem of the American people, the ideological imperative of E Pluribus Unum, the intensely felt need to create a union from the disparate groups that formed their country.

## The Problem of National Identity

Much has been said and written about Americans' pride in their unique heritage, but before being transmogrified into a

---

1. Jefferson Papers, Firestone Library, Princeton, MS. #45052.

the conspicuous differences among the people
tates caused much uneasiness. Americans knew
f a commonwealth was one king, one church,
and one tongue, and certainly colonial leaders had striven to
achieve that organic unity. The Revolution offered patriots the
rhetorical opportunity to treat America's social diversity as a
summons to a new kind of nationhood, but old sensibilities
lingered on. What a successful War for Independence could not
supply were the shared sentiments, symbols, and social explanations necessary for an integrative national identity. Much of
the bombast about America's unique calling to nurture freedom
for the entire human race should be heard as rather nervous
whistling in the dark or, more accurately, whistling through
the graveyard of failed republics unable to secure the unity and
solidarity that monarchies imposed.

Scholarly preoccupation with political history has encouraged the view that national integration was largely a matter of
muting the autonomous tendencies of thirteen once-sovereign
states or of working out compromises among antagonistic sec-
tions of the United States rather than one of creating a common
identity to undergird the whole. The Westward Mill Library
Society presents the situation in its most mundane form: could
a people split into a dozen religious denominations, shedding
the social forms that separated mechanics from militia majors,
divided between native-born and naturalized citizens, unify?
And if so, on which and whose terms? Could Americans will
themselves into a national culture as they had willed themselves
into a War for Independence?

As one might expect from an activity which distributed
social power, fashioning a national self-image became itself a
contentious process. The fighting of the War for Independence
had not turned Americans into a united people. Rather it had
created the problem of nationalism—that imperative to form a
more perfect union once the practical tasks of fighting a common enemy and securing a peace treaty no longer exerted cen-
tripetal pressure. The citizens of the United States at the end of

the Revolution had not only *not* lived long in their land; the land they lived in wasn't even theirs. Until recently much of it had belonged to other people. Indeed, the domain they coveted beyond the Appalachian Mountains still remained part of the ancestral holdings of Amerindians.

Caught geographically between native Americans and Europeans, Americans were also betwixt two rationales for the social use of land: the European doctrines bestowing land to countries capable of "effective occupation" and the Indians' belief that human societies could no more own land than they could own the sun and air. The apologetics for conquest which had served a European power like Great Britain had little usefulness to the independent United States. In the age of exploration, European navigators, enjoying the patronage of monarchs, had sallied forth from metropolitan centers where their right to conquer was recognized at home and their might made right abroad. Their religious evangelical traditions accommodated—even encouraged—the subjugation of heathen peoples while their hierarchical political forms greatly facilitated governing others in distant lands. Uniquely situated, the new American nation was an alien European outpost perched on the Atlantic shelf of a vast continent, its legal link to Great Britain severed by rebellion. An alternative line of reasoning was required to explain why the new republic should send its people to dislodge the native inhabitants of the vast North American continent.

The thirteen now-independent states represented a hodgepodge from which to form a nation. Only retrospectively can historians assign to their similarities more prominence than their differences. The commonalities that did exist among them—those of language, law, and institutional history—all pointed in the wrong direction, backward to the past, toward an association with England, whose utility as a contemptible oppressor could not easily be done without. Their common Protestant heritage looks homogeneous only retrospectively. At the time a dozen or more denominations and sects warred against each other, most claiming for their doctrines an exclusive orthodoxy. There was one common and inspiring document—the Declaration of Independence—but its self-evident truths that all men were created equal proved more divisive than conciliating, in a society of slave-holders.

The American Revolution had not produced a nation, much less a unified people. The Constitution provided new institutions for national governance, but its very success in removing power from local majorities worked against the forming of a popular, patriotic culture. Even the Philadelphia delegates who gathered in 1787 to consider strengthening the central government made the case for a more perfect union not through appeals to symbol and sentiment, but in a lawyerly fashion that emphasized procedures and structures. They built their argument for a reconstructed national government on reasoned discussions about defensive strategies against foreign powers and interstate cooperation for trading purposes.

Despite the openness of the ratification process with its specially elected conventions in the states, the fifteen-hundred-odd delegates who debated the constitutional plan during 1787 and 1788 represented an extension of the revolutionary elite. They earned their offices in free elections while retaining the political mores of a closed ruling body. Theirs was a nationalism of practical wisdom. Outside their circles of political conversation, there were few shared assumptions operating at the intimate level of human experience and a paucity of positive symbols easily recognized from one end of the Atlantic shelf to the other. Theirs was a nation without a national ideology, save the shared understandings of its leaders. Indeed, the Founding Fathers offered a neocolonial answer to the problem of unity—direction from the center exercised by officials deliberately holding themselves aloof from the people.

Americans' self-congratulation at their success in establishing a new and more powerful federal government did stimulate enthusiasm for their new career in self-government. The return of prosperity after a postrevolutionary depression also strengthened confidence in the republican experiment, but the working out of the content of American identity did not take place until the mid-1790s, when the events of the French Revolution converged with new development in American domestic politics.

Quite unexpectedly, the proclamation of the French Republic called forth a new cohort of American radicals, most of them too young to have engaged in the protests against the British. They took up the French cause as their own, finding in the destructive fury of 1793 a confirmation of the portentousness of the moment. The French Revolution opened the way for a reinterpretation of the American Revolution as the initial act in a historic drama of liberation, now sweeping Europe. The French embrace of newness itself suggested that the novelties of American society were harbingers of things to come rather than egregious examples of raw provincialism.

Long uprooted from their European past, American citizens could plant themselves in the imaginative soil of a visionary future. The rhetoric of Republican France roused political passions in the United States at the very time that members of Washington's administration were congratulating themselves upon having achieved stability through the workings of an energetic central government. The hoped-for deference from ordinary voters dissolved into a round of public demonstrations in support of French military victories. Political clubs formed in flagrant imitation of the Jacobins, and Republican newspapers were founded for the sole purpose of attacking the government.

In an unusually probing analysis of the social basis for elite power, the new radicals—who called themselves Republicans—precipitated a divisive controversy about popular political participation itself. Thus disputes about specific issues brought to light even more profound disagreements about the nature of democratic governance. Their denunciatory attacks on the established authorities continued unabated until the election of Thomas Jefferson in 1800. Jefferson won the presidency in an exuberantly contentious campaign which sharply defined the choices between gentry rule and popular power, changing forever the nation's political culture and fixing the character of participatory politics in the United States for the next sixty years.

At the same time, America had entered into a period of great commercial prosperity—in part a consequence of its role in shipping as a neutral carrier for the belligerent nations of Europe. This prosperity promoted the construction of roads, the extension of postal services, and the founding of newspapers in country towns. A dense new communication network vastly increased the resonance of partisan disputes. The control over information and opinions once exercised by an elite had been wrested away by articulate critics of the elite. Male literacy outside the South approached the 90 percent level, with female literacy following the same upward climb. The tactical advantages that accrued to an upper class small enough for concerted action were now overpowered by the mobilization of popular majorities through print campaigns.

### History and National Identity

In retrospect one can see that the French Revolution enabled Americans to liberate themselves from the Eurocentric orientation of their colonial past, but it was a socially specific liberation. The Federalists' defeat at the polls predisposed many elite families to withdraw from national politics and leave the issue of nationalism for others to define. The rambunctious politics of the 1790s brought disillusionment to a number of cultural nationalists like Noah Webster, Charles Brockden Brown, and Samuel Latham Mitchill who had expected the free institutions of America to promote literature, science, and scholarship. Their nationalist fervor had been nourished by fantasies of American greatness in areas marked out by the high civilization of metropolitan Europe. For them the outburst of revolutionary passion from uneducated men had proved the conservatives right: when the pot boils the scum rises. The political rejection of the Federalists reflected more than a change of personnel; it marked the defeat of a venerable conception of authority while creating a new sense of what it was to be American.

Those who were liberated from America's traditional orientation to Europe were the ordinary men and women who sought affirmation of their tastes and values in the celebration of what was distinctively American: its institutional permissiveness, its pervasive practicality, its reforming zeal, above all its expanded scope for action for ordinary people. In the decades that followed Jefferson's election, the meaning of a democratic political order became manifest. People did not just want to vote; they wanted to experience full social participation—gathering in quasi-public meetings, debating matters of policy, mobilizing fellow citizens, and forming groups based on the affinities of conviction. The single most striking feature of the early republic's social life came from the spontaneous generation of thousands of voluntary associations, a phenomenon that announced the arrival of an American public, a body of men and women actively committed to participating in the life of the nation and to interpreting the significance of the United States.

The formation of new voluntary associations was only limited by the reigning social imagination. There was even an Association of American Patriots for the Purpose of Forming a National Character, started in 1808. Organizations formed to build circulating libraries, like the Westward Mill Library Society that had written to Jefferson, abounded. The zeal for self-improvement found outlets in debating and study clubs, a particular favorite among young adults. Fire societies multiplied with the growth of cities along with other mutual benefit associations. Almost all religious denominations had auxiliaries. Women were unusually active in this new associational life as the principal organizers for the provision of charity, founding female domestic missionary societies and homes for friendless women in every town.

The most common impulse promoting voluntary clubs was

the urge to reform society—often prompted by a religious revival. First and most enduringly there was the temperance movement, then reform of prisons and hospitals, sabbatarianism, later nativism, and, most productive of reforming zeal, the antislavery movement. There were literally hundreds of antislavery societies, many flourishing in the South. These multifarious voluntary associations revealed an efficiency in mobilizing recruits and in circulating information that far exceeded anything done by public authority.

Where the educated elite had wished to establish national identity upon the basis of America's distinctive contributions to established realms of achievement, the reformers and revivalists were expressing a different sense of nationhood. For them the United States represented a new kind of social existence in which personal fulfillment came through public initiatives. The activists' optimism about concerted efforts to eliminate slavery, correct the treatment of the insane and criminal, reorganize charity, and raise the tone of public morals became a part of American character. Solidarity in this highly mobile society would be fashioned from the outpouring of energy devoted to social betterment. Defeating the establishment's presidential candidate, mobilizing volunteers for a dozen reform activities, asserting a right to define the content of Americanism, the public spokesmen who emerged in the 1790s saw well that they could build their own national structure on the revolutionary foundation.

During these same years, nationalism became a powerful force throughout Europe, not just in the United States. Swept up by the revolutionary momentum begun in France, more and more people began to think of themselves as citizens with new responsibilities to assume in the public realm where science was fostered, history written, and social policy determined. The new industrial order began luring people to factory jobs in burgeoning cities, breaking up the intimate communities of an older, agrarian world. Industrialization also promoted literacy and cheap printing, which meant that newspapers and journals designed for a large reading public became widely available. Shared information, shared stories, shared symbols invisibly pulled adult readers into a new association dependent upon the mutual ties of language, commerce, and governance. With these common reference points, people could form what Benedict Anderson has called an "imagined community" to take the place of the intensely real rural communities they left behind.[2]

Sensing that written records of the American Revolution could supply the deficiency of venerable traditions, religious uniformity, and common descent, the aging witnesses of the Revolution took up their pens in the closing years of the eighteenth century. Moved by their own awe at the momentousness of the events of the 1770s, they wrote their country's first histories, filling the "imagined community" of American nationalism with the details of heroism and virtue generated by the war itself. Most ambitious in this exploitation of memory were a half-dozen men and one woman who embarked on multivolume studies, almost all of them drawing on personal experience. John Marshall found time from his duties as Supreme Court chief justice to write a life of George Washington, whom he had first encountered at Valley Forge when he was a twenty-one-year-old Virginia regular. David Ramsay and Hugh Williamson had served as surgeons in the Continental Army; Edmund Randolph accompanied Washington to Boston as an aide-de-camp before he became a Virginia delegate to the Continental Congress. The historians Jeremy Belknap, Benjamin Trumbull, and William Gordon, all Congregational clergymen, preached to the troops in the field. Mercy Otis Warren, whose brother and husband were famous Boston patriots, wielded a pen in part because her sex denied her the opportunity to take up "manly arms" against the British.[3]

Writing from both sides of the rancorous divide of the

2. These themes are developed in Benedict Anderson, *Imagined Communities* (London, 1983).

3. Lawrence J. Friedman and Arthur H. Shaffer, "Mercy Otis Warren and the Politics of Historical Nationalism, *William and Mary Quarterly*, 48 (1975): 194–215.

1790s, these historians showed a remarkable disinclination to fan the flames of partisanship, preferring to use history to create artificially the "mystic chords of memory" the nation lacked. Ardent nationalists themselves, they constructed a common past which projected the national distinctiveness of the United States into the future, more specifically the republican character of the new government and the country's destiny to be, as Warren wrote, "an enviable example to all the world of peace, liberty, righteousness, and truth."[4] A history of fresh beginnings and founders' intentions quickly took shape as patriotic writers created a compelling historical narrative which interpreted the Declaration of Independence as the culmination of a long colonial gestation period.

These original efforts served as a template for successive reworkings of the story of American nation-building. Its fundamental assumptions were not challenged for over a century. America, the infant of enlightened European parents, struggled for a new birth of freedom and clung to its principles rather than let "the last, best hope of mankind perish from this earth."[5] When Americans began self-consciously constructing a national identity, they emphasized those American practices and values which distinguished their society from the mores and institutions of old-regime Europe. In doing so, they became partisans in the raging battles between the defenders of hierarchical tradition and the champions of radical reform. Since the Enlightenment ideals which Americans called upon were themselves the objects of a long and contentious struggle over the nature of truth, Americans found themselves locked into a way of seeing themselves which was strongly derivative of European cultural wars. As we have already seen in the first chapters, two intellectual enterprises, history and science, had fused to form a powerful new philosophical synthesis in the closing decades of

4. Warren, *History of the Rise, Progress and Termination of the American Revolution* (Boston, 1805), vol. 3, p. 435.

5. The phrase comes from the eighteenth-century French statesman Anne-Robert-Jacques Turgot.

the eighteenth century. Both became part of the self-awareness of the citizens of the new nation. For Americans, democratic nationalism came to represent the principal vehicle of social progress. Blending the intellectual and nationalistic challenges of the Enlightenment, Americans looked at the history of the United States as a great predictor, foretelling the future of the world's oppressed people who would one day throw off the yoke of oppression and come into their full human estate.

In the United States, the circulation of popular, consensus-building ideas and values was particularly critical in the absence of a patriotic folk culture. Detecting no conflict between their zeal for truth and their love for their own country, nineteenth-century writers provided the "imagined community" of the new nation with a history that was both patriotic and scientific. The growing conviction that democracy had a scientific foundation, e.g., that it was the only governmental form congruent with the known characteristics of human nature, encouraged Americans to think that theirs was a pathbreaking course which the rest of the world would follow. Yet the compatibility between nationalism and science could endure only so long as the search for meaning and the search for truth led to the same understanding of reality.

The explicit political philosophy of the Declaration of Independence suggested a mythic history in which individuals created government in order to secure their inherent rights. At the time, however, it took a highly imaginative reworking of historical materials to turn the Declaration into the logical termination of America's colonial experience. People who lived through the Revolution knew with what sudden conviction Americans had chosen independence. While hardly novel in its propositions, the Declaration represented an unexpected eruption in the thirteen discrete histories of the colonies. Few people had earlier thought that these separate societies could or would want to unite as a nation; fewer still would have named an abstract philosophy of natural rights as the reason for their union. Colonial history had ended abruptly with the formation of the United States. That was certain, but turning this event into a destiny implicit in the original seventeenth-century settlements was a narrative invention.

If the Declaration was made to appear as the natural end point of colonial developments, then the independence of the United States could be understood as the climax to a long and heroic sequence of events. A story that tied the intentions of the first settlers to the fulfilling acts of the Revolution and Constitution could also create the bonds of union among the disparate groups that had rebelled against British rule. Within a generation, a powerful interpretive tradition had formed that did exactly this. Like a cluster of tributaries pouring into a mighty river, the discrete colonial pasts became part of a destiny tied to the expansion and power of a nation dedicated to nurturing both individualism and democracy. In this Benjamin Trumbull's history was a model, integrating the diverse accounts of colonial origins into a single national narrative.[6] Taught to successive generations of children and immigrants, this history enabled white Americans to orient themselves at home and abroad. Equally important, the history worked out in the early decades of the nineteenth century acquired the force of an uncontested truth.

In successfully shaping historical memory to these ends, personal and national identity were powerfully fused. One became an American by exhibiting the autonomy implicit in the natural rights doctrine. Collectively Americans loved their country because it promised to the world—in the words of the Gettysburg Address—"that government of the people, by the people, for the people, shall not perish from the earth."

There was no place in the first American histories for examining the variety of complex reasons that had brought Europeans to the North American continent, much less for taking stock of the enslavement and expulsion of peoples whose cultural values called into question the claimed universality of

---

6. Trumbull, *A General History of the United States of America* (Boston, 1810), iii, as cited in Friedman and Shaffer, "Mercy Otis Warren," pp. 213–14.

American ideals. Instead the intentionality of individuals was deduced from the general spirit of a free and independent nation. The convictions showcased by the Declaration of Independence and Constitution formed the glue that American nationalists used for pasting together the country's component parts. In histories for students, the American Revolution was presented as the next most important event to the birth of Christ; as Ruth Elson concluded from a survey of nineteenth-century schoolbooks, "God both decreed and directed the American Revolution."[7] Meanwhile ministers and authors like Parson Mason Weems produced the myths appropriate for a national pantheon of heroes which an eager reading public consumed with enthusiasm. A new and compelling absolutism about national origins had been put in place, not to be dislodged for a full century.

Fortuitously, the doctrine of natural rights offered a justification for the conquest and subjugation of Amerindians. Because the native inhabitants repelled the efforts of Presidents Washington and Jefferson to get them to adopt the white man's ways, they were placed outside the charmed circle of progress. Their indifference to American definitions of individual liberty and productive pursuits disqualified them from the unfolding plan for human improvement which science and history disclosed. They figured in the popular imagination as savages, but as superior, noble savages because they were the original occupants of the American continent.[8] Historians fashioned a story that emphasized the determination of the original settlers to lay the foundation for an independent nation. The 169 years of colonial life became a prologue for the nation that was to be, a rendering of the past equivalent to our interpreting the present through the aspirations of those who will live in the twenty-second century.

With the writing of American history, the open-ended search

7. Ruth Miller Elson, *Guardians of Tradition: American Schoolbooks of the Nineteenth Century* (Lincoln, Neb., 1964), p. 62.

8. Ibid., p. 70.

for information about the past collided with the vigilant censors of patriotic pride. If the United States was to represent the fulfillment of precious political ideals, its founders must be presented as people with a mission, animated by enlightened intentions and intrepid spirits. The anthropologist Mary Douglas has described very well how history and democratic nationalism serve each other's purposes: "Any institution that is going to keep its shape," she has said, "needs to control the memory of its members." Hence an institution—in this case a nation—causes its members "to forget experiences incompatible with its righteous image and it brings to their minds events which sustain the view . . . that is complimentary to itself."[9]

During the nineteenth century, most of what really happened in the colonial era was forgotten because it conflicted with the imperatives of nation-building. Looking back upon the colonial era one discovered profoundly different concerns engaging people's attention. The self-conscious crafters of American identity took great pride in religious freedom, but the colonial groups like the Puritans of New England openly embraced orthodoxy—banishing dissidents, whipping Baptists, even executing four Quakers. "Tolerance stinks in God's nostrils," the Puritan divine Nathaniel Ward announced. And so it went with free speech. Congress composed a Bill of Rights guaranteeing free speech, but colonial magistrates had been much more likely to jail their critics. And then of course there was the adoption of slave labor and the elaboration of slave codes by colonial legislators. How were those decisions to be integrated into the story of a peculiarly free people? This imaginative legerdemain became the work of America's first historians, a category that includes the participants in the Revolution and the preservers of eyewitness accounts as well as those taking on the task of reconstructing events for nineteenth-century schoolchildren.

What the colonial period did have to offer the nineteenth century's self-conscious nationalists were a few heroes like Roger

9. Mary Douglas, *How Institutions Think* (Syracuse, N.Y., 1982), p. 112.

Williams and Benjamin Franklin, ancestors worthy of their descendants, along with some memorable scenes. A deep forgetting fell over the twenty thousand Puritans who came to America to build a city on the hill for the spiritual edification of their European brethren. Instead the appealing picture of several hundred humble Pilgrims sitting down to dinner with Wampanoag Indians in mutual respect and general thanksgiving came to stand in for the whole gallery of disputatious colonists. The colonial period also yielded a wonderful line: "God sifted a whole Nation that he might send choice Grain over into this wilderness."[10] Although it was spoken to honor the Puritan founders, it anticipated a major motif of American selfunderstanding in the first century after independence.

## Natural Rights as an Ideology

Like all moral truths, the thrilling affirmation of inalienable rights in the Declaration of Independence involved behavioral entailments. Its high-minded Americanism exacted a price in the form of a collective uneasiness about institutionalized slavery and covetous territorial ambitions. The flagrant contradiction between slavery and the principle of equality led to the nation's first emancipation movement as one after another of the Northern states abolished slavery in the waning years of the eighteenth century. With these remarkable acts, the old surveyors' line which Messrs. Mason and Dixon ran between Maryland and Pennsylvania became the symbolic division between freedom and slavery. The nation that sought a unifying doctrine found itself divided along an utterly new axis of labor systems. By freeing themselves from the onus of slavery, Northerners could expatiate on the meaning of freedom, but as this became a significant identifier of national purpose it ominously added ideological momentum to the slow differentiation taking place between North and South.

Ironically it was a slaveholder, Thomas Jefferson, who first

10. As quoted in Perry Miller, *The New England Mind: From Colony to Province* (Boston, 1953), p. 135.

envisioned an "empire of liberty" when as president he purchased Louisiana in 1803. The national quality which Jefferson
coveted for Americans was not the chaste liberty of eighteenth-
century constitution-writers but the robust liberty of assertive
go-getters finally free to put their lives in tune with nature's
rhythms. The eighteenth century's beau ideal of liberty as the
corollary of order yielded to the nineteenth century's liberty as
release from custom. Always an enthusiastic expansionist, the
young Jefferson had been the major architect of the land policy
that eventuated in the Northwest Ordinance of 1787. Mary
Douglas's injunction about a nation's controlling the memory
of its members comes to mind in contemplating Jefferson's
accomplishment in the Continental Congress. All Americans
probably "remember" that slavery was banned in the Northwest Ordinance, but have forgotten—that is, were never taught—
that there was also a Southwest Ordinance which opened the
deep South to slavery's spread. One looks in vain for references
to the Southwest Ordinance in American history textbooks,
but the knowledge of the Northwest Ordinance has been planted
in the reconstituted memory of us all.

The West was the screen upon which Jefferson projected
his vision of a nation both democratic and enterprising—hostile to privilege and authoritative meddling, supportive of innovative, individual effort. The Declaration could also elevate
the significance of America's Revolution if natural rights were
converted into universal aspirations. A born phrasemaker, Jefferson did just this, using striking rhetorical flourishes to sketch
a picture of ordinary men working out their destiny as curious,
vital, productive, and aspiring human beings. He even turned
the Garden of Eden into the seedbed of democratic nationalism: "I would have seen half the world desolated. Were there
but an Adam and Eve left in every country and left free, it would
be better than it is now."[11]

11. Jefferson to William Short, January 3, 1793, in Adrienne Koch and William Peden,
eds., *The Life and Writings of Thomas Jefferson* (New York, 1944), pp. 321–22.

Jefferson pointed Americans, geographically and temporally, toward the West with its promise of a continental future for the United States. We have so long taken for granted this orientation that it comes as something of a surprise to learn that an astute political leader like Alexander Hamilton actually opposed the Louisiana Purchase, declaring it the wisdom of all governments to prevent the dispersion of their people. Behind Hamilton's dictum lay the belief that only in close-knit communities did men and women learn their place and how to stay in it. Order was achieved by prescription. Fighting against the physical and spiritual immobility of such political prudence, Jefferson considered repressive what Hamilton thought was the common sense of the matter. The fear of disorder, for Jefferson, became an intellectual ruse used to arouse opposition to the exercise of freedom by ordinary folk. He went so far as to incorporate social obligation into men's natural endowment. "So invariably do the laws of nature create our duties and interest," he wrote, "that when they seem to be at variance we might suspect some fallacy in our reasoning."[12] Men did not need to stay put and learn their duties from their betters and elders; they knew them intuitively and fulfilled them as they pursued their natural inclinations.

Directing his appeals to the independent family farmer of the North, Jefferson left slavery in a conceptual limbo. It was free men, free land, free institutions, free choice that America stood for and that—historians now began to say—it had been tending toward since the Mayflower Compact. African-American men and women fell afoul of the historical apotheoses of ordinary white men and their families. Children's schoolbooks taught that Negroes were "a brutish people, having little more of humanity but the form." Despite the vigor of the abolitionist attack, slaves themselves were condemned by their blackness, the reigning assumption that darkness of skin color accompa-

12. Jefferson to J. B. Say, February 1, 1804, in *Writings of Thomas Jefferson*, ed. Andrew A. Lipscomb and Albert Ellery Bergh (Washington, D.C., 1903–5), vol. 11, pp. 2–3.

nied weakness of intellect being routinely inculcated in classroom teaching.[13]

Without writing histories himself, Jefferson became the font
of inspiration for the historical consciousness of the nineteenth
century. His role as the prophet of American nationalism is
unique. In his declining years, both Henry Clay and Andrew
Jackson came to ask his blessing for their competing campaigns
for the presidency. A generation after his death, the founders
of the Republican Party chose their name in tribute to him,
which means that both of the country's major parties claim him
as their founder, even divvying up the label, Democratic Republican, by which Jefferson's own movement was known. The
political philosophy which he expressed in his speeches and
letters affirmed both liberty and equality, the grand themes of
party platforms and national histories.

The incompatibilities between the liberty and equality that
Jefferson extolled generated the tensions of American political
life for the next two centuries. Most people experienced these
as problems in reality rather than as the two sides of a contradiction lodged deep within their moral traditions. It took an
outsider, Alexis de Tocqueville, to see that the equality of condition he found in the United States actually posed a threat to
liberty, or at least to the aristocratic ideal of liberty as the expression of courage and excellence. Highly conscious of the invidious comparisons Europeans made between their traditions and
the raw spirit of democratic nationalism, Tocqueville embedded his critique of the United States in a fascinating sociological
account of how opinion formation, voting, ordinary ambition,
and even geographic mobility contributed to the tyranny of the
majority in a nation dedicated to freedom.[14]

For Americans, their history became the history of the
progress of normative political and economic institutions. God

13. John M'Culloch, *Elements of Geography and Astronomy* (Philadelphia, 1789), p. 30,
as cited in Elson, *Guardians of Tradition*, p. 87. See also p. 88.

14. Alexis de Tocqueville, *Democracy in America* (New York, 1835), vol. 1, pp. 258–71;
vol. 2, pp. 99–105, 240–43, 336–47.

had sent choice grain into the wilderness, and now there were fruited plains from sea to shining sea. Effortlessly the intentionality of the Almighty merged with the intentionality of all men, that is, if they were left free to choose. Colonial seeds flowered in the universal manhood suffrage, continental expansion, and material abundance of the nineteenth century. Materialism and morality coalesced to create a new imperative for the human species. Although many people—African-Americans, women, Catholics—were excluded from the full promise of this creed, they generally found it more satisfying to attack the hypocrisy of the white male citizenry than to disavow the political principles of those in charge. Indeed, the American creed and the history of its origins became the major resource for dissenters, radicals, and reformers.[15]

Jefferson's was an understanding of American history replete with accessible images. Appealing to the sense of worth in the actual pioneers of the trans-Appalachian West (one-third of Americans lived in new communities by 1810), it also stirred the imagination of those in the East who could relive the accomplishments of their forebears. The progressive and selective development of the economy acquired a moral foundation from the footings laid down by intrepid frontier families. Out of this history came a new model of human behavior—actually male behavior—*Homo faber,* man the doer, whose activities in the world are enlarged by a generous nature. The American moral imagination seized upon the productive ideal, investing the unceasing doing and making of things with transcendent value. Land then became the means for men's achieving, with womanly assistance, their natural potential. Voluntary cooperation, mutual forbearance, spontaneous order—these were the human possibilities revealed in America. "We can no longer say there is nothing new under the sun," Jefferson wrote the philosopher Joseph Priestley. "For this whole chapter in the his-

---

15. This theme is explored in David Thelen, ed., *The Constitution and American Life* (Ithaca, N.Y., 1988).

tory of man is new. The great extent of our republic is new."[16]

Here Jefferson again caught the sentiment that made this account of America so potent in the nineteenth century. An unimportant country of several million people separated by thousands of miles from any major civilization had written itself into the foreground of human destiny. Americans could only transcend their isolation by universalizing and exalting what was peculiar to them—their success in establishing free institutions, their cultivation of the wilderness, their liberation of the ordinary ambitions of ordinary men. What might be construed by Europeans as uninterestingly vulgar was elevated by the Americans' historical imagination to a new chapter in the history of mankind. The historical narrative which Ramsay, Warren, and Turnbull first wrote and Jefferson came to exemplify focused upon American values to cement a fragile political union and, ironically, created an understanding of American nationalism which impeded historical consciousness. Cruising above this popular and self-congratulatory national history was an account of human purpose that connected the political and economic initiatives of bustling, busy Americans with the epic march of the human species toward social improvement.

It became the grand theme for America's first major historian, George Bancroft, whose *History of the United States,* written during the middle decades of the nineteenth century, fully documented how American greatness arose from its citizens' commitment to democratic virtue.[17] Himself a product of the German historical methods championed by Leopold von Ranke, Bancroft introduced both scientific research methods and romantic motifs into American historiography. As a doctoral candidate in Germany, Bancroft had come in contact with the most

16. March 21, 1801, in *The Writings of Thomas Jefferson,* ed. Paul L. Ford (New York, 1892–99), vol. 18, pp. 54–56.

17. Bancroft, *History of the United States,* 3 vols. (Boston, 1834–40). For a fascinating discussion of the imperviousness of revolutionary history to critical attack, see Sydney G. Fisher, "The Legendary and Myth-Making Process in the Histories of the American Revolution," *Proceedings of the American Philosophical Society,* 51 (1912): 53–75.

advanced centers of historical scholarship, but his grander theme was to exalt the American nation by revealing in its history the course of a universal democratic spirit. Enveloping the history of the revolutionary era in a mist of veneration, Bancroft established a patriotic orthodoxy in the 1830s which was often at odds with his legacy of innovative research. After the celebration of American grandeur in his best-selling histories, it became increasingly difficult for Americans to accept more modest portrayals of their past.

Like Jefferson, Bancroft was both an upper- and lowercase democrat, but unlike Jefferson's, Bancroft's democratic fervor was laced with a Christian sentimentalism that blurred the lines between religious and political ideals. Bancroft rolled up intuition, sentiment, reason, grace, and a belief in the equal endowments of human beings into an all-purpose force propelling Americans toward their progressive goals. Using natural imagery and appealing to instinctual powers, he described the expansion of the United States across the continent as a kind of democratic folk movement serving both God's and the nation's purposes. The individual and the race were simultaneously ennobled by the liberation of the human spirit from the shackles of poverty, superstition, and tyranny, in Bancroft's account. A contemporary of Charles Darwin, Bancroft published his last three volumes during the same years that *The Origin of Species* and *The Descent of Man* appeared, but there was no trace in them of the mordant spirit of Darwin's evolutionary theories, with its presentation of nature "red in tooth and claw." Rather Bancroft's blend of religion and rationalism embellished his romantic notions of historical causation. Powerful as a stimulus of national loyalty, Bancroft's *History* helped insulate the nation's past, particularly the nation-building acts of the Revolution and Constitution, from scholarly scrutiny, despite his role in bringing German training in critical scholarship to the United States.

Like most educated Americans, Bancroft felt keenly the disparity between the achievements of America and those of Europe. In the immediate aftermath of the Revolution, expectations were high that the free institutions of America would promote excellence in literature, science, and scholarship. Indeed, nationalist fervor had been nourished by fantasies of American greatness in the areas marked out by the high civilization of metropolitan Europe. As these expectations were confounded by reality, many Americans began to define their country by its actual political liberties and economic advances rather than its anticipated cultural contributions. Bancroft had insinuated that European accomplishments were the product of an overripe society, thus maintaining the credibility of the United States as the standard-bearer of the human race. By Bancroft's time—two generations after the Revolution—an invidious comparison with Europe had become a staple of patriotic prose, which had the effect of subtly linking the world of letters and arts to decadence.

Far from telling a straightforward story, early-nineteenth-century historians explained to Americans why their nation was both unique and a model for the world. More ominously, their emphasis upon progress provided the rationale for displacing the Shawnees, Cherokees, Seminoles, Creeks, and Choctaws whose ancestral lands lay astride the settlers' path. William Henry Harrison, a military hero and territorial governor destined to become president of the United States in 1840, conveyed this sentiment well with a rhetorical question posed to the Indiana territorial legislature in 1809: "Is one of the fairest portions of the globe to remain in a state of nature, the haunt of a few wretched savages, when it seems destined by the Creator to give support to a large population, and to be the seat of civilization, of science and true religion?"[18] Here was an inexorability beyond human agency; Americans' move across the continent could be construed as nothing more than the workings out of

18. William Henry Harrison to Legislative Council and House of Representatives of Indiana Territory "Annual Message," November 12, 1810, in Logan Esarey, ed., *Messages and Letters of William Henry Harrison,* in *Indiana Historical Collections,* 7 (1922): 492–93.

human progress, a thought so congenial to them that they readily accepted their conquest of northern Mexico as a "manifest destiny."

Expressed by significant participants like Harrison, this sense of a grand design in American affairs drew distantly on the old Puritan ideal of building a city upon the hill for all to imitate, but its immediate inspiration came from the more recent claim that the United States was the flagship of democracy. The democratization of American politics was effected by the efforts of ordinary citizens, whose exertions in the electoral campaigns of Jefferson and his two successors, James Madison and James Monroe, led to their celebration as humble foot soldiers in the war against aristocratic pride and privilege. When they improved their worldly standing, commentators interpreted their rise as proof of the naturalness of social mobility. In what has proved to be an enduring association, democracy and prosperity were linked together, both construed as the natural entitlement of independent men.

American writers made the settler families of the land west of the Appalachian Mountains the carriers of a new and vibrantly democratic civilization. They were never depicted as invaders even though blood was always spilled in violent contestation with the Indians before any territory was opened up for settler occupation. The iconography and literature of the westward movement instead evoked a peaceful tableau in which the sunburned and hardy pioneer father walked beside his Conestoga wagon, Bible in his hand, his rifle at the ready should any hostile force attempt to repel his "castle on wheels." The history of these migrations served both American democracy and American nationalism, the former by celebrating the courage and fortitude of ordinary white citizens and the latter by justifying the seizure of territory long occupied by native Americans.

The histories of the nineteenth century had discursively woven together a nation of strangers and newcomers, but the price to be paid for this national fabric was the suppression of cultural differences. The reigning metaphor for the nationalizing process was the melting pot—compulsory mixing at high temperatures. (No one ever suggested the colorful patchwork quilt, seamed into a whole.) The descriptions of self-sufficient men and women sending down roots in virgin soil and sprouting the towns that would nurture Harrison's "civilization, science and true religion" stirred the imagination. Whether operating as a theoretical safety valve or reflecting the actual opportunity to purchase homesteads, the idea of a vast continent inviting the simple exertions of house raisings and land clearing elicited nearly as much loyalty as the accessible land itself. Moreover, depicting American history as the repeated new beginnings of an industrious people provided a picture compelling enough to eclipse the memory of the uprooted Africans brought across the Atlantic in leg irons or of bedraggled and reluctant immigrants cast out of their European homes.

### Frederick Jackson Turner's Frontier Thesis

The nation's material and social advances were actually counted every ten years from 1790 when the census was taken. Each decade the agricultural output increased and the size of manufacturing establishments became larger and more complex. Every census confirmed the remarkable increase of population and cleared land and fortified Americans' predisposition to turn statistical measures into confirmation of a grand design. Every ten years the census report also pointed out the location of the frontier line inching westward across the map of North America. The acquisition of California and the opening of the Oregon Trail in midcentury made it possible for settlers to pass through the semiarid lands of the Far West and head for the Pacific Coast. The decadal westward creep of the frontier line bounced to the coast. Charged with indicating the frontier line, the superintendent of the U.S. Census in 1890 looked at the scattered settlements, threw up his hands in despair, and declared that the frontier era had come to an end.

This cartographical decision from the census head prompted one historian, Frederick Jackson Turner, to reflect upon the significance that the frontier had played in the American past. Writing at a time when his fellow citizens were coming to terms with their new situation as members of an industrial nation, Turner wrote a history of the frontier which ministered to people's nostalgia about a simpler era. He also defined as American those democratic and egalitarian values which justified the bloodletting of the Civil War just a generation earlier. To the frontier, Turner said, America owed not only its consolidation as a nation but its characteristic intellectual traits—and he went on to catalogue them: "coarseness and strength combined with acuteness and inquisitiveness; that practical, inventive turn of mind . . . that masterful grasp of material things, lacking in the artistic but powerful to effect great ends; that restless, nervous energy, that dominant individualism with the buoyancy and exuberance which comes with freedom."[19] Following Bancroft's romantic invention of the American people as the collective agents of change, Turner anthropomorphized the whole nation by converting it into a single individual—not even an individual really, but a type—standing in for the country as a whole.

The shared American understanding that history told the story of progress helped Turner dispose of the Indians, whose presence on the frontier could not be neglected entirely. Without being hostile or deprecatory toward the indigenous population, Turner suggested a reason for its disappearance which removed all moral responsibility for the many violent acts that had swept the Indians from the path of the settlers. He began by professing to be at a loss to explain why the trading stage of frontier life had yielded so quickly to the advancing column of pioneer families and then handed the topic over to theorists: "In this progress from savage conditions lie topics for the evo-

19. Frederick Jackson Turner, "The Significance of the Frontier in American History," *Annual Report of the American Historical Association for the Year* 1893 (1893), pp. 199–227.

lutionist." Next the Indian presence was saluted as a consolidating agent; their contribution to America, Turner wrote, was as "a common danger, demanding united action." Still twelve lines further the Indians figure even more obliquely in passages stressing the importance of the frontier as a military training school, "keeping alive the power of resistance to aggression."[20] Reflecting a kind of Darwinian resignation in the face of processes now deemed inexorable, Turner attributed the ejection of successive Native American tribes to natural forces. In the space of one page, he used evolutionary theory to explain the eradication of the indigenous peoples and then evoked their presence to demonstrate the frontier contribution to American unity, only to conclude by reversing the moral stance of settlers and Indians by claiming that the endemic warfare on the frontier prepared Americans to resist aggression!

### Capitalism, the Constitution, and American History

At the very time that Turner was writing to celebrate the moving frontier that had spread family farms across the North American continent, farming itself had become an increasingly precarious way of life. As farm incomes plummeted, most young men and women from rural America had to seek their fortunes in the newly sprouted factory towns. But frontier farms, in Turner's assessment, had produced something more important than crop yields; they had fostered American character traits. So while those who clung to their farms were battered by declining prices, tight credit, and rising freight costs, the frontier heritage of independence, productivity, and initiative furnished a spiritual link between America's agrarian past and its industrial future. Despite his celebration of an era that had come to an end, Turner's message about Americans' "inventive turn of mind" and "masterful grasp of material things" spoke directly

20. Ibid., pp. 226–27.

to his contemporaries, in part because these qualities were deemed so important to the entrepreneurship that was reshaping the United States into a powerful industrial nation. Far removed from steel-fabricating plants and bituminous coal mines, Turner's history of the frontier nonetheless provided distinctive American roots for the capitalist economy which had emerged to dominate national life.

In the early years of the twentieth century, scholars introduced the notion of capitalism into the history of the American nation, and then in a highly unflattering way. The debased living conditions in factory towns had called forth a fresh generation of reformers who aroused the nation's concern about the widening gulf between the new industrial plutocrats and their overworked, underpaid workers. Capitalism thus entered American historiography as part of a polemic. Only recently has the word shed some of its negative associations because of the collapse of the Soviet regime. Although strictly speaking a reference to a specific economic system, the word tends to direct attention to one aspect of the system, the economic power in capital itself. Since such a concentration of power is at odds with democratic values, Americans have maintained an ambivalent attitude toward capitalism. Far different is what might be called the subliminal culture of capitalism—those images of individual fortitude, prosperity, agricultural abundance, open opportunity, hard work, free choice, inventive genius, and productive know-how. As Turner's work suggests, the culture of capitalism has thoroughly permeated the nation's historical consciousness. More to the point, this self-understanding which history has furnished Americans has played a critical role in promoting actual capitalist development.

At first sight the American economy seems to be straightforwardly driven by the dynamics of market production, mediated only by the private decisions of property owners. In other words, capitalism seems confined to impersonal processes and personal events. This view is tenable, however, only if one assumes that human beings naturally know how to work and save, take risks, make wise choices about resources, and adapt to constant innovation and change. But in fact it is culture that furnishes models of behavior and distributes honor and shame to indicate the appropriateness of individual actions. In a market economy, dependent upon voluntary efforts, the cultural element is critical, because it is through explicit social values that people are given the personal ambition and essential knowledge to keep the system going.

Thoroughly privatized, the American economy only moves in response to personal initiatives to invest in productive enterprises, to mobilize resources for work, and to save or spend according to individual dictates. Because decisions like these are guided by deeply internalized values, our culture acts as the invisible engine driving the free market. Particularly important to this culture of capitalism have been the meanings and values Americans have invested in their history, their laws, and their literature. As recently as twenty years ago, social scientists would have denied the centrality to the economy of anything as elusive as culture, but the experiences in Eastern Europe have forcefully demonstrated how important popular understandings are to the workings of an economy. The cultural models that sustain the American economy were long ago insinuated into the nation's history books and through them into the consciousness of the people. American children learn their most basic economic truths through stories, sermons, movies, and the adult injunctions that follow them from home to school and school to community. History texts have provided American children with exemplary models of trailblazing initiatives, disciplined efforts, and individual sacrifices for progress. Beginning with the accounts of nation-building in the revolutionary era, national history has imparted the kinds of moral lessons that have enabled capitalism to flourish, but like the roots of a plant this vital cultural sustenance is hard to see.

One of the distinguishing features of a free-enterprise economy is that its coercion is veiled. This is an absolutism that works without visible constraints. The apparently voluntary nature of commercial transactions creates the illusion that participants are free to choose. The fact that people must earn before they can eat is a commonly recognized connection between need and work, but it presents itself as a natural link embedded in the necessity of eating rather than as arising from a particular arrangement for distributing food through market exchanges. Despite the fact that men and women must buy and sell in order to live, the optional aspects of the market remain most salient. It is the individual who makes choices, takes risks, and suffers or enjoys the consequences. Presented as natural and personal in the stories people tell about themselves, the social and compulsory aspects of capitalism slip out of sight and out of mind. Yet learning to participate in American economic life requires years of preparation, not only in acquiring skills, but also in creating that self-possessed individual who accepts as just the outcomes of market transactions. Far from being natural, the cues for market participation are given through complicated social codes. Indeed, the illusion that compliance in the dominant economic system is voluntary is itself an amazing cultural artifact.

Americans came to think of their economic responses as natural largely because of the way their history was framed. Already well established in colonial America, the mores of the market economy—the cultivation of enterprise, the receptivity to innovation, the alertness to market signals—acquired political overtones when they were connected to the story of personal liberty. Linked to a national destiny to turn the American wilderness into a "fruited plain," economic liberty became one of the principal elements of American self-understanding. Indeed, the market—conceived abstractly—suggested a better solution to the venerable problem of order. Its capacity to enlist people in productive activities offered an alternative to the overt social direction of magistrates and ministers. In the presumed naturalness of self-interest lay the key for considering the market economy—in fact, a very sophisticated social arrangement—as a natural system whose principles, like the laws of gravity, could be uncovered by scientific research.

Political philosophy had long discussed the human predicament of having to invest power in government in order to secure order, but then having to live in fear of the disordering possibility of the government's abuse of that power. The conventional American understanding of this conundrum was that men (and it was a male concept) yearned for freedom, particularly the freedom to look out for themselves, but that they also used and abused other men's freedom in the pursuit of their own. Only liberty and competition—in both the political and economic realms—could accommodate the needs and nature of the self-willed individuals who formed civil society. Thus the imperative that connects economic and political freedom is assumed to be rooted in the structure of the human personality. The status of these assertions as hypotheses disappeared in a historical record that treated them as facts. And Americans continued to look at the past for evidence that the natural principles of society were working themselves out in the time and space that belonged to the United States.

A key component of this understanding of political and economic freedom was the presentation of the United States Constitution in history texts. Before the Civil War, the Constitution had been a bone of contention between the Northern and Southern states. Northerners, following John Marshall's lead, wished to consider the Constitution in Hegelian terms, as a particular manifestation of eternal principles of justice. Southerners resisted this interpretation as part of their general rejection of the concept of nationhood, preferring to see the union as a contract freely entered into by the diverse states. Central to the South's defense against antislavery reformers was the claim that the Constitution was a dissolvable compact. So successful was the South in using the Constitution to prevent interference that abolitionist leaders publicly burned copies of the Constitution to dramatize their commitment to a higher law.

Among the many fruits of victory that the North garnered in 1865 was the opportunity at last to depict the United States Constitution as the organic law of the land, understood both as a sublime expression of popular sovereignty and the embodi-

ment of true principles of civil order. Without further jurispru-
dential challenge from the South, Northern scholars after the
Civil War fashioned a history that linked the Constitution to
ancient concepts of justice and traced its transplanting from
Teutonic forests and heroic English documents to the Mayflower Compact and New England town meetings.

After the Civil War, historians were also able to tie the
intentions of the Founding Fathers to the actual emergence of
the nation as a mighty industrial power. In this interpretation,
the Constitution became the embodiment of natural law because of its protection of life, liberty, and property. No longer
obliged to consider Southern constitutional thinking with its
emphasis upon the contractual nature of the union, Northern
jurists and scholars were free to elevate the Constitution far
above statute law. An invidious comparison between the "Supreme Law of the Land" and the laws of elected legislators gave
a peculiar twist to American democracy. Historians presented
the Constitution as an inviolable fundamental law. Its framing
and ratification elicited reverential encomiums to popular sovereignty, while the daily practice of democratic power by the
president and Congress acquired the odium of vulgar politics,
conducted largely for the benefit of politicans. Democracy came
to be associated with the capacity of equally enfranchised ordinary white men to ward off government intrusions. Citizen
action in the pursuit of common goals lost whatever glory its
association with democracy had provided because the activities
themselves had been deflated to mere politics.

Behind these representations of political institutions lay the
model of the market understood as a nexus of voluntary associations limited only by the demands of open access. Because
American history stressed that liberation from oppressive authorities of all kinds would lift the dead hand of the past to the
benefit of humanity, nature, and progress, the Constitution was
glorified as the guardian of that liberation. In the decades bracketing the turn of the nineteenth century, this Northern interpretation of the Constitution aroused the ire of a new group of

critics, the Progressives. When interpreted as prescient because it anticipated America's industrial future and sublime because it embodied eternal principles of justice, the Constitution could be used to block new social policies like those enunciated in state laws protecting working women and children from the worst perils of the factory system.

The British historian Lewis Namier once commented that the Enlightenment was dead everywhere except the United States. In this observation, Namier turned the Enlightenment into a shorthand reference to a cluster of powerful ideas that came to dominance at the end of the eighteenth century: faith in progress, commitment to free inquiry, belief in the rational capacities of man, tolerance of religious diversity, respect for individualism, and insistence upon equality of rights. When the American colonists plunged into unexpected conflict with Great Britain, they found in the Enlightenment reconfiguration of political order a justification first for prosecuting their rebellion and second for declaring themselves an independent nation. By taking as their motto *Novus ordo seculorum*—a new order for the ages—Americans were paradoxically forming an enduring alliance with a troubled European reform tradition. The American example made the goals of Europe's radicals appear realizable just as their admiration for the new nation turned the American Revolution into an epochal event in world history. In subsequent generations what had been fluid and immanent in these expectations of progress froze into the conviction that the United States was the embodiment of reform ambitions. The Enlightenment lived on in the United States, as Namier noted, because it provided the philosophical womb for American nationhood, itself now at risk from just the kind of revolutionary thinking that had originally inspired it.

The United States could serve as an ideal for humanity only if human aspirations were funneled into the vessel labeled "autonomous, hardworking, self-reliant man." Here becomes apparent the troubling contradiction in a history which glorified freedom and went on to assert that the only thing people were free to do was engage in relentless self-improvement. Through all these years while schoolchildren learned to celebrate their country's undoubted achievements, they were conditioned to accept unquestioningly the implicit values of individual responsibility and decision-making. They were also taught to think within a cultural frame of reference that was predominantly male in gender, white in color, and Protestant in religious orientation. Making, doing, building, increasing, growing—these were compulsory virtues.

At the center, then, of American history was an undersocialized, individualistic concept of human nature set in an overdetermined story of progress. Deeply etched into the collective imagination, this history distributed social merit and public attention—and through them political authority. Shoring up the frail unity of thirteen rebelling colonies, it assumed the absolutist character of a mythic tale of origins for a mighty industrial nation. In time its imperviousness to change stifled curiosity about America's past because it could not explain the real problems of living people: the turbulence of the Civil War, the dislocations of immigration, the source of imperial ambition, and the reconfiguration of the American economy. Vibrant processes—totally alien to the world of the Founding Fathers—were rapidly transforming the country into a modern industrial giant, and as they did so, the first generation of twentieth-century Americans began searching for new interpretations of their national past, their capacity for critical thought stirred by the modern absolutisms generated by science, social theory, and nationalism.

PART TWO

———◇———

# Absolutisms Dethroned

$\diamond 4 \diamond$

# Competing Histories of America

URING THE EIGHTEENTH CENTURY the absolutist state came to represent all of the ills of society. Castigated as hierarchical, intolerant, repressive, and implacably opposed to all change, the old-regime monarchies furnished most of the targets for reform literature. In contrast to these moribund institutions, Enlightenment writers imagined a free and open social world where citizens, savants, and statesmen would reason together to encourage enterprise, expand the ambit of liberty, foster learning, and promote the interests of humankind. In the United States the Enlightenment program passed quickly from theory to practice. Through most of the nineteenth century, American citizens viewed their nation as the embodiment of Enlightenment ideals as well as the template for social advances that would one day come to all peoples.

Even in Europe, where the radical reforms of the French Revolution were blunted by a powerful reactionary movement, science, technology, and industrialization marched together toward impressive material and intellectual accomplishments. Pacing this record of mastery were the ambitions of philosophers who envisioned a coordinated assault upon the mysteries of nature, society, and human behavior. The positive laws of social development revealed for their believers a future of beneficent change. The abuses of the new industrial system, like the enduring miseries left uncorrected from past times, came to be categorized as parts of an unfinished agenda, mere examples of cultural lags rather than intractable aspects of the human condition. During most of the nineteenth century, success sealed off the prophets of progress from exactly the kind of scrutiny which their predecessors had brought to bear on traditional institutions. And so the enlightened enemies of absolutism ended up by erecting a new kind of absolutism—only now it reigned in science, philosophy, and enlightened public policy. History came to play a major role in propagating this modern orthodoxy, particularly in the United States. And just because their national history was so integral to Americans' identity, the new orthodoxy became a part of the political conflicts generated by industrialization.

The appalling destruction of the Civil War remained a vivid memory during the closing decades of the nineteenth century, the carnage itself being replicated when the Union Army moved west to wage savage campaigns against the Plains Indians. In the South the white supremacist Redeemers used selective violence and systematic terror to drive freed men and women back to a state of servile dependence once federal troops were removed with the end of Reconstruction in 1877. Lynch law became the law of the land for African-Americans, with lynchings reaching a cumulative total in the thousands in the early years of the twentieth century. Historians after the Civil War dropped a discreet veil over this discreditable record, focusing instead upon the valor of the white soldiers which had made the Emancipation Proclamation possible. Abrading the sensibilities of white Americans more than violence against Indians and blacks were the threats posed by immigration, labor unrest, and declining profits in farming, all traceable to the profound restructuring of the American economy.

American industry revealed its astounding potential for growth between 1880 and 1920. A new breed of national leaders emerged—the winners in an utterly unprecedented competition for control of entire trades like meat packing, sugar processing, and oil refining. Swiftly the myriad of locally owned enterprises disappeared into giant national firms, leaving the new institutional leviathans—the corporations and trusts—with centralized control over the economic lives of the farmers, mechanics, and shopkeepers dispersed across the continent. Increasingly the future for their children meant leaving the countryside to join the swelling population of factory workers.

What had once been islands of manufacturing enterprise became national networks drawing labor and resources to new hubs of economic activity. The private decisions of bankers and manufacturers created complex, interlocking systems of industry, commerce, and finance which pushed to the margins of national life the country's rural communities. Maintaining the concept of an undifferentiated people—so long a resonating theme in America's self-understanding—proved impossible. The rich were not only getting richer, their conspicuous riches advertised a new, more modern, and more menacing era. Journalists raided the lexicon of aristocratic societies and found "tycoon," "magnate," and "robber baron" to label America's triumphant industrialists. Since references to feudal Europe uniformly evoked the thought of a privileged class lording it over hardworking ordinary folk, talk of the nation's new robber barons called into question the permanence of America's revolutionary legacy.

Evidence of material progress abounded, but opportunities for individuals to connect independently with the country's economic expansion declined during its sudden industrial transformation. The minimalist government which had been the proud manifestation of the Jeffersonian faith in the ability of ordinary men and women to run their own affairs now appeared hopelessly outmatched by the giant corporations. The possibility that there might be material improvement concurrent with the corruption of democratic practices threatened to sever that ideological link between materialism and morality that had enabled Americans to interpret their prosperity as proof of their superior values.

Philosophy too seemed to have turned against the United States. The optimism about man's rational capacities—and it always was man's—which characterized attitudes at the nation's founding had been supplanted by a tough-minded skepticism about the power of thought to affect the larger forces shaping human existence. The mechanistic depiction of the genesis of *Homo sapiens* in Darwin's evolutionary theory published in *The Origin of Species* in 1859 had struck a blow at the Judeo-Christian foundations of the nation's culture. By the end of the nineteenth century, Europe again was providing intellectual ammunition for an assault on the new absolutism grounded in the natural laws of progress. Only this time it would be liberalism itself that fell under the analytical gaze of scholars. Marx's radical reinterpretation of the root causes of social action, Darwin's subversion of Christian dogma, and Freud's startling disclosures about infant sexuality—all of these critical investigations of human nature and society—acted like enormous boulders thrown into waters that had been calmed by Enlightenment confidence in man's mastery of the universe.

Outside the realm occupied by philosophers, the lives of millions of men and women on both sides of the Atlantic were being wrenched out of familiar agrarian patterns by the relentless progress of economic development. By the end of the nineteenth century, Darwin's bleak depiction of the struggle for survival imposed on all living creatures offered a grim analogy to actual social developments in the United States. Mines, foundries, sweatshops, factories, and tenement houses sprawled across the urban landscape, while suburbs were laid out to shelter the families of the well-off from the stench of progress. Industrial advance came with lightning speed to an America barely recovered from the devastating bloodbath that had pitted North against South. The bounteous nature that had been so profligate with its gifts to America's charter settlers had yielded to Darwinian laws that explained how the scarcity of goods forced people to fend for themselves in the great scramble of life. Where, within this biological dynamic of chance and destiny, was there a place for the United States, whose national history orbited around the twin stars of liberty and equality? More to the point, how was the American legacy going to be distributed in an industrial society of dispossessed farmers and deracinated immigrants?

It is one of the great strengths of ideologies that they defy logic and hence are able to weld together incongruous, even conflicting, ideals. The American identification of national mission with the clean slate of the frontier West is a case in point. The opportunity for free men and their families to fashion their own lives was deemed generally fulfilling because of desires embedded deep in all human hearts, while the nation's bounty of undeveloped land was accorded the specialness of a divine dispensation. The universal and particular fused. All men and women wanted the fresh start America offered. This uniform yearning lifted American history above the specificity of time and place. Still for the world, as for most of the citizens of the United States, the West was more inspirational than real. Its invitation to quit established settlements created a kind of psychic space in which men and women could fantasize about other possibilities in life while its actual awesome emptiness and exotic indigenous peoples possessed more appeal as subjects for dime novels than as future homesites and neighbors. When the superintendent of the U.S. Census announced that there was no longer a frontier line, he cut off one of the escape routes of the American imagination, and he did so at the very time that a host of other changes challenged the nation's collective capacity to adapt to industrialization.

By 1893 when Turner offered his frontier thesis as a way of understanding the American character, the very idea of an American people had become problematic. What challenged it was the unexpected arrival of millions of uprooted Europeans. Beginning in the 1870s and swelling with each succeeding decade until the outbreak of World War I, people from Greece, Italy, Ireland, Croatia, Serbia, Germany, the Baltic states, Poland, and Russia streamed into America—fifteen million in the first fourteen years of the twentieth century alone. Many of these new arrivals were Catholics and Jews, whose alien religious practices stirred deep prejudices in the native-born white population. Bred to believe in toleration, the predominantly Protestant citizens of the United States were sorely perplexed by their own intolerant responses to the immigrants' peculiar ways. What became quite evident was that America's religious diversity had been pretty much confined to the Protestant strain of Christianity, and within that strain common folkways had ameliorated the friction from divurging patterns of faith and worship. Whether they were Catholic or Jewish, the conspicuous differences in the immigrants' looks, behavior, and patterns of sociability disturbed American Protestants. They drank beer in the parks, enjoyed boxing matches, followed religious rituals in foreign tongues, and crowded into makeshift tenements. Their very cultural diversity implicitly challenged the universal validity of American norms, just as their dark coloring brought to the surface the contradictions between Americans' ideals and their racial prejudices.

Despite the nation's commitment to religious liberty, the preponderant descendants of the white American colonists were highly sensitive to variations from their own mores even when they were sanctioned by a religious denomination. The Mormons, for instance, were subject to persecution in the 1840s. In a largely unself-conscious way the oldest white immigrants—a group often referred to now as WASPs—had defined as universal values which, in fact, came from their Protestant background. The love of individual liberty that they extolled along with self-reliance were qualities closely identified with the Protestant side of that great divide in Christendom created by the Reformation. Thrift, disciplined effort, and the deferral of pleasure were such conspicuous traits of early modern Calvinists that the German sociologist Max Weber labeled them the Protestant work ethic. Even the "invisible hand of the market" which Adam Smith had evoked to describe the uncoerced operation of a free economy owed far more to the Protestant orientation of the British people that he observed than to any universal tendencies in human nature.

American Protestants tended to treat these personal dispositions as natural endowments rather than social characteristics. These qualities emerged particularly strongly in the United States, they argued, because it took a free environment to cultivate man's natural tendency toward individual autonomy. Even though these personal traits have to be carefully instilled at childhood, it has only been in our own time that the cultural component of behavior—the learned behavior that requires models and mentors—has been thoroughly explored. In the nineteenth century, American history, like American intellectual life in general, pivoted around the successful male white Protestant, whose features were turned into ideals for the entire human race. When lacking, their absence indicated an unnatural deviation, except in the case of women, who were viewed as naturally deficient and hence dependent upon men.

The middle class's unacknowledged universalizing of Protestant values became conspicuous in its public denunciations of the mores, politics, and religion of the recent arrivals. For the American WASPs whose lives spanned the turn of the twentieth century, the foreigners flooding into their cities represented a threat just because they were so un-American. The southern and Eastern European origins of the new immigration stirred fears of a mongrelization of the native stock, leading to calls for congressional restrictions on immigration. The very term "mongrelization" evoked images of a civilization-destroying animality. Darwin's theory of evolution with its sociological corollaries gave nineteenth-century Europeans and Americans, already acutely aware of the divide of race, a scientific rationalization for counting others as inferior.

The idea of progress lent itself to these preoccupations, for if one assumed that human society was inexorably improving, then some explanation needed to be given for the relative indifference to material and social innovations among those outside Western Europe and America. Evolutionary theory, applied to entire societies in the world, provided an answer. Melding the physical with the social, scientists announced a new hierarchy of racial types which ranked human beings according to their group's measurable advance toward progress evident in the West.

These prevailing anthropological theories invited an intense scrutiny of faces, body types, and intelligence quotients for signs of inferiority in the immigrants coming to the United States. Disposed to think in these terms, public commentators concluded that the new immigrants were not so much different as backward. Stressing as they did genetic endowments, evolutionary theories were used to add a specious scientific underpinning to the hostile passions of prejudice. A virulent new form of racism took root in the country at large, leading many to declare blacks, Indians, and the new immigrants unfit for American citizenship.

Added to these tensions was the powerful sense of national failure in the effort to "reconstruct" the Old South following the Civil War. Not only did the federal government withdraw effective protection from the millions of freed men and women in the South, but many Americans on both sides of the old Mason-Dixon line came to accept as routine the attacks on black Americans. At the same time, the vaunted independence of American farmers crumbled before the economic muscle of the trusts while the industrialists' voracious demand for labor insistently lured Europe's own dispossessed peasants to the United States. The sense of an organic nation, which at best had always been fragile, collapsed altogether.

By the beginning of the twentieth century, the conventional history of the American people as the heroic champions of democracy had lost much of its credibility—not because Americans had abandoned their belief in progress, but rather because conditions in the United States at the time mocked the high moral purposes embedded in that faith. Something had clearly gone wrong. The patriotic history that had originally worked to unify a disparate people had been turned into an icon of conservatism used to ward off criticism of the political institutions now firmly under the control of a wealthy elite. Fears about declining economic opportunities with the closing of the frontier mixed with anxiety about the loss of democratic virtue and the dilution of the nation's old bloodlines. A new generation of historians, following Karl Marx's lead, stopped talking about the whole American people, as Bancroft had done, and began discussing class. Unwilling to grasp the nettle of American race prejudices, this scholarly cohort was ready to examine the role of class conflict in the American past just as a new group of Progressive reformers emerged to take on the plutocrats whose exercise of power was making a mockery of American democracy.

### Progressive Historians' Revision of American History

Ever since the Revolution, Americans had believed in progress, but the dominant school of historians in the opening half of the twentieth century were the first to be called Progressive historians, largely because of their efforts to reform American politics. The preeminent Progressive historian, Charles Beard, laid out the agenda for a thorough revision of national history in 1913. He himself began by smashing the pedestals upon which the Founding Fathers had stood for over a century. Getting these revered nation-builders at ground level, Beard then proceeded to go through their pockets and found—to the Progressives' delight—that they were stuffed with government bonds which everyone knew would increase in value with stronger fiscal policies should the Articles of Confederation be superseded by a new frame of government. This proved to Beard that the Constitutional Convention had brought together in Philadelphia in 1787 not an assembly of demigods, as Jefferson had called them, but self-interested politicians like those so conspicuous in his day.

Beard's *An Economic Interpretation of the U.S. Constitution* demonstrated in a new and powerful way just how crucial history is to democratic nationalism. Availing himself of new social theories and unexploited archival records, he stiffened his findings with the starch of science and revolutionized the way his contemporaries thought about their Constitution. Beard revealed, as no one had before, that history could be a mighty weapon of reform. By writing colloquially about the Constitutional Convention and the mixed motives of its delegates, he penetrated the sacred penumbra that had enveloped the document and brought into historical consciousness the Constitution as a political act.

Formerly presented as the embodiment of ideals of justice going back to the Greeks, the U.S. Constitution now took its place in history texts as the achievement of a proto-capitalist elite whose aversion to sharing power with ordinary Americans was matched by their farsightedness in preparing for the industrial nation that was to come. Because American entrepreneurs had used the Constitution to block intrusive legislation designed to improve the working conditions of their employees, Beard's critical examination of the framing of the Constitution became immediately relevant to the decisions being made by the Supreme Court. By successfully demystifying the Constitution, Beard had called into question the validity of the entire historiographical tradition surrounding the Constitution that had flourished since the Civil War.

Attacking the notion that the Constitution represented the pinnacle of the country's revolutionary achievement, Beard separated the Constitution from the Declaration of Independence by describing it as a reactionary document calculated to blunt the genuinely democratic forces unleashed by the Revolution. Class conflict became for the Beardians the engine driving American history. Linking the self-interested actions of the Founders to the subsequent industrialization of the United States meant tying America's origins to the course of world capitalism. Although Beard did not actually draw upon the controversial nineteenth-century writings of Marx, he nonetheless injected the Marxist categories of material interests and class conflict into the nation's historical consciousness. Moving beyond a simple interjection of rough reality into a celebratory historical tradition, he thoroughly scrambled the central message of American ideology by redefining the people as members of a powerless majority. For the first time, the nation's professional historian parted company with the guardians of American exceptionalism.

Finally released from the vow of silence imposed by patriotism, Beard's followers had a field day locating interest groups in the American past. From their research came the debtors and creditors, Westerners and Easterners, farmers and merchants, manufacturers and laborers who have confronted each other in history textbooks ever since. Beard himself had a prodigious output, and with his wife, Mary Ritter Beard, he wrote a comprehensive history of the United States which exposed the power of economic forces so long cloaked by patriotic rhetoric. The Beards revised the history of the Civil War by turning it into a second American Revolution—a veritable replay of the confrontation between farmers and capitalists which had brought forth the Constitution. Construing the North as a society run by nascent industrialists, the Progressives explained the war as a triumph of the modernizing North over the resolutely traditional Southern planters. Once again, the nation's problems were resolved through violent conflict, only now the power of propertied men had been so greatly magnified by the course of industrial development that the future of American democracy was at risk.

Working with different assumptions about the nature of historical change, the Progressives revamped the topics, the story line, and the tone of American history-writing. They believed not only that economic interests determined people's personal loyalties but also that those interests were divisive. Hence social conflict was inevitable. Even more profoundly revisionary was the way Progressives treated the influence of ideas in historical developments. Since economic interests were not openly acknowledged—particularly in a society committed to high-toned political values like equal rights—the Progressives believed that historians needed to look beyond the surface rhetoric of politics in order to find the true motives animating people.

With this methodological assignment, scholars approached the nation's rich political literature about justice, truth, free choice, checks and balances, women's rights, universal suffrage, and religious tolerance as so many smoke screens behind which the real reasons for seeking and using power were negotiated. Long-term goals, concern for the good of the whole, lofty ambitions for the nation—these were dangerous abstractions in the eyes of the Progressives, created to divert naive observers from the real springs of human action. As Beard himself wrote, "Man as a political animal acting upon political as distinguished from more vital and powerful motives is the most insubstantial of all abstractions."[1]

Applying these historical insights to the patriotic effusions of nineteenth-century history books proved exhilarating for a generation of early-twentieth-century scholars. The men who ran the United States could no longer count on professional historians to present their acts as contributory to American greatness. Not coincidentally, Beard's readers drew parallels between the Founding Fathers' efforts to check the popular will and the exercise of power by the nation's new robber barons. The debunking *élan* of the Progressives roused the ire of the industrialists and financiers who had just settled into enjoying the country they had so recently bought, but rank-and-file Americans named Beard, who taught at Columbia, one of the ten most influential men in the United States. Nicholas Murray Butler, the redoubtable president of Columbia, suffered the discomfort of being the buffer between Beard and his critics, many of them university donors. Walking across Morningside Heights one day, Butler was reportedly hailed by a faculty member who called out to him, "Have you read Beard's last book?" "I hope so," Butler replied, "I hope so." He had not, of course. Beard and his fellow scholars published a stream of new work. They also succeeded in making American history a fascinating subject for the sophisticated reading public.

By the 1920s the Progressives had won the battle to control the nation's collective memory, in large part because their depiction of historical action seemed more believable to a generation weaned on the strife of industrialization. Still, by stressing the predominance of economic interests, the Progressives actually continued that part of the American historical tradition which had emphasized that progress came from material advances. For them, America's revolutionary democrats struggled for free land and access to the nation's abundant resources, whereas their own contemporaries fought for higher wages and better working conditions. The Progressives denied that there had always been an identity of interests among Americans, but they retained the conviction that history revealed a progressive struggle of ordinary men against the power of privilege. Hardheaded in their depiction of interest-group conflicts, the Progressives never doubted that aspirations for personal freedom and economic opportunity represented core human drives. As much an activist as a scholar, Beard along with the radical economist Thorstein Veblen and the philosopher John Dewey founded the New School for Social Research, the first American institution to open up higher education to adults who did not possess the customary qualifications.

The idea of progress had created for the United States a central place in the evolution of human society. Denied a venerable past, American historians had turned the revolutionary origins of the nation into a prologue for the future of human beings. Of necessity this kind of elevated history, written to illuminate broad philosophical trends in the unfolding destiny of the human race, lost contact with the actual people of the past. Because progress itself provided a script for why people did things, historians could be indifferent to the immediate values and plans which engaged women and men, nor was any curiosity bestowed upon those people or events off the beaten path. There was only one kind of maverick deserving attention—the individual who was ahead of his time. Even the Progressive historians who began as the unmaskers of the patriotic and celebratory histories they had inherited never moved far from the central question of American historiography: had the nation kept faith with its democratic promise and enlightened principles?

## Perry Miller's Rehabilitation of the Puritans

In the 1930s a young scholar named Perry Miller boldly set out to study colonial America independent of its later connection with the United States. Probably this century's greatest historian, Miller chose a most unsympathetic band of colonizers, the Puritans, to carry the burden of a different message about the meaning of English settlement in the New World. Miller viewed with scorn Turner's apotheosis of "the ruling and compulsive power of the frontier." It failed Miller's test of credibility, because it suggested that mindless conditions, not mindful men and women, made history. Depicting mere circumstances as the cause of social action amounted to a regression into the womb of irresponsibility, Miller said, and he pointed to Turner as the foremost victim of the American fallacy of thinking "that things rather than forms define reality."[2] This was bold stuff, introducing philosophical considerations that went against the assumptions that had controlled the writing of American history for a long time. Without raising the issue of Marxist interpretations of history directly, Miller's insistence upon both human agency and the predominant influence of ideas in causing change pushed American historical writing decisively away from the Progressives' essentially economic agenda.

Rejecting the idea that pecuniary interests or material forces

2. See David Hollinger, "Perry Miller and Philosophical History," *History and Theory,* 7 (1968).

directed social change, Miller maintained that ideas and purposes shaped the course of events. Human beings could not
move without a thought in their heads, he noted, and those
men and women that moved others did so with well-articulated
thoughts. Their plans might involve national glory and territorial domination, or economic enterprise and mastery of nature,
or the preservation of a sacred form of life, but whatever the
goal, it required intellectual framing. Someone had to describe
the vision, address its implications, and chart the course of
actions for its attainment. Nor were ideas equal in Miller's eyes:
some had the power to propel people across an ocean; others
failed to stir a whisper of response in the popular imagination.
It was, in Miller's view, the obligation of historians to search
for the motives and incentives present in the historical moment.
It was an abrogation of that responsibility to assume that there
were universal drives like economic self-interest or political state-
building that could account for the historic transformations of
modern society.

Miller chose to study the Puritans because their clarity of
vision revealed the human will at work fashioning institutions
and imposing form upon the inert material of the physical environment. His contemporaries, having only very recently freed
themselves from their "puritanical" heritage, were not exactly
ready for a sympathetic reading of Puritan ideas. The popular
satirist H. L. Mencken had made the Puritans the butt of American humor. A Puritan, Mencken said, was a person haunted by
the fear that somewhere, somehow, someone was having a good
time. The times were not propitious for Miller's rehabilitation
of the Puritans. So secular had American culture become that
another wit suggested that the nation's religious history should
be taught as the passage from "Sinners in the Hands of an
Angry God" to God in the hands of angry sinners.[3] But he took
all this on and transformed the sin-hating Puritans into the bold

3. "Sinners in the Hands of an Angry God" is the title of a famous sermon preached by
Jonathan Edwards in which he compares the fate of the damned to that of a spider
falling into an open fire.

protagonists in a drama of stirring spiritual ambitions and paradoxical outcomes.

Miller adroitly conceded to the Puritans' critics every crabbed quality they despised: his Puritan divines were dictatorial; their devoted followers obsessive salvation-mongers. Cotton Mather he described as "the most nauseous human being that ever lived."[4] However, by imaginatively participating in the Puritans' courageous aspiration to be in the world of sin but not of it, Miller turned these decidedly un-American characters into dauntless tightrope walkers of the soul, as courageous in plumbing the depths of their own unworthiness as Turner's pioneers had been in confronting unseen adversaries in the wilderness. Using his great gifts as a historian, Miller read between the lines of the Sunday sermons not for evidence of economic interests but rather for the passionate commitments that these intrepid pioneers of the spirit poured into their Christian devotions. He also made the Puritans' anguish accessible to twentieth-century readers by revealing them searching for the naked truth about the fate of humankind as they scraped away the barnacles of philosophical blathering from their sacred texts.[5]

Whatever came from God, the Puritans observed, was perfect; whatever came from human beings was fragmented, marred, broken, compromised. Faith, they taught, sprang from the very core of personal conscience—the sense of responsibility, the feelings of guilt, and the longing for forgiveness. As one scholar expressed it: "No man [or presumably woman] if he grows to maturity, escapes these experiences. Every man, sooner or later, feels himself rightly exiled from paradise and looks for a return. Puritanism is the elaboration of this theme, and the inculcation

---

4. Perry Miller, *The New England Mind: The Seventeenth Century* (Boston, 1939); *The New England Mind: From Colony to Province* (Boston, 1953), p. 269.

5. See especially George Marsden, "Perry Miller's Rehabilitation of the Puritans: A Critique," *Church History,* 39 (1970).

of its stern implications: some things are better than other things and the discovery of the best is of paramount importance."[6]

Approaching the Puritan settling of New England as a dramatic script, Miller was able to invest the clerical infighting over religious policies like the Half-Way Covenant with the theatrical suspense usually reserved for Napoleon's entrance into Moscow. His Puritans were God-intoxicated dreamers of a Bible Commonwealth. They also were the ruthless destroyers of the Pequot Indians. Like modern men, they were full of angst. Like modern women, they were deeply suspicious of the unleashed virility of natural man. Miller's Puritans were articulate opponents of most things liberal, from toleration and novel-reading to personal liberty and practical virtue. And most disruptive of American sensibilities, the Puritans were losers. They had lost to the Enlightenment's faith in human reason; they had lost to the revolutionary generation's infatuation with secular progress. Still, for those Americans who were struggling to comprehend the horror of the Holocaust in the years after World War II, it was reassuring to at last find ancestors who had more than a passing acquaintance with evil.

The advance of progress had provided an overarching theme for the histories written about the United States from the Revolution to the Second World War. But Miller's story of the Puritans drew heavily upon the Judeo-Christian tradition. It told of Biblical promises, human sinfulness, divine punishment, promised redemption, and repeated failures. Placed at the true beginning of the history of the American people in the early seventeenth century, it reversed the story line of American progress completely. Hope—exalted hopes for a people covenanted with God—came first, followed by disappointments and unexpected twists of fate. From this perspective, the nation-building acts of revolution and constitution-writing looked more like compromises than climaxes. An inescapable

6. Ralph Barton Perry, *Puritanism and Democracy* (Boston, 1945), p. 627.

conclusion from Miller's account was that there was a decided
lowering of goals at the founding of the United States. As
critics of modernity, Miller's Puritans made more intelligible
the dissenting voices of Jonathan Edwards and Henry David
Thoreau.

Students of American history now had to confront the fact
that the men of the seventeenth century had not been grooming
themselves to be forefathers of a democratic nation, but rather
came on their own mission of restoring the unity and purity of
European Christendom. This really was a liberating, if subversive, idea. So too was the recognition that though the colonial
experience had little to say about progress, it was rich with
other truths about living with hope and loss and guilt, about
sustaining communities against the ravages of change, about
defining decency, facing death, accepting failure, and enduring
the success of one's enemies.

## Social Historians Transform
## Historical Research

Miller's historical approach exercised its greatest influence
in the decades after World War II, when American historians
were working out an interpretation of their country's past which
explained why the United States had diverged so strongly from
the totalitarian regimes spread by communism and fascism. In
these same years, a whole new generation of social historians
set out to reconstruct the details of how ordinary Americans
had once lived. Interest in this new research in social history
can be partly explained by the personal backgrounds of the
cohort of historians who undertook the task of writing history
from the bottom up. They entered higher education with the
post-Sputnik expansion of the 1950s and 1960s, when the number of new Ph.D.s in history nearly quadrupled. Since many of
them were the children and grandchildren of immigrants, they
had a personal incentive for turning the writing of their disser-

tations into a movement of memory recovery. Others were
black or female and similarly prompted to find ways to make
the historically inarticulate speak. While the number of male
Ph.D.s in history ebbed and flowed with the vicissitudes of the
job market, the number of new female Ph.D.s in history steadily
increased from 11 percent (29) in 1950 to 13 percent (137) in
1970 and finally to 37 percent (192) in 1989.[7]

Although ethnicity is harder to locate in the records, the GI
Bill was clearly effective in bringing the children of working-
class families into the middle-class educational mainstream.[8]
This was the thin end of a democratizing wedge prying open
higher education in the United States. Never before had so
many people in any society earned so many higher degrees.
Important as their numbers were, the change of perspective
these young academics brought to their disciplines has made
the qualitative changes even more impressive. Suddenly graduate students with strange, unpronounceable surnames, with
Brooklyn accents and different skin colors, appeared in the venerable ivy-covered buildings that epitomized elite schooling.
Their parents didn't own stock; many did not even own their
own houses. Where Perry Miller had confronted the absolutism
of the inexorable workings of progress by insisting upon the
primacy of ideas in social action, these scholars approached the
Enlightenment orthodoxy with the skepticism all outsiders feel
for the ideology of the insiders.

The effect of the influx of new graduate students could be
seen almost immediately in the topics of their doctoral disser-
tations. Between 1958 and 1978, the proportion written on
subjects in social history quadrupled, overtaking political his-

7. We are grateful to the American Historical Association for providing these statistics.

8. In 1975 3.9 percent of doctorates in history were earned by minority students; in
1990, 6.9 percent. But these figures represent percentages of those willing to identify
their ethnicity (more than 90 percent of respondents). *Summary Report 1990: Doctorate
Recipients from United States Universities* (Office of Scientific and Engineering Personnel, National Research Council, Washington, D.C., 1991), pp. 40–41, 88.

tory as the principal area of graduate research.[9] Like the Boston Brahmins who formed the caste of gentlemen scholars of the nineteenth century, these young researchers looked for their ancestors in the American past, but they found them in most unlikely places for historical personages—shop floors, slave quarters, drawing rooms, relocation centers, temperance meetings, barrios, sod houses, rice fields, and tent revivals. Their radically different perspective on the American past—so understandable in the light of their backgrounds—threw into sharp relief the standards of significance which earlier generations of gentleman scholars had assumed when they concentrated upon statesmen, generals, diplomats, intellectuals, and elite institutions.

Equipped with computer skills and excellent eyes, the young scholars of the 1960s began poring over long-ignored records of births, marriages, deaths, probate inventories, land titles, slave purchases, city plans, and tax assessments. From these forgotten sources, they ingeniously mapped out the patterns of life and death, marriage and mobility, opportunity and outcome in the American past. They also illuminated the lives of those men and women who had been cast into the shadows by the conventional spotlight thrown on pathbreakers and heroes. Digging away in the public archives for thirty years now, social historians have discovered tales of frustration and disappointment which cannot be easily assimilated to the monolithic story of American success.

To reconstruct the character and structure of ordinary life was not easy. There was first of all deciding what was typical, a quality that could be determined only by examining the long-run records of large numbers of people. Unlike diaries and letters, such records do not speak for themselves. They can only answer questions that have been carefully posed by expert in-

9. Robert Darnton, "Intellectual and Cultural History," in Michael Kammen, ed., *The Past Before Us: Contemporary Historical Writing in the United States* (Ithaca, 1980), P. 334.

vestigators. And these kinds of questions require testable hypotheses. Did colonial Americans marry young and have many children? And if their population dynamics differed from time to time and place to place, what were the mechanisms that accounted for shifts? Did family patterns change when an agrarian way of life gave way to industrial labor? If so, what were the factors mediating between the external economy and the personal choices of farmers and servants? If workers were in demand in the New World, what factors determined which external source of labor supplied the deficiency? Or more specifically, did Virginians turn to slave labor when white immigrants ceased to come to the New World or because the decline in the mortality rate made it worthwhile to invest in the entire life of a laborer or because the growth in the number of planters buying slaves created an incentive to slavers to bring their ships to the Chesapeake? Which immigrants went to what cities? Did cities attract immigrants because they offered employment or did a pool of immigrants drawn to a particular city by ethnic ties attract manufacturers looking for cheap labor? Questions like these inspired fresh research; they also transformed into evidence the inert notations on documents buried in public record offices and private account books. And from this evidence came the stuff of new narratives about the American past.

The social sciences—particularly sociology and economics—had long been engaged in tracking patterns of behavior, so these disciplines were able to furnish historians with theories and models. With well-framed hypotheses to test, scholars could afford to lavish months, even years, calculating the relative fertility of black women in Jamaica, Barbados, and Virginia or the proportion of tenant and farmer-owned acreage in selected counties of Iowa. These new methods also enabled historians to move away from the exploits of the exceptional leader and determine instead the norms of the unexceptional plain members of society. Since their new sources of information yielded more numbers than words, researchers had to become proficient in statistics. Soon a new vocabulary made its appearance in history books with references to gini coefficients, bell curves, and guttman scaling. Long the guardians of the particular, historians now found themselves talking about the repetitious. They took on board a new lexicon filled with words like "norm," "pattern," "process," "structure," "organization," and "system." Quantitative researchers—familiarly referred to as "number crunchers"—brought history closer to the social sciences, much to the dismay of those who maintained that history was a literary art.

At the same time that daily newspapers were introducing contemporary Americans to demographics, scholars began studying population dynamics in the past. Historical demographers arduously reconstituted families from the scribbled entries in seventeenth-century parish registers and nineteenth-century vital records. Unlike the genealogists, however, these social historians were not seeking distinguished ancestors, but rather the most intimate details of ordinary life. It is hard now to appreciate how little was known twenty-five years ago about the fundamental facts of life and survival, life and life chances in historical America. And, as Perry Miller had already shown, a different encampment in the American past necessarily led to different truths. This was strikingly the case with those social historians who investigated the behavior of groups and reported their findings by talking about patterns and processes deduced from averages, means, modes, and standard deviations. The importance of the systematic had finally been flushed out of America's historical records. At last historians could see a system—or more ominously, the system—controlling access to opportunity and categorizing the worth of men and women while distributing the nation's cultural and economic goods.

Looking at the life cycle of average Americans, social historians necessarily found out more about groups than about individuals. They even made precise the nature of that group dependency which native-born white Americans had found so threatening in the "wretched refuse" of Europe's teeming shores. In their scholarship, the archetypal American—that autonomous pathbreaker—was replaced by the community member, deeply socialized and fervently bound to kith and kin. Once located and studied, the historical experiences of women, of children, of laborers, of ethnic neighbors, of slaves, and of Indians could become part of America's historical consciousness. Yet scholarship alone would not accomplish this act of inclusion. New interpretations were needed, for much like the relation of bricks to blueprints, discrete pieces of research rely on design for incorporation in a structure—in this case, a structure of meaning. Accustomed to a celebratory account of the American past, many historians found it awkward to describe those lives that had been marked by struggles without success. The newly reconstructed narratives about "the other Americans" fit ill with stories of progress or analyses that began with uniform economic drives.

There was more than an armory of anticelebratory values in the new social history. There was life—Irish, Italian, and Jewish immigrants recoding the culture of the block as they moved through neighborhoods; pioneer women pouring the grief of separation into their prairie diaries; freed slaves miraculously reconstituting their dispersed families in the heady days after Emancipation; Polish housewives juggling their New World choices against their husbands' opinions about women's place. Black Americans, so long hidden under the blanket rubric of slaves, came alive when they were encountered as persistent carriers of their indigenous culture or intrepid self-liberators (a term which jars readers into seeing how the language of the masters controls perception of their workers).

It would be hard to exaggerate the dissonance between a historical account told through the doings of an individual— the American Adam, the innovative pathbreaker, the solitary dissident—and history built up with the modular units of group experience. Whether the historians' subject was the charter families of Germantown, Pennsylvania, the enslaved Ibos of South Carolina, the Dust Bowl migrants of Oklahoma, or the political leaders of the Progressive era, the story had a different ring when the actors were approached as members of a group.

## The Implication of Social History
## for Multiculturalism

History, like literature, speaks directly to curiosity about human experience, but it takes concrete details to open the door into an imaginative recreation of the past. Philip Greven reports that fathers in Andover, Massachusetts, prevented their sons from marrying until their late twenties by barring their access to land.[10] A few statistics about wills, ages at marriage, and land conveyances and the reader could fill in the social reality of parental control and filial submission. Would the reader chafe under these constraints? Did *they*? What kind of satisfaction was there in being part of a lineal family, manuring the fields that generations to come would plant? The effect of this new capacity to vivify the characteristics of countless mundane lives is moral. It sparks a human connection. There is an enormous difference, for instance, between knowing that there were slave quarters and being able to gaze at a floor plan, calculating living space while imagining young children playing within or perhaps even the hulking figure of a black man aching with the pain of a flogging. What the history of ordinary life delivers is the shock of recognition—my kind is humankind.

Looked at this way, it is clear that social historians put their research on a collision course with the conventional accounts of the American past, which had relied in turn upon the inevitability of progress. They worked with different subject matter, and they brought to their topics different assumptions about human nature. The undersocialized concept of man that we identified as characteristic of earlier national histories ran headlong into the oversocialized concept of men and women which emerged from work in the social sciences. That old, familiar tale of the pioneer alone with his family on the frontier, or the Protestant alone with his God, or the rights-bearing man alone with his conscience, only made sense within a frame of reference celebrating the individual over the group.

10. Philip Greven, *Four Generations* (Ithaca, N.Y., 1970).

The conviction that society got to the individual first and stamped her or him with a group identity raised a number of troubling questions about the older belief in universal human traits. Qualities that had been assumed to be natural might possibly be social in origin. The insistence of social historians that the historical experience of women be taken seriously also challenged the easy equating of universal standards with those which were merely male. Historical research on women's lives revealed differences which threw into sharp relief just how gender-specific was the male ideal that had dominated Western letters since the Greeks. Perhaps nothing made clearer the exercise of power involved in the writing of American history during the first two centuries than the exclusive focus upon male interests and achievements.

The new histories made salient yet another unexamined assumption of traditional American historiography: the idea that human nature itself was the source of the motives for action. As long as it was believed that human beings had been endowed with universal behavioral drives, there had been no need to consider the specific meaning attached to the motivations of historical persons. But if particular societies shaped their members' intentions through culture, then it became necessary for historians to examine the matrix of meaning behind human motives as a separate factor, because human nature could no longer be seen as supplying the invisible springs of action and desire. Here the theoretical insights of social historians converged with the idealist emphasis of intellectual historians like Miller. In addition, the richly textured scholarly work of cultural anthropologists gave social historians a theoretical framework for discussing how societies integrate values into their workaday way of life. All rejected the Enlightenment conviction that universal human struggles for liberty had supplied the motive power for historical changes which were moving expeditiously forward on the greased track of inexorable improvement. In this emphasis on the shaping force of social values, the social historians were following in the footsteps of the African-American sociologist W.E.B. DuBois, who had powerfully demonstrated in his 1903 masterpiece *The Souls of Black Folk* how racial hostility supplied the grist for the Southern mill of segregation.

More and more it appeared likely to historians that culture gave form and meaning to people's lives and that only by exploring a particular group's values could their actions be understood. It was not enough to identify a human emotion like ambition or jealousy and let it explain an action. Rather, from a cultural perspective, emotions would be structured in distinctive ways varying with time and place. If one believed, as students of culture do, that particular societies provide the channels for expressing emotions and interests, then that specificity would become the object of historical curiosity. If every baby has to be taught how to think and act like a member of her or his group, then only the reconstruction of that prescribed behavior could open up the world of motivation and meaning to the historian.

The social history research of the past twenty years has lifted from obscurity the lives of those who had been swept to the sidelines in the metahistory of progress. It has also pierced the veil of those hidden systems which regulated the flow of opportunities and rewards in the United States, demonstrating how their functioning influenced the personal outcomes of success and failure. Those disinherited from the American heritage had at last found advocates at the bar of historical justice. Because this scholarship concentrated on the past experience of undistinguished Americans—many of them long subjected to bias and harassment—it has been criticized as a thinly veiled attack on American institutions themselves, just as the social historians' avidity for the obscure details of past lives has been decried for trivializing the grand themes of national history.

The relationship of history to American citizenship had been flushed out from its cover behind the conventional historical record of high politics. As Mary Douglas said, nations need to control national memory, because nations keep their shape by shaping their citizens' understanding of the past. Yet in practice it is the historians who do research on the past, write the histories, and teach the nation's youth. It is they who lock up and unlock memory. Close to one-eighth of all Americans between the ages of twelve and twenty-one right now are enrolled in a course on the history of the United States. Whether democratic leaders like it or not, historians fashion the nation's collective self-understanding, but they do it without thinking of themselves as agents of the state. Thus, the political imperatives embedded in the uses of national histories are complicated by the dispersal of authority in a democracy. The simple sociological truism about the need to control national memory is fraught with problems for the investigators who are committed to the integrity of free inquiry.

History is a disciplined inquiry about past events, separate from what the guardians of nationalism might want its citizens to believe. Moreover, public officials and history teachers are not the only ones involved. A democratic perspective includes far more than the government's point of view, embracing as it does all the different groups with their divergent opinions within the society. The idea that nations control the memory of their citizens pushes to the fore the question of which persons are in charge of the nation. They may be virtuous leaders, cultural elites, locally powerful minorities, pluralistic coalitions, triumphant interest groups, or the winning competitors in the latest electoral donnybrook. Whichever they are, they are manifestly not the whole people. So to speak of the nation as an institution working assiduously to forget experiences incompatible with its righteous self-image is to fudge the issue of whose experiences must be forgotten and for which group's benefit. A democratic nation—particularly one with as many different ethnic groups as the United States—embraces a citizenry much fuller than its official representation.

Conflicts of interest abound here. National leaders try to control the collective memory in order to forge a civic identity, while other groups in society recount particular stories to build solidarity, often in defiance of those seeking a shared past. Dif-

ferently situated still, historians—when they are true to the
ideals of truth-seeking and objectivity—seek to expand and
complicate the collective memory beyond the utilitarian limits
of consensus-building. In doing this they may well turn up
information that undermines a nation's self-congratulatory image or challenges a group's cherished beliefs about its past. It is
also the case that historians can take on the role of social critic,
eschewing the cold facade of scientific fact and pointing their
research toward moral lessons. These clashes make the writing
of the history of one's own country different from other historical work, for with it, a relatively open-ended scholarly inquiry
collides with the vigilant censor of national self-interest and the
group pressure of celebratory self-fashioning. And when this
happens, historians are made acutely aware that they are also
citizens who believe that what their country represents is inte-
grally connected to what one thinks the country has done in the
past.

From the historical review in these first four chapters it
should be clear that the ideals embodied in the Declaration of
Independence came to reflect the highest aspirations of an as-
cendant West as it moved to conquer both the world of nature
and those people classified as "backward." Its affirmations re-
sonated with eighteenth-century Americans, providing them
with an ennobling identity as a nation. Over time, these principles precipitated divisive issues about how best to live up to
the national goals, as the slaughter of the Civil War so agoniz-
ingly demonstrated. Then and today, America stands for a set
of abstractions pointing to the superiority of individual freedom, restrained government, open opportunity, mutual tolerance, and diplomatic support for free nations. Honestly
embraced, these ideals raise expectations that bear on citizens
and officials alike; demoted to patriotic bombast, they threaten
the cohesion of the nation and its connection to the cause of
democracy worldwide. Having chosen to knit themselves together as a people with the propositions of liberal democracy,
Americans initially turned their history into a record of national
cohesion.

The ferocity of the current argument about how United States history should be taught reveals the important fact that the stories recounted about the past have power. Indeed, the rendering of the American past—told and retold in textbooks, sermons, and campaign literature—has played a major role in the course of the events themselves. This grand narrative, worked out in scholarly and popular writings, powerfully influenced the invisible process that mobilized resources and distributed rewards. The values it propagated determined the character of American ambition and established the magnetic poles of virtue and vice, attention and indifference, success and failure. From the Revolution to the early twentieth century, this history came from a small, well-established subset of the nation's population, and it invariably flattered the members of this elite. In these histories, their social preferences have been embedded in stories of the nation's achievements, leaving children with a set of values that were male in gender, white in color, and Protestant in cultural orientation. They used the striking prosperity of the United States, in comparison to the poverty of other countries, as incontestable evidence of the superiority of capitalism with its legal deference to private ownership and its moral aversion to social planning. Opposition to these inferences, particularly the conflation of democracy and free enterprise, has animated dissenting historians since the beginning of this century.

Eighty years ago, Charles Beard and the Progressives attacked the veneration of the Constitution by pointing out the pecuniary interests of the Founding Fathers and the perdurability of interest-group conflict. Believing that the patriotic view of the nation's founding acted as a bar to contemporary reforms, they used historical scholarship to strip away sentimentality and revive curiosity about more authentic human motives. Social historians during the past three decades have concentrated upon the experience of America's outsiders—the poor, the persecuted, and the foreign. Their scholarship has revealed the fragility of community in an economic order which promotes competition for jobs and money and exposes working-class families to the inevitable ups and downs of the business cycle. The structural punishments of capitalism, they argue, have been denied through a presentation of reality which ascribes poverty to character flaws and bad luck. To tell the story of striking miners, Southern sharecroppers, or factory-working mothers, as they have, does more than give voice to the previously inaudible, it exposes the costs of capitalism.

Because social historians have set out to explore the linkages between conventional national history and the maintenance of the status quo, they have aroused the ire of patriots who claim that today's university faculty is filled with the middle-aged and tenured radicals whose political values were forged in the caldron of the fiery sixties. Offensive to them also has been the cultural wedge driven between contemporary Americans and their illustrious forebears. The documented differences between the worldview of America's revolutionary generation and that of the present generation have made it difficult to believe that the Founding Fathers existed to bring forth the American nation of the twentieth century. Like ourselves, eighteenth-century men and women now appear to have responded to contingent events as they moved into an unknown future. Reattaching the Founding Fathers to their own time has simultaneously detached them from the grand narrative of progress, making it all the harder to believe in a national destiny in which the United States carried the torch for all mankind.

Like John Donne, critics of the new social history have lamented, " 'Tis all in pieces, all coherence gone."[11] And indeed, it seems as though the new scholarship about ordinary people has produced more history than the nation can digest. This research that has continued unabated since the 1960s has fundamentally altered the relationship between history and democratic nationalism. There has been an avalanche of information—much of it unassimilable into any account written to celebrate the nation's accomplishments. This raises very forcefully the disturbing possibility that the study of history does

11. John Donne, "The Anatomy of the World."

not strengthen an attachment to one's country. Indeed, the reverse might be true, i.e., that open-ended investigation of the nation's past could weaken the ties of citizenship by raising critical issues about the distribution of power and respect.

Ruminating on the hardship and heartbreak of human life, a youthful Richard Niebuhr wondered how the Puritan message could ever have been portrayed as having been defeated— it had been ignored, maybe, but what, he asked, could ever render irrelevant the Puritans' convictions about "the precariousness of life's poise, or of the utter insecurity of human society, just as ready to plunge into the abyss of disintegration, barbarism, and the war of all against all as to advance towards harmony and integration." Here Niebuhr anticipates why late-twentieth-century Americans have responded to the sermons of Puritan divines while recoiling from the simplistic oratory of a Daniel Webster whose speeches schoolchildren once committed to memory. Miller's recovery of the stern Puritan message and social historians' discovery of the pain and hardship of not being in the charmed circle of success have struck resonating chords with a generation of Americans concerned about nuclear war, the population explosion, the decline of family stability, the AIDS epidemic, the rise of drug dependence, the disappearance of endangered species, and the depletion of the ozone layer.

Almost two centuries ago, historians began looking to the past for the laws of social development. Confidence in this enterprise has now yielded to a profounder skepticism that questions whether such laws exist. Indeterminacy about human processes seems more believable today than the determinacy of inexorable processes. Human agency, contingency, roads not taken—once the inspiration of novelists and poets—have returned to intrigue the historian. Uncoupled from the quest for general social knowledge, history has found itself linked to a new set of public issues—those connected with the dawning appreciation of America's multifaceted past and its multicultural heritage.

° 5 °

# Discovering the Clay Feet
## of Science

OF ALL THE CERTAINTIES inherited from the eighteenth
and nineteenth centuries, the heroic model of science
has proved to be the most enduring. Even radicals
and skeptics considered science an essential tool in
the dismantling of old absolutisms. Throughout most of this
century, American historians in the Progressive tradition, from
Beard and his followers to the new social historians of the
1960s, found an ally in pure science. With methods they labeled
scientific, the twentieth-century reformers of the American historical consciousness shattered old icons about the nation. The
result has been the creation of competing, multicultural visions
of the American past.

Understandably, those with a liberal or reformist persuasion recoiled at dismantling the model of science which had
served them so well. For a long time the intellectual and material benefits derived from science appeared so unmitigated by
bad side effects, unintended consequences, or environmentally
dangerous applications that the heroic model of value-free science seemed the only way to guarantee the certainty of knowledge about the human condition, past or present. Then, rather
suddenly, the reticence to criticize it vanished. In the postwar
era the heroic model of science came undone.

In the history of Western science, as in much else, Hiro-
shima marked a major and frightening turning point. In the

decades that followed, nuclear science, cloaked in the mantle of disinterest and neutrality, served the interests of all Cold Warriors while the nuclear scientists and bomb-builders worked for any government that needed them. To no one's surprise, at the end of the Cold War some nuclear scientists and technologists faced with imminent unemployment seemed capable of taking their skills to any tyrant or potentate, or simply to the highest bidder. As military goals came increasingly to shape the contours of postwar science and technology, people became anxious about the uses to which the new technology might actually be put.[1] To the fear of nuclear war was added concern about environmental damage. In this menacing setting, the notion of value-free science, ready to be taken up by whatever government or cause, seemed not just amoral but potentially immoral.

Cold War anxieties and disillusionment with the heroic image of science encouraged historians and philosophers to interrogate scientists and their practices. Immediately after World War II, historians of science, many of whom had seen war service, resumed their investigations with the encouragement of the scientists. But the history of science now took on a new mission. Some of its promoters had also been at the very center of the American wartime effort to build the nuclear bomb. With the end of the war the question became who would control nuclear technology. In 1945 many feared that if nuclear science and technology were not brought under firm civilian control, the power of the military might undermine democracy, scientific freedom, and international stability. Among the four or five most important American administrators of the American wartime nuclear program was the chemist and president of Harvard, James B. Conant. With various liberal allies he joined

---

1. Ann Markusen, Peter Hall, Scott Campbell, and Sabina Deitrick, *The Rise of the Gun Belt: The Military Remapping of Industrial America* (New York, 1991), p. 3. And for prescriptions, Ann Markusen, "Dismantling the Cold War Economy," *World Policy Journal,* Summer 1992, pp. 389–99. See also Arnold Thackray, ed., *Science After '40* (Chicago, 1992) and Stuart W. Leslie, *American Science and the Cold War* (New York, 1992).

a national campaign to promote the civilian control of nuclear power. Scientists like Conant did not want to see postwar nuclear policy set secretly by the military; they also wanted to foster international cooperation and arms control. Within the framework of these prescriptions, a citizenry knowledgeable about science through its history would become indispensable supporters of Conant's cause.

From the podium provided by the presidency of Harvard University, Conant made the case for civilian control and scientific freedom along with a revitalized study of the history of science. Science had to be made accessible if it was to be understood. Its traditions and rational procedures had to be appreciated by laymen, whose task in a democracy was to exert firm civilian control over all matters in domestic and foreign policy. Recognizing that much of twentieth-century science was so complicated as to be daunting, Conant urged that science be taught to nonspecialists through its history. He called for the creation of whole new disciplines to study science and to teach about its centuries of achievement to a new postwar generation of American undergraduates.

Led by the Harvard initiative, the history, sociology, and philosophy of science emerged after 1945 as distinct disciplines with new departments established at a number of major universities. At Harvard, historical case studies were used in courses about science in order to illustrate its extraordinary progress. In other universities, history departments once content to teach nothing but political, diplomatic, and military history hired their token historian of science. In the 1970s the history of technology also emerged as a distinct discipline.

At the heart of Conant's vision for the history of science lay value-free, progressive science. That model prevailed in most history of science courses right into the 1960s. In the previous decade, John U. Nef, a leading historian of industrialization, explained that Western science alone could be distinguished "from all science of the past . . . [by] the rigour with which the scientists have confined themselves in their inquiries . . . to the objective analysis and examination of matter, space, time and motion." For Nef the freedom of the human spirit "was the principal power behind the scientific revolution."[2] His contemporary the Cambridge University historian Herbert Butterfield insisted that the history of science should be the bridge between the arts and the sciences. In 1948 he offered a series of general lectures about the Scientific Revolution to students at Cambridge and assured them that "since the rise of Christianity there is no landmark in history that is worthy to be compared with this." He also believed that living in the postwar era gave the historian a unique understanding of the historical importance of science in Western culture since the eighteenth century. To this day Butterfield's lectures remain the most readable general introduction to the Scientific Revolution that has been written in English.[3]

But by the 1970s everything Conant, Butterfield, and their generation had in mind when they urged that science be taught through its history had unraveled. Instead of illustrating the wonders of scientific rationality and objectivity—the obstacles met and conquered by the heroes of science—a new history of science challenged the heroic model. Some suspected that rather than making students more knowledgeable about the West's most distinctive cultural achievements, Conant and his allies had unwittingly created a sinister Trojan horse concealing irreverent critics. Once released, they would trample irresponsibly through the academic groves and damage the reputation of the science in which Conant's generation had so fervently believed.

## The Kuhnian Trojan Horse

Ironically, it was one of Conant's followers at Harvard, Thomas S. Kuhn, who brought the horse into the center of public controversy. A teacher in the new history of science

2. John U. Nef, *Cultural Foundations of Industrial Civilization* (Cambridge, England, 1958), pp. 23, 64.

3. Herbert Butterfield, *The Origins of Modern Science 1300–1800* (New York, 1957), p. 201.

curriculum there, Kuhn developed a thesis that relied upon social factors to help explain the origins of scientific revolutions. In *The Structure of Scientific Revolutions*, published in 1962 and prefaced by a statement from Conant, Kuhn argued that each scientific field is organized around an overarching, or paradigmatic, theory. In normal, everyday science the social networks and community experiences of scientists in laboratories and professional associations help reinforce the dominant paradigm. Sealed off in their working enclaves, scientists routinely try to explain away any anomalies that their research might turn up. Only when forced by mounting evidence to confront these anomalies will some scientists—they are always rare—make a sudden mental shift which permits them to break with normal science. This is how scientific revolutions occur. The paradigm shift, from one theory to another, permits scientists to break away from the assumptions taken for granted in old theory governing everyday normal science. Again according to Kuhn, social factors keep scientists tied to normal science, while theory shifts let them escape.

Nothing in this account seems either sinister or suggestive of a Trojan horse.[4] But when it first appeared, Kuhn's book was blamed for introducing the notion of social conditioning into the way in which scientists routinely proceed, and thus conceivably into the way they break with existing paradigms. In retrospect, it is possible to see Kuhn's book as a sign of the times, an example of the growing effort, originally encouraged by Conant and others, to understand the nature of scientific knowledge because it had become increasingly and disturbingly important.

Notice what Kuhn's book did and did not say. In the Kuhnian model, scientists most of the time are sequestered, not only from rival theories, but also away from larger social, economic, and political interests. In that situation and under the guiding influence of their paradigm, they routinely do normal science.

4. The following essay offers a similar analysis of what Kuhn said: Steve Fuller, "Being There with Thomas Kuhn: A Parable for Postmodern Times," *History and Theory*, 31 (1992): 241–75.

Only a dramatic, theoretical innovation, the now famous paradigm shift, will shake them loose from their theoretical moorings and permit the emergence of new, revolutionary science. Kuhn did not say that these shifts occur in opposition to the methods of science or without regard for empirical work.

Kuhn did not intend to open the door to relativism. His model remained true to essentially realist assumptions about the relationship between what the scientist can know and how scientific laws mirror nature. For the classic philosophical realist, it is possible to imagine a tight, uncomplicated fit between the language of science and nature. In the Kuhnian model the paradigm shifts permit the scientist to adjust the angle from which the mirror is fixed on nature. The emphasis on paradigm shifts leaves the impression that at moments the mirrors can get a little fogged over by habits and clubbiness; but, in the Kuhnian model, science works because it corresponds to what is in nature, *more or less*. In contrast to a naive version of human knowing which conceives of the mind as a blank slate upon which sense data drawn from nature write, Kuhn saw the mind organized by theories, reinforced by social conventions. Kuhn did not believe, however, that the disclosure of the workings of theories or social conventions invalidated the scientific enterprise. It just made it a little more human.[5]

No amount of realism saved Kuhn from being blamed almost immediately for the rising skepticism about science. For even mentioning the social, he was accused of rendering the once objective into the hopelessly subjective. Because he said that scientific change is frequently the result of paradigm shifts made by small groups of scientists, critics said he made it seem that the "adoption of a new scientific theory is an intuitive or mystical affair, a matter for psychological description," rather than a matter of evidence and logic, pure and simple.[6] In the last thirty years *The Structure of Scientific Revolutions* has been

---

5. We owe our emphasis here to Ruth Bloch.

6. Israel Scheffler, *Science and Subjectivity* (New York, 1967), p. 18.

translated into many languages and has sold over 750,000 copies worldwide. Kuhn's sociological vision of science became synonymous with retreat from the heroic model of scientists with their special purchase on truth. That retreat was, however, neither swift nor steady. Before it occurred, one final philosophical barrier had to be breached.

In the eyes of Kuhn's generation, the generation that fought and won World War II, heroic science had seemed both philosophically correct and morally necessary. Even the threat of nuclear destruction could not shake their conviction that science and its history provided, as Conant put it, "the basis for a better discussion of the ways in which rational methods may be applied to the study and solution of human problems."[7] As to what might be concluded from the history of twentieth-century nuclear science once the story got to the nuclear bomb, Conant assured Americans that its destructive power might just be "the price we pay for health and comfort and aids to learning in this scientific age."[8] Believing that science laid the foundations for progress and rationality in the West, Conant and his generation of historians and scientists were not about to sacrifice it on the altar of social explanations. As Western scientists had done ever since Descartes, believers in heroic science grouped behind the barrier provided by philosophy. They were convinced that the social represented the irrational, and that only the mantle provided by logic and reason, philosophically understood, would save science from contamination.

## The Philosophical Armor of Heroic Science

Historians and scientists of the generation of Conant and Butterfield institutionalized the history of science in American universities because they believed that its history, as they under-

7. James B. Conant, *On Understanding Science: An Historical Approach* (New Haven, 1947), pp. xii–xiii.
8. Ibid., p. 5.

stood it, underwrote the Enlightenment's vision of science. They also possessed a powerful moral armor in academic philosophy as it was taught from the 1940s onward. Its positive approach to science stressed that science, alone among the various forms of human inquiry, worked because of an inherent rationality. At the core of science lay logical rules upon which a few of the early geniuses of science had first managed to stumble. Right into the 1980s, in some quarters of public and academic opinion the legend of science had it that "successive generations of scientists have filled in more and more parts of the Complete True Story of the World."⁹ It had been that simple and that positive.

The roots of a positive philosophy of science go back to Comte and the early nineteenth century, but more immediately to Vienna during the 1920s. There, one of the most influential philosophers of science in this century, Karl Popper, first published on the logic of scientific discovery. Forced to flee Austria and Germany in the 1930s because of Nazi persecution, Popper and his philosophical associates went to major English-speaking universities on both sides of the Atlantic. From those institutional bases their positive vision of how science works influenced historians, many of whom had been combatants against the evil that Popper and his colleagues had fled.

Buoyed by Popper and his associates, the latter sometimes called logical positivists, these philosophers taught that only a positive—and we would argue an essentially ahistorical—understanding of science could reinforce the barrier of reason in a century where reason had been in short supply.¹⁰ Popper emphasized that cooperation among disinterested scientists makes for objective knowledge. If it cannot be falsified, this knowl-

9. Written with irony by Philip Kitcher, *The Advancement of Science: Science without Legend, Objectivity without Illusions* (New York, 1993), p. 3.

10. In the interest of brevity we have necessarily elided the differences between Popper and many logical positivists. We take Popper as the emblematic figure because of his enduring interest in the questions that concern us here; cf. Robert Proctor, *Value-Free Science? Purity and Power in Modern Knowledge* (Cambridge, Mass., 1991), pp. 209–12.

edge is true forever. In Popper's telling, the job of the philosopher was to understand how the game of science is played, how the scientist probes "into the unknown reality behind the appearances, and [is] anxious to learn from mistakes."[11] Allied to science, the philosopher explicates the philosophical logic working in it. The logic of science is distinctive, and the discipline provided by scientific experimentation and mathematical reasoning rivets the mind on nature. The positive, unrelenting logic of science, the armor that girds Western truth-seeking, stands as the model for the methods of all other disciplines.

Popper's faith in the logic of science had been forged amid a bitter reality. Throughout much of this century the assault on rationality has been associated, quite rightly, with totalitarian political systems. Popper and his fellow refugees from Nazism saw its irrationalities as further support for their belief in the intimate link between the neutrality of science and the possibility of rational thought and action. Only the Nazis, they believed, had sought to manipulate science, and they of course were the great enemies of both reason and objectivity. The point was not lost on British and American intellectuals of the 1940s. They had watched with horror as fascism took hold in the heart of scientifically advanced industrial countries. Suddenly the Western enterprise with its commitment to scientific rationality seemed fragile at best. Added to its fragility came the threat posed by Soviet communism. Both before and after the war, the emergence of communism and Nazism provided very good reasons for preserving every aspect of the Enlightenment legacy. The generation that fought against totalitarianism and won World War II needed heroic science. Because those of that generation knew that totalitarianism was inherently immoral and its premises irrational, they naturally believed that science in totalitarian societies could not be rational.

The generation of Conant, Butterfield, and Nef viewed science through lenses that had been focused by Popper and his

11. Karl P. Popper, *Realism and the Aim of Science* (Totowa, N.J., 1983), p. xxv. Much of this was written in the 1950s, but publication was delayed into the 1980s.

followers. Some of these philosophers believed that the methods of science and in particular its search for the laws of nature could be transferred to the social sciences and to the study of history. Historians should look for the laws of historical development. As late as the 1960s, students in American graduate schools of history were asked to read articles about the nature of history's "covering laws." That no historian had ever been able to find a single historical law that worked universally left the logical positivists unmoved.[12] Generally, and perhaps mercifully, most of them ignored history, regarding it as irrelevant to the task of explicating philosophically the rationality and neutrality of science. Their enterprise recalls the agenda set by those positivists of the nineteenth century, Comte and his followers. They too had named science—pure, simple, unadulterated—the last, positive stage of human inquiry.

Into the 1970s, Karl Popper was still arguing that the purpose of his philosophy of science had been to justify the rationality of science and to counter intellectual and moral relativism, which he saw as the main philosophical malady of the time. Popper worried about the renewed danger of relativism revived by Kuhn's book and the implications drawn from it by a rising generation of social historians. Of course, Popper had always thought that historical arguments would lead to relativism, and here it was back again, alive and well (even if hiding in the Trojan horse) in the work of Thomas Kuhn.

Popper took the highest ground he could find against a social reading of science by appealing to metaphysics. Imagine the contempt in his voice when he said: "I do not regard methodology as an empirical discipline, to be tested, perhaps by the facts of the history of science."[13] So much for the social history

---

12. In saying there are no universal laws of history, we do not seek to deny the possibility of there being patterns of cause and effect that may even on occasion be replicable. For covering laws, see C. G. Hempel, "The Function of General Laws in History," *Journal of Philosophy*, 39 (1942): 35–48; and for a discussion of Hempel's position, see Louis O. Mink, *Historical Understanding*, eds. Brian Fay, Eugene O. Golob, and Richard T. Vann (Ithaca, N.Y., 1987).

13. Popper, *Realism*, p. xxv.

of science, at least as far as Popper and his followers were concerned. Instead Popper wrapped science in a mantle he described as metaphysical realism. Scientific method rested on the rules of logic, on the testing of theories, not simply upon fact-gathering. The relative success or failure of any empirically focused exploration of natural phenomena did not determine the rationality of science.

When Popper invoked metaphysical realism, he was trying to move the terrain right out from under the feet of the new social history of science. But he also wanted to be sophisticated and cautious about the way he mounted his philosophical rescue operation. As seen in the earlier discussion of heroic science, philosophical realism lies at the heart of its claim to represent nature exactly in its laws. When the scientist speaks, whatever the vernacular, his words are really about the eternally true, or the eternally unfalsifiable in Popper's important modification. Unlike all previous science, which barely deserves the name, true science depends upon the mirrors that the scientist flashes on the world.

But as Popper well knew, there are dangers in a naive version of the realist argument. What if accepted, everyday science gets it wrong and is overthrown by new, better science? Was Ptolemy doing bad science, or no science at all, when he postulated the earth in the center of the universe, an error which Copernicus and his followers caught only centuries later? Does progress in science render nonscientific everything that went before the latest discovery? To argue that science *is* nature in the sense that its laws correspond to what is actually going on in nature opens up as many philosophical problems as it seeks to close down.

Popper argued instead that the realism of science lies not in a naive correspondence between the empirically tested world and the mind of the scientist, but in the rules of logic, in falsification and verification. He preferred the term "metaphysical realism," because it suggested a model of science evolving by its own internal logic—a logic that transcends history—and leaves open the question of just how tight the fit need be between the laws and the there out there. Placed in opposition to the social history of science, metaphysical realism claims that there are "purely scientific revolutions that are not connected with *ideological* revolutions." In Popperian logic, ideology equals impurity, and both equal the illogical, and hence neither has anything to do with the actual thought processes of the scientist. Popper tried to save the scientific baby by taking it out of the historical water altogether before the skeptical social historians could come along and drown it in historicity. By contrast, we will argue that scientific revolutions are also ideological revolutions but that the ideological dimension does not undermine the validity of the scientific breakthrough. Science can be historically and socially framed and still be true.

## The Generation of the 1960s

Right up to the 1960s the understanding of science taught in American universities had stayed close to the triumphant story told by Andrew Dickson White at Cornell in the 1890s. The history of science had been written by men with strong backgrounds in science and little training in historical methods. In the history of medicine up to the 1960s the situation was similarly skewed toward doctors who also practiced history. Then a new generation of young women and men came to White's Cornell from the big East Coast cities, from parochial and public schools, from parents who had seen war service as ordinary soldiers, sometimes in segregated units, or who had immigrated from Eastern and Western Europe in this century. To their skepticism about elite culture was added the moral turmoil induced by the Vietnam War and the civil rights movement. Professionalization accompanied democratization. In perhaps the final irony of all, science fell under the gaze of science-inspired historical methods wielded by a new generation more interested in writing true history than in preserving the truth of science.

In nearly every field the new social history described in Chapter 4 challenged and dethroned the inherited intellectual absolutisms. When the same thing happened in the history of science, an icon of Western culture was undermined. The challenge ignited a war, what we will call, in honor of the terminology used at the time, the War between the Internalists and the Externalists. The so-called Internalists took an essentially Popperian position with regard to science. Its historical development occurred as the result of empirical work and the unfolding of the rules of logic. Basically the history of science had nothing to do with the social. The heroes of science got put up on their pedestals because they were true heroes, smarter and more creative than everyone else.

Under the influence of social history, a new generation of so-called Externalist historians of science looked for the larger interests and values at work within communities of scientists. The Externalist position—the term misleadingly predetermines what is inside and what must therefore be outside—vastly extended the definition of the social. Whereas Kuhn confined it to networks of scientists, the generation of the 1960s made it the universe beyond the laboratory or university. With the battle cry "social context," the Externalists took up arms against the Internalists. The war was waged, not surprisingly, around the pedestals of the scientific heroes.

Born under the shadow of the bomb, the generation of the 1960s took a very different approach to science from that of most of its predecessors, Kuhn included. Like the Progressive historians of an earlier era, they developed new methods and asked new questions in an effort to understand the role of interests and ideologies in the making of science. Given the strength of social history by the 1960s, the history of science, not surprisingly, took a turn toward the social, now broadly defined. In centuries where most men and more women were neither literate nor leisured, it was relatively easy to find the scientists among elites, sharing their social outlook and political interests. Looking in private letters and diaries, social historians of sci-

ence found the heroes of science immersed in the power relations of their time, willing to adopt or abandon theories for
many complex, and not always disinterested, reasons. The new
social historians sought to understand scientists in relation to
governments, churches, religious beliefs, political ideologies,
even with regard to their gender identities and their material
assets and property.

In the expanded social understanding of science associated
with the Externalists, the interests, values, linguistic conventions, even pride and greed of scientists shaped their understanding of nature. In effect, the definition of what should be
considered internal to science changed dramatically. The heroes
of science tumbled off their pedestals, their statuesque feet upon
closer inspection seemed more clay than marble. Perhaps Popper had been right after all. If those mirrors in the heads of the
heroes and founders of Western science could be shown to have
been made by society, surely all of human knowledge could be
revealed as socially constructed. The position was paradoxically
a remake of the older realist, mirrors-in-the-head version of the
scientific mind common among the positivists. The positivists
and Internalists said that the scientists had mirrors always trained
on nature; the extreme Externalists said that if so, those mirrors
were the products of society. Thus trapped in the thicket of
linguistic conventions, modern science succeeds only by using
words like "nature" and "society" in ways that are entirely the
result of linguistic moves made by seventeenth-century scientists like Boyle and Newton. They invented the modern meaning of "nature," and thereby tailor-made for themselves a world
which they and their successors could in turn investigate.

Such a dramatic paradigm shift in the way historians understood science now requires inspection. The generation of Conant, Butterfield, and Nef would have been horrified by the gap
that has opened between the few remaining defenders of heroic
science and the social historians of science. Among Conant's
generation, the great teachers of the postwar history of science,
Henry Guerlac, I. B. Cohen, and Richard Westfall, never imag-

ined that their discipline could even remotely challenge the truth and status of science. In the 1950s they began programs to train the next generation to study science historically. But once again, history intervened and a process we have described as the democratization of higher education began in earnest. By the time their programs were well established an explosion had occurred in the demand for college teachers and hence in the number of graduate students seeking higher degrees. Once trained and placed in the academy, the rising generation of historians turned to the heroes.

### Reevaluating the Heroes: Newton and Darwin

Beginning in the 1960s, historians of science began to put the great icons of heroic science back into their social context. Not surprisingly, they look remarkably different when placed under a broad, social lens. The seventeenth-century English scientist Robert Boyle turned out to have formulated his law of gases while deeply involved in political and religious issues.[14] Worse still, his contemporary Isaac Newton was discovered in his laboratory practicing alchemy—nothing is as external to heroic science as magic—while a century and a half later Charles Darwin put together the theory of natural selection with one eye on the impoverished classes. The history that produced these findings was never what Conant, or even Kuhn, had in mind. It was close, however, to fulfilling Popper's fear that the study of ideology at work in the mind of scientists would lead to philosophical relativism. Could science still be true when it resulted from such a messy, seemingly irrational process of thought?

Venturing into seventeenth-century England to discover the social lair inhabited by the great geniuses of science can be a formidable excursion. Concepts like "matter theory" or definitions of pantheism do not readily spring to mind. Even defin-

14. James R. Jacob, *Robert Boyle and the English Revolution* (New York, 1977).

ing an Anglican, never mind a Leveller or a Digger, taxes the historical memory. Yet those were household words to the age when Newton lived. If you want to understand someone born in 1642, there is no escaping a brief journey into baroque metaphysics and religious sectarianism. Broaching the new social history of science requires some general history. Consolation may be found in knowing that after Newton, Darwin cannot be too far away.

Once, Westerners had a tidy picture of Newton, the rationalist. It seemed that nothing would ever destroy it, but in the 1930s new evidence about Isaac Newton, who had died two hundred years before in 1727, surfaced in the form of thousands of unpublished manuscripts. When they came up for auction in 1936 at Sotheby's in London, many were discovered to be of a decidedly "unscientific" character. Few bidders could be found for the hundreds of theological and alchemical manuscripts in the collection. At bargain prices, they dispersed to every corner of the globe, some probably lost forever. It was only in the 1960s with the professionalization of the history of science that anyone bothered to take a serious look at Newton's private writings. What historians found turned out to weaken further the model of science beloved by the logical positivists and their many followers. New evidence sometimes gives rise to anomalies, for both historians and scientists.

Reexamining the writings, both published and unpublished, of the titan of the Enlightenment revealed an Isaac Newton radically at odds with the secular hero. Newton can now be shown to have rejected certain philosophical positions not simply because the science they supported was wrong, but also, and perhaps primarily, because he believed that those positions would lead to atheism. Good seventeenth-century Protestant that he was, Newton rejected Descartes's theory of matter because it led to the denial of God's activity in the universe, and hence in Newton's mind to atheism. The Cartesian universe worked because it was completely filled: bodies moved by constantly colliding with each other; all motion resulted from the mechanical push-pull interaction between bodies, whether large or minuscule like an ether; no spiritual agency was necessary.[15]

Newton's unpublished writings, now housed in libraries from California to Israel, show him to be horrified by the religious implication of the filled Cartesian universe. To him Descartes's universe appeared not only self-regulated but also self-perpetuating, and hence godless. Here religious conviction reinforced scientific and mathematical calculations. In direct opposition to Descartes's busy, filled universe, Newton also saw from his mathematical model of the universe that no "pull" or "drag" on the motion of the planets seemed to exist; if there were extra matter, however ethereal, then his mathematical formulae would not work as well as they did. The Cartesian universe filled with swirling vortices implied extra matter of measurable weight apart from the planets. But how to abandon mechanical push-pull, the central achievement of the new science as formulated by Descartes, and not fall back into magical or teleological notions of motion as simply there because in the very nature of bodies?

The new socially focused scholarship on Newton saw religious values at work in his rejection of Descartes, and the new scholarship also revealed Newton's fascination with alchemy. The question loomed large: had Newton, one of the founders of modern science, in fact reneged on the central commitment of the new science, to pursue nature through experiment and not through magical shortcuts? Did Newton sacrifice science on the altar of his religious convictions? If historians frame the questions in ways that reflect their definitions of what science must be like, refusing to suspend belief in those definitions, then even Newton fails the test.

Religiosity approached historically held the key to explaining how Newton understood nature and science. Because of his belief in the supreme power and authority of God, as expressed

15. See A. Rupert Hall and Marie Boas Hall, trans. and eds., *Unpublished Scientific Papers of Isaac Newton* (Cambridge, 1962), pp. 142–43.

through spiritual agents and immaterial forces at work in the universe, Newton was able to escape the trap set by magic on one side—seen as fostering a kind of atheism because it made nature and magicians into forces independent from the deity—and on the other move beyond the prevailing science of his day, the Cartesian model. Newton postulated a universe with empty space dominated by spiritual forces: God, angels, "active principles," even Christ. Space became, to use his metaphor, the sensorium of God wherein He established contact with His creation. In Newton's view, the matter of the universe was dead, "brute and stupid," moved only by immaterial forces. With this model, Newton could abandon contact action between bodies as the key to motion in the Cartesian universe. He could also devote a good portion of his working life to alchemical experiments. To him they revealed the presence of invisible forces derived from an all-powerful creator. Whether Newton was studying planets or minuscule portions of chemical substances, he sought to demonstrate definitively God's creative force and continuing power.

Without the religious element in his life, Newton could not have articulated the law of universal gravitation. Newton's social universe, as it worked into his science, lay just as much in the chapel of Trinity College, Cambridge, as it did in his laboratory. Religious conviction enabled him to conceptualize universal gravitation. Divinely implanted, gravitation operates as a force in a universe composed of planets at motion in a vacuum. The physical truth of the mathematical law could finally be possible for Newton because of his religious and metaphysical convictions.

The social history of science only began with Newton's religious and philosophical writings. In search of the context of those writings it expanded outward from chapel and laboratory to his childhood and beyond, to revolutionary England during the middle and late seventeenth century. When barely twenty in 1661, the first year of the restored monarchy and reestablished church, Newton went to Cambridge University as a scholarship student who waited on the tables of his betters. In the aftermath of the Puritan revolution, Cambridge had become an ideological minefield where students and faculty picked their way through bitter doctrinal and sectarian battles. Bent upon purifying the university, churchmen sought to root out heresy even among their own kind. More tolerant Anglicans, like Newton's teachers, were willing to compromise with former Puritans, and as a result they were persecuted by the less tolerant; even the new science, because associated with the Puritan cause, was suspect. No single ideology or cultural stance or religious position determined the content of Newton's science. But cultural and social forces did set limits and give permission to certain theories and not others. Influenced by the churchmen who taught him, Newton could not countenance any theory of matter that would make it alive, dynamic, and self-regulated, or the master of its motion. Such beliefs were associated with the pantheism and materialism of the radical sectaries of the revolution. Going further than even Puritans who had started the revolution, the radicals used philosophical arguments intended to level the clergy, indeed to level society. Radicals like the Levellers argued for voting rights for all males except servants, and for property redistribution. A sect known as the Diggers wanted the communal ownership of land; the Quakers let women preach publicly before congregations. The religious beliefs of the radicals focused on the sanctity of this world, and their philosophical doctrines collapsed the separate spiritual realm back into the world of everyday things. All these beliefs amounted to atheism, according to the orthodox defenders of social order and hierarchy.

Newton's idea of the absolute, eternal truth of every aspect of his science followed from his belief in his God and his concomitant fear of atheism. With God in place, Newton knew there could be order in the universe, possibly also in society. There could also be absolute Truth which existed in a higher spiritual realm into which the world offered only occasional moments of insight. The kind of transcendent truth that Newton believed his science to possess, and that he bequeathed to the Enlightenment, started with a transference. He transferred divine authority to the laws of science. Three centuries after the first major revolution in the West it is possible to see the origins of the modern belief in the transcendence of scientific rationality in those distant seventeenth-century struggles to maintain the transcendence of the deity, to assert the supremacy of orthodox Christianity over heresy and disorder.

But Newton's historical legacy remains relevant in another way. Research in Newton's papers has even made standard notions of rationality problematic. His private alchemical writings reveal that like many of his scientific contemporaries, Newton was a practicing alchemist. Even then, but more so now, many people have defined alchemy as magic, and magic, so it is believed, could not be rational. Newton, however, practiced alchemy as a vital element in his religious and scientific enterprise. As he watched mercury begin to make gold swell, he wrote in his manuscripts how its appearances "fascinate me everyday." [16] He hid the experimental work in alchemy; its extent only came to light during the Sotheby's auction back in 1936. Many of Newton's contemporaries associated alchemists, astrologers, and magic in general with radical political movements active during the midcentury revolution. Throughout the seventeenth century the activities of alchemists were seen to be potentially subversive—imagine what it does to a currency if ordinary metals can be converted to gold—and they were also regarded as engaged in a form of deception. Alchemists were infamous for their elixirs and love potions, and when caught selling them they were routinely arrested and jailed in some countries. [17]

Once examined in the postwar era, Newton's voluminous manuscripts suggest that in the privacy of his laboratory he took

16. Betty Jo Teeter Dobbs, *The Foundations of Newton's Alchemy* (Cambridge, England, 1975), p. 253, quoting from his manuscript "The Key."

17. Prefecture of the Police, Paris, Aa / 5 / 218, the arrest (c. 1704) of Marie Magnan.

his alchemy as seriously as he took his physics. Indeed, Newton's reading in the alchemical literature may have reinforced the philosophical underpinnings of the law of universal gravitation, for it depended upon being able to imagine the force of invisible actions occurring at a distance between the planets even through the vacuum within space.[18] The distinction between science and magic, once believed to be so clear and universal, was foreign to Isaac Newton. The Newton revealed by modern research perceived nature both scientifically and philosophically in ways that were deeply influenced by the political and cultural world in which he lived. Newton remains a mathematical genius, and his method, as his notes demonstrate, was indeed rigorously experimental and extraordinarily wide-ranging, encompassing physics, optics, mechanics, and even alchemy. Nevertheless, just at the moment when Western travelers were berating the Chinese for their backward magical practices, the laboratory in Newton's rooms at Trinity College was the site of a busy, methodical, and secret effort to convert base metals into gold.

Their religious and philosophical roots buried in his private papers, Newton's laws bequeathed to the Enlightenment an understanding of nature as mathematical, ordered, and harmonious. With the assistance of some of Newton's closest associates, the *Principia* was also used against the atheists, to argue that God had designed the Newtonian universe. But gradually and ironically, the immediacy of Newton's God faded out of the Newtonian universe, and deism became the commonplace creed of many an educated person in eighteenth-century Europe. The invisible hand of the ordering deity became increasingly remote, and in the nineteenth century under the impact of Darwin's writings it became irrelevant.

In the Newtonian universe constructed by Christian

18. We are indebted here to Betty Jo Teeter Dobbs, *The Janus Faces of Genius: The Role of Alchemy in Newton's Thought* (Cambridge, England, 1991).

churchmen, the order ascribed to the planets, sustained by the deity, had been presumed to characterize biological and geological development as well. Belief in an ordered development of the earth and in the fixed nature of the species that inhabit it was entirely compatible with the belief that the act of creation described in the Bible had been a real moment in time. As told in Genesis, both the earth and humankind were created more or less as they have been known since recorded history began. Early in the nineteenth century, one aspect of the Newtonian vision of order and harmony came undone as evolutionary theory drastically reformulated the Western understanding of human and animal origins.

Obviously a break of such importance fascinated the new generation of social historians, who predictably focused their methods on the key figure in the transition, the great nineteenth-century British naturalist Charles Darwin. Born in 1809 into an elite family enamored of science, Darwin (another Cambridge man) knew and yet rejected the arguments for divinely engineered order and design as applied to biological species and geological formations. Developed during his student years, his fascination with living organisms led him to take a remarkable and harrowing five-year voyage halfway around the world. In the Americas and Africa he observed species never before recorded. The experience of "fine corals, the warm glowing weather, [and] the blue sky of the tropics" made him "wild with delight."

Upon his return to England in 1836, Darwin tried to make sense out of the "the gradual birth and death of species," the confusing evidence of his geological and biological observations. His linguistic colleagues taught him that the artifacts of nature were like the words then being so avidly investigated by philology, the new science of hermeneutics. In a passage that Darwin liked to quote, one of the leading advocates of hermeneutics explained: "Words are to the Anthropologist what rolled pebbles are to the geologist—battered relics of past ages often containing within them indelible records capable of intelligible interpretation." But how does the scientist hear amid the silence of these newly discovered artifacts? [19]

Darwin's wide familiarity with economics and social theory through the writings of Adam Smith, Auguste Comte, and especially Thomas Malthus facilitated his development of an explanation for what he had seen on his voyage. A generation earlier in his *Essay on Population* (1798), Malthus had formulated a law of population development which stated that while the food supply increases arithmetically, as one plus one, people increase exponentially, two times two. To curtail the growth of the masses and thus to obviate the necessity for this struggle, Malthus recommended sexual abstinence, particularly for the lower orders, whom he regarded as almost a separate race. The Malthusian perspective reinforced policies toward the poor being advocated by middle-class reformers. They would make the poor work and force them to compete, rather than remain tied to the charity of their betters. Many of these same liberal reformers were also freethinkers, eager to reform science, to make it less subservient to Christian doctrine and the influence of the clergy. It too should stand on its own, not shackled by the tyranny of dogma.

As a liberal Whig with industrialists in his family, Darwin sympathized with the reforming impulse. His recent biographers describe his circle as a place where "politics, science and literature were all of a piece." [20] Reform suggested that the present was better than the past, that in effect the superior drove out the inferior. In addition, the idea that struggle was at the heart of the development of a species, the Malthusian vision of population survival of the strongest with containment of the weakest by plague and famine, set Darwin to thinking. Before

19. Adrian Desmond and James Moore, *Darwin* (New York, 1991), p. 215, quoting Herschel. The quotation about his delight is on p. 140 and comes from a letter Darwin wrote to a friend. The mention of the "gradual birth and death of species" comes from his notes taken on the *Beagle* and refers to his reading of Lyell (p. 159).

20. Ibid., p. 216.

him lay the evidence he collected of fossils and birds which suggested that species had replaced other species, or that in certain geographical conditions only species with certain characteristics survived.

The fossil evidence came from his years of travel, and with it uppermost in his mind Darwin sat in his London study reading among scientists as well as theorists of market society. Perhaps the constant pressure for survival experienced by variants within an animal or human population wedged them into certain niches from which they might perish or develop. Out of the variants new species would emerge. Perhaps species are not fixed after all, simply God-given. Did he not live in a society where the poor were manifestly weaker, struggling to survive? Did it not appear that the obviously superior Europeans, heady from technological and imperial pursuits, had evolved because of certain characteristics that made it seem ridiculous now in the present that they would ever again fear barbarians? [21] Did it not seem that the reform movements of the 1830s signaled the evolving progress and improvement of society and government? These were questions alive in Darwin's intellectual circle but also in the larger society.

Darwin needed the social ideas of Malthus and others, for without them he could not have formulated the explanatory and theoretical mechanism of natural selection. Randomness—the random mutations of species—could work toward their survival or extinction, and it lay at the heart of Darwin's model. But randomness was incompatible with any belief in the divine oversight of fixed species or with a moment for special human creation. Newton's God could not have permitted the natural world seen by Darwin. Darwin needed a different metaphysics, his slowly, even painfully, acquired and very privately held atheism and materialism. Now with access to Darwin's diaries listen

21. David R. Oldroyd, "How Did Darwin Arrive at His Theory? The Secondary Literature to 1982," *History of Science*, 22 (1984): 325–74; on the barbarians, see Charles Darwin, *The Descent of Man, and Selection in Relation to Sex*, vol. 1 (London, 1871), p. 239.

to him say, almost offhandedly to himself, "It is an argument for materialism, that cold water brings on suddenly in [the] head, a frame of mind, analogous to those feelings which may be considered as truly spiritual." Hardly the sentiments of a Christian, or even of a theist. Almost incredulous, Darwin wondered to himself if it wasn't "a little remarkable that the fixed laws of nature should be 'universally' thought to be the *will* of a superior being." [22] Newton would have been horrified if he had ever peered into the heart of Charles Darwin.

The social attitudes of an imperial and market-oriented society in which continuous reform seemed possible were woven through Darwin's science. On one hand Darwin the materialist could conceptualize human equality—simply the equality of all atoms—randomly selected; the inheritance of acquired characteristics was incompatible with random selection. But Darwin the British gentleman could also effortlessly imagine that moral superiority, a characteristic so fortuitously acquired by Westerners, particularly by men, might even be inherited: "the low morality of savages . . . their insufficient powers of reasoning . . . weak power of self-command . . . this power has not been strengthened through long-continued, perhaps inherited habit, instruction and religion." [23] Darwin's racial and sexual views permeated his discussion of the origin of species and especially of the descent of man. His contemporaries were shocked by the notion that human beings had evolved from the primates. Now many people are shocked by his racism.

### Truth and the Consequences of Social History

Back during the War between the Internalists and the Externalists, the social history of science lay at the heart of the

---

22. Paul H. Barrett, Peter J. Gautrey, Sandra Herbert, et al., eds., *Charles Darwin's Notebooks, 1836–1844. Geology, Transmutation of Species, Metaphysical Enquiries* (Ithaca, N.Y., 1987), pp. 524, 535. Both excerpts were written in 1838.

23. Darwin, *Descent of Man*, vol. 1, pp. 225, 97.

fray. Inspired by it, a small group of philosophers said that they could provide a "strong programme"—the phrase, complete with British spelling, became a battle cry—for showing the socially determined or constructed nature of all scientific inquiry.[24] Although they caused a stir and agitated the philosophical heirs of logical positivism, the social constructionists could not explain the way in which technical problems, or new natural phenomena like viruses, set whole research agendas. They did, however, manage to start a philosophical discussion that encouraged some significant historical research.

This research suggests that something closer to social framing—a bracketing and limiting rather than a simple constructing—seems to occur in science. Social factors—like Darwin's attitudes toward his imagined inferiors—blend into the assumptions and values that scientists bring to their research practices. The social insight illustrated by the Newton and Darwin stories does not, however, underwrite the more extreme claims of strong programmers who have never offered an adequate theory to address the complexity of circumstances and situations that produce reasonably true human knowledge. Recent philosophers of science talk about a "hard program" and—with deliberate whimsy—challenge the macho of the strong programmers. They advise admitting failure, the dead end of social constructionism and relativism, and trying a harder task, that of understanding how the social and the cognitive cohabitate and interact.[25] As in the final section of this book, they suggest new understandings of how objective truth can be produced by deeply subjective people.

The social perspective on both Darwin and Newton enriches the history of Western science and renders into human

24. One of the main papers is by B. Barnes and D. Bloor, "Relativism, Rationalism and the Sociology of Knowledge," in M. Hollis and S. Lukes, eds., *Rationalism and Relativism* (Oxford, England, 1982).

25. W. Schmaus, U. Segerstrale, and D. Jesseph, "Hard Program: A Manifesto," *Social Epistemology. A Journal of Knowledge, Culture and Policy*, 6 (1992): 243–65. In the same issue is a particularly helpful response by Helen Longino.

scale even its greatest practitioners. But nothing in these histories denigrates the inescapable need that Darwin had for his fossils and finches or Newton for his mathematical creativity and cautious experimental rigor. It is also the case that deeply held values undergirded and even intruded into the science practiced by both Newton and Darwin. Yet much of their science was also reasonably true to nature, and remains in use. The practice of science which can be value-laden, subjective, gendered, theory-oriented, and also metaphysically informed still occasionally leads—through contention, dispute, and testing—to reasonably true statements about nature. Whether engaged in a search for knowledge about the human past as a scientist or as a historian, evidence has to be gathered, weighed, and examined. Theories have to be formulated that bear relation to the worlds around them, both natural and social. There are no blinkers in the mind filtering out the one or the other. Built into the understanding of evidence, whether it be fossils, planets, or old documents, are ideas and ideologies drawn from lived experience, identities, values, and prejudices. And not least, scientists as well as historians have metaphysical views. When Darwin formulated his theory of evolution he was an atheist and a materialist, and these religious convictions enabled him to seek purely random explanations for the origin, as well as the natural selection and fluidity, of species.[26] On the question of God's existence neither Darwin nor Newton were "objective" or value-free.

The new historical knowledge about the social framing of modern science poses an interesting philosophical problem. More precisely, the social history of science has exacerbated a philosophical problem present since the early nineteenth century. At that time scientists stopped including God as an explanatory mechanism in their thought processes about nature. Until then, most disciplined inquiry into the human or natural

26. For a good discussion of Darwin and many of the philosophical issues raised by the social history of science, see David L. Hull, *Science as a Process: An Evolutionary Account of the Social and Conceptual Development of Science* (Chicago, 1988), pp. 1–37.

condition presumed that meaningfully true things could be known about objects because the metaphysical, metahistorical realm wherein Newton's God dwelt ultimately guaranteed truth. Human beings had a chance at finding the truth, however enfeebled they might be by evil or self-absorption, because God existed and oversaw the natural and human world. In other words, the first Western scientists were able to agree that science occupied a higher platform from which to search for truth because their intense theism, their particular definition of the Judeo-Christian God, allowed them to anchor science in a divine order. They were fitting their laws to God's creation, set by Him who would not deceive. English Protestants and American Puritans especially latched onto the Baconian injunction to study God through His word and His work.

By the nineteenth century one did not have to be an orthodox religious believer to hold a similar kind of position. Late-eighteenth-century pantheists and materialists such as Darwin's grandfather Erasmus Darwin, who was also an atheist, made an interesting linguistic move. The elder Darwin said that Nature is God, and capitalized the word to make the point. In a stroke—or a word—even eighteenth-century atheists managed to save the truth status of the metaphysical and hence physical realm. They simply invested Nature with all the attributes of transcendence that made eighteenth-century scientific truth and the objective posture needed to search for it possible.

In the twentieth century, neither God nor Nature has been allowed as an admissible explanation for the truth in any scientific (or for that matter in any political) debate. In effect, the metaphysical platform bequeathed by the early modern theologies—even by old-fashioned pantheistic materialism—was conveniently detached from the being that permitted its erection. In the past, human beings could discover absolute Truth because God (or Nature) guaranteed it for their knowing. While politicians may piously invoke God, in practice a candidate would be run out of town for telling voters that the recession was over because God had answered his prayers of the day.

Similarly, a scientist who proclaimed that God had revealed the existence of quarks would have a hard time getting published. To avoid relativism, modern men and women cannot jump back to the seventeenth century and embrace Newton's God. He is gone forever, ironically undone by the power unleashed by Newton's science.

The social history of science needs to be put near the top of a list of factors that hastened the demise of one of the West's most tenacious absolutisms. But its findings have remained confined to the occasional quarrels that erupted in the philosophical literature about science, their relative obscurity matched by the fate of historical studies of Western science. Rather than becoming a mainstay in the educational experience of the citizenry, the history of science became the subject of specialized courses taken by a small minority of students. The new departments were small, and their clientele, not being required to study the history of science (or indeed by 1970 not being required to study much of anything), opted for physics for poets instead of "From Galileo to Einstein." Likewise, in American colleges science itself attracts a smaller percentage of students than once it did.

## Relativism Redux

Since the 1960s, American universities have established whole departments devoted to the history of science and technology and have awarded annually about thirty Ph.D.s in the history and philosophy of science.[27] Professionalization and democratization combined with increased funding for the social history

27. *Survey of Earned Doctorates, Sponsored by Five Federal Agencies: National Science Foundation (NSF); National Institutes of Health (NIH); U.S. Department of Education (USED); National Endowment for the Humanities (NEH); and the U.S. Department of Agriculture (USDA); and conducted by the National Research Council (NRC),* available from the National Research Council, Washington, D.C. Covers the period from 1940 to the present and shows that the doctorates in the field of the history of science were not disaggregated from history degrees until 1967 and since then have averaged fewer than thirty per year.

of science from the National Science Foundation contributed decisively to the triumph of the social turn taken by the discipline. Within the postwar context, all these innovations in American universities encouraged a break with the Enlightenment faith in heroic science which had prevailed since the eighteenth century. By the last quarter of the twentieth century the Enlightenment's vision of disinterested, unfettered, value-free truth conquering superstition and ignorance, and always in the service of human progress, no longer appeared entirely relevant or even credible. Effective challenges to the neutrality of science shattered a once innocent faith. Critics saw science and technology not as enterprises in the service of humanity, but as disciplines whose content reflected the interests of government sponsors, military projects, or more generally, the needs of Western men, women having largely been excluded from the laboratories.

Influenced by this same disillusionment with the universalist claims of science, by the 1960s historians looked back at the history of Western science and found a very different story from what had been believed throughout much of this century. In the very sinews of heroic science they located concepts of masculine domination as well as biases toward women and non-Europeans.[28] In the eighteenth-century colonies of the European nations, for instance, historians discovered scientists and doctors in the age of Enlightenment eager to apply their methods and treatments in the interest of extracting more and better labor from their slaves.[29] Then there were the horrors of their own century. New research on German science during the Third Reich revealed an even more disturbing paradox. Once the believers in value-free science had said that all Nazi science had been pseudo-science, but historical research showed that the Nazis did indeed have their natural and social sciences which

28. Londa Schiebinger, *The Mind Has No Sex? Women in the Origins of Modern Science* (Cambridge, Mass., 1989).

29. James E. McClellan III, *Colonialism and Science: Saint Domingue in the Old Regime* (Baltimore, 1992). Slaves owners included the king and many clergymen.

served the ideological and military needs of the regime right to its end.[30] Nazi science could be both quite good in scientific terms and singularly evil in political and moral ones. Some cynical critics have even tried to argue that the second was a consequence of the first.

To the acknowledgment of Nazi science was added a new awareness about the workings of science and technology in the former Soviet Union. Suddenly at the end of the twentieth century, the rest of the world discovered its relative backwardness. As true believers in heroic science (even Marxism was supposed to be scientific) the Soviets had built the largest scientific and technological establishment in the world, and still managed to be industrially and environmentally backward.[31] The conclusion becomes inescapable: the inevitable progress promised by the model of heroic science does not fit with reality. The strong programme or social constructionist approach offered relativism in response, but most historians and philosophers of science, although accepting the importance of social context and social framing, did not find that relativism could adequately account for the truths found in science. The solution that seemed to make the most sense entailed understanding the historicity of science, of scientists and scientific texts, while at the same time recognizing the interpenetration of rational and social processes.

The implications of the Internalist/Externalist War and of social constructionism have been missed or ignored by innovators in other fields of history, in hermeneutics, and especially in theory. On the face of it, the history of Soviet physics, or steam engines and turbines would not seem to have much to say to people reading Sartre, or later Foucault and the postmodernists. Yet saying, as some theorists do, that science is part of the West's uniquely universalist and hegemonic discourse does not

---

30. Alan Beyerchen, "What We Now Know About Nazism and Science," *Social Research*, 59 (1992): 615–41.

31. For background see Paul R. Josephson, *Physics and Politics in Revolutionary Russia* (Berkeley, Calif., 1991).

adequately address the knowledge it offers and represents. It may seem liberating to assert, and claim as feminism, that "the subject of technique and its technologies is the *ego cogito*—Man in history." [32] The argument implies that because the Cartesian prescriptions for truth-seeking were offered primarily to men, the enterprise of scientific knowing cannot have a universal meaning. The method of doubting and investigating nature in the search for usable knowledge is relative only to the seventeenth-century men for whom it was primarily intended, and late-twentieth-century women should liberate themselves from these conventions.

Relativism does not help us understand the power of some methods and the knowledge those methods are capable of producing. Sometimes gendered human beings working in laboratories, enveloped in linguistic conventions and cultural matrices of values and beliefs, can solve a problem in such a way that it need not be reopened. Put another way, although he feared atheism and irreligion and cherished a baroque metaphysics while practicing alchemy along with mechanics and optics, Newton came up with a physical and mathematical formulation—compatible with his beliefs and values—which became for him and subsequent generations in all cultures the law of universal gravitation.

Perhaps, in a curious way, the heroic model of science helped to breed contemporary relativism because its heroic conception of scientific rationality served so many masters, because it was used to undergird standards of right and wrong, along with the self-serving and imperial belief in Western and male superiority. The absolutist defenders of scientific truth thought that if heroic science did not hold up, then relativism would be the only position logically available. Ironically, the old positivists sound much like the new postmodern relativists. Both deal in absolutes; neither can imagine the complexity of a human situation

---

32. Alice A. Jardine, *Gynesis: Configurations of Woman and Modernity* (Ithaca, N.Y., 1985), p. 73.

in which workable truths appear as the result of messy, ideologically motivated, self-absorbed interventions undertaken by myopic people whose identities may be vastly different and distant from one's own. Both absolutists and relativists seem uncomfortable when asked to address simultaneously the historicity and the successes of human inquiry.

As disillusionment with the scientific model of historical truth has grown among historians, an option imagined as new has attracted adherents: why not embrace the historian's version of a strong programme and take up philosophical relativism? But if embraced, the resulting relativism fails to address adequately the search for historical truths, and the need for causal explanations and narratives. Once again relativism fails the needs of historians just as it skirts the possible existence of truths in science. Every time people go down the relativist road, the path darkens and the light recedes from the tunnel.

## Truth Without the Heroes

The social history of science suggests that people create knowledge in time and space. Such truths do not permit access to the transcendent realm that Newton believed his science could reveal. This limitation constrains science, making it neither very heroic nor grand, but leaving it both rational and powerful. Indeed, unheroic truths even have their philosophical advocates. Since the early nineteenth century and the writings of the German philosopher Hegel, Westerners have been able to articulate a human situation in which truths occur in history, in which forms of knowledge are invented by human beings trapped in time, deeply influenced by the social and natural worlds around them.

Historicizing science has rendered it the work of human beings; it becomes truth-seeking and truth-finding without the possibility of transcendence. Despite what Newton, and even Hegel believed, there can be no dwelling among the gods. But Popper also got it wrong when he thought that historicity makes relativism inevitable. It is possible to have scientific revolutions influenced by both technical problems *and* ideologies. The one need not exclude the other, now or in the past.

Historians of science sometimes get the defenders of science very mad because they think that historical reconstruction suggests the futility of believing that science can produce a workable, practical truth. They assume that the social historians are the new relativists who would deny the possibility of articulating laws reasonably true to nature. They wrongly presume that historians embrace what can be called, somewhat ironically, an absolute, as opposed to a methodological, relativism. The method of relativism draws upon Descartes's prescription "I imitated the skeptics who doubt only for doubting's sake . . . in order to find rock or clay." [33] Skepticism, or relativism, by this method becomes a means toward the end of finding a more workable truth. In other words, to do the history of science, the historian begins with a willing suspension of belief. If you presume that Newton was simply right, it becomes harder to ask what he thought he was doing and why he did it. Historically situating any body of knowledge, including science, is how historians go about the job of discovering, describing, and explaining the past. But did not the methods of science help shape the practices of modern historians? Some might say that in the course of applying their critical methods, especially to the truth claims of science, modern historians have become an ungrateful lot.

The charge of ingratitude should not be dismissed lightly. Watching the assault mounted in this century against truth and the search for objectivity by various forms of totalitarianism, some people have concluded that putting history back into science will undermine its truth and the achievements of its practitioners. But it is not necessary for the historian to endorse that conclusion in order to see the larger issue. Given the status and achievements of modern science, its relativizing would be the ultimate goal in any project to destabilize the search for

---

33. René Descartes, *Discourse on Method and The Meditations* (New York, 1968), p. 50.

truths or the endorsement of objectivity. Because the study of history, as well as the entire enterprise of Western learning, has been tied to science since the Enlightenment, the demise of heroic science has implications for all historians. Denying the possibility of truth produces a relativism that makes it impossible to choose between ethical systems. And since the demise of Newton's God, epistemological and moral relativisms are always a possibility; indeed, they are even once again fashionable.

But relativism need not be the only option. Just because science, like everything else, has a history does not mean the end of truth. It does mean that the nineteenth-century philosophers attributed far too much to its power, and then in the process tried to make history be like it. In the nineteenth-century sense, there is no scientific history, nor is there even scientific science. But it is possible to know some things more rather than less truly. In their respective realms, both history and science seek to do that. Given the issues about truth and relativism that have been raised late in this century, historians cannot pretend that it is business as usual. It is essential to rethink the understanding of truth and objectivity. Faced with what is known about the interaction of the social and the scientific, philosophers of science are groping their way through the thicket, and so, too, must historians and scientists.

Philosophers can offer historians some help in the debate about relativism. Most of them have moved beyond the positivist / social constructionist dichotomy. Their approach to the problem of truth-seeking is relevant to any discipline coming to terms with the social, gendered, temporal, and linguistic nature of human knowledge and with the concomitant challenge of relativism. Historically informed philosophers argue, for instance, that the social nature of scientific work is part of its essence, not simply the aftermath of too much conference-attending. In other words, the social is essential to scientific truth-seeking. "Scientific knowledge cannot be reduced to the knowledge of an individual and cannot be understood in terms of processes in principle individualistic, such as the simple additive accumulation of the individual's knowledges."[34] Social perspectives such as these do not seek to deny the existence of truths hard won by reasoned inquiry and contestation (even if the struggle appears to be largely private, resembling Newton's dialogue with Descartes). Rather they point toward renewed understandings of objectivity, of how reason works in complex ways. They imply that the objective does not simply reside within each individual, but rather is achieved by criticism, contention, and exchange. Without the social process of science—cumulative, contested, and hence at moments ideological—there is no science as it has come to be known since the seventeenth century. Criticism fosters objectivity and thereby enhances reasoned inquiry. Objectivity is not a stance arrived at by sheer willpower, nor is it the way most people, most of the time, make their daily inquiries. Instead it is the result of the clash of social interests, ideologies, and social conventions within the framework of object-oriented and disciplined knowledge-seeking. Encouragement to continue seeking comes from truths discovered in time, a temporal process preserved by memory and history for all time.

An argument emphasizing the social character of scientific research points directly toward the history of democratic practices and institutions in the West. The emergence of a relatively free social space for discussion and contention depended upon the creation of civil society. Still other aspects of the Enlightenment's legacy are germane. Hermeneutics, the art of interpreting the world through its texts, applies to both scientific and historical truth-seeking. There is a hermeneutics within science. Scientists give meaning to objects; they too are bound by linguistic conventions, by discourse. Even experimental and experiential knowledge has to be expressed by languages which

34. Helen E. Longino, *Science as Social Knowledge: Values and Objectivity in Scientific Inquiry* (Princeton, N.J., 1990), p. 231.

can embody theoretical presuppositions and social values. "Facts," before they can be discussed, must be named.[35] Such arguments should not undercut the ability to say meaningfully true things about the world. Regardless of language and human linguistic conventions, nature, whether in the form of planets or microbes, would still be real, out there and behaving in predictable ways, even if there were no way of saying so.[36] Colliding with a moving object repeatedly could, however, only illicit a growl and never the law of inertia.

From this philosophical perspective the scientist's language, or the historian's language, becomes actively involved in the knowledge created. When Newton used the word "matter" he had to have in his mind an entity without life or will before he could have conceived of a separate dynamic, gravitational force in the universe. And the words "force" and "universe" and "God" all had to have meanings distinctive to his mind and hence to his time. This does not mean, however, that no longer believing as Newton did that matter is "brute and stupid," twentieth-century people cannot understand or refine the law of universal gravitation. Or take Darwin. When he saw the evidence for species that had perished he could imagine random survival partly because of the harsh circumstances of survival he witnessed in the social world that nurtured him so comfortably. Neither historical insight undercuts the truth of evolutionary biology or Newtonian mechanics; both offer a historical perspective on the hermeneutics through which truths were discovered. Truths hard won by human beings, however mired in time and language, can make for consoling allies. In the darkest moments of this century they have kept many people from despair. Historicizing any moment need not, should not, sacrifice the truths people discovered in it. Indeed, histo-

35. Joseph Rouse, *Knowledge and Power: Toward a Political Philosophy of Science* (Ithaca, N.Y., 1987), p. 47.

36. See Charles S. Peirce, "Critical Review of Berkeley's Idealism," in *Values in a Universe of Chance: Selected Writings of Charles S. Peirce*, ed. Philip P. Wiener (New York, 1958), p. 84.

ricizing entails imitating their quest, searching for other kinds of knowledge, for historical knowledge.

Precisely as a consequence of that search, the absolutist, heroic science bequeathed to the twentieth century by the true believers of previous centuries came under fire. In the postwar era, given the role played by science and technology in war-making, the very nature of science had to be dissected and reevaluated. No body of knowledge of such power, no group of men (or women) with such command of resources—some kept secret from public inspection—could be allowed to go unexamined and unchallenged. The icon of heroic science found its iconoclasts. Yet not despite but because of all that is now known about the unheroic, deeply social nature of scientific truth-seeking, science still stands at the center of the enterprise of knowing. A democratic society with roots in the Enlightenment depends upon the positioning of science, upon the affirmation it gives to the human ability to reason independently and successfully about objects outside the mind, while recognizing the social and ideological dimension of all knowledge.

# ◇ 6 ◇

# Postmodernism and the Crisis of Modernity

ROM THE 1960s ONWARD, new trends in the writing of history combined with larger social and political transformations to dethrone many of the long-standing absolutisms about the nature of the American nation and the certainty provided by the heroic model of science. Social history challenged American unity by telling about competing and conflicting ethnic and racial groups whose experience could not be fitted easily, if at all, into a single story line glorifying an essentially white Protestant nation. In growing numbers the new social historians also subverted the happy tale of the self-reliant, ever-entrepreneurial individual who made his (always his) own choices and thereby fortuitously contributed to the strengths of the American capitalist economy. Similarly, social histories of science showed that even the heroes and geniuses of science had lived lives fully enmeshed in the social and political relations of their time. Newton and Darwin would not have articulated theories of such universal breadth without the push and pull of religious, political, and social interests. Suddenly, science, like the forging of the nation, only made sense in a social context.

As might be expected, the social historians' challenge to the foundations of America's (and more generally the West's) faith in itself has provoked attacks, particularly from the political right. Defenders of the traditional views about American history and Western culture berate the new generation of historians for their supposed cynicism about national and Western values. The new historians' critical stance, it is alleged, prevented them from telling an edifying national saga and from explicating transcendent Western values. Gertrude Himmelfarb, for example, took social historians to task for "devaluing the political realm" and thus denigrating history and even reason itself. Their "revolution in the discipline" undermined the rationality inherent in the historical enterprise, she claimed. They did this by focusing on the irrational and nonrational infrastructures of life—ranging from the economic interests of legislators to the eating habits of ordinary folk—rather than on "the constitutions and laws that permit men to order their affairs in a rational manner."[1]

In her report to Congress in 1988, the chairwoman of the National Endowment for the Humanities, Lynne V. Cheney, stopped just short of attributing the recent decline in the number of history majors to social history itself. Students no longer grasp the importance of studying history, she asserted, because the increasing specialization of the disciplines and the enthusiasm for quantitative techniques—both central to the development of social history—had undermined the necessary sense of a unified educational purpose. The "crisis" in the humanities the "isolation" and "disarray" she found among scholars had been caused, she concluded, by politicization. The humanities had been reduced to "arguing that truth—and beauty and excellence—are not timeless matters, but transitory notions, devices used by some groups to perpetuate 'hegemony' over others."[2] Social history was thus deeply implicated in the whole debate on Western culture.

These attacks stung but they did not kill. Social history had been predicated on the assumption that more was better; if more was known about the lives of ordinary people, workers,

1. Gertrude Himmelfarb, *The New History and the Old* (Cambridge, Mass., 1987), pp. 18–23.

2. "Text of Cheney's 'Report to the President, the Congress, and the American People' on the Humanities in America," *Chronicle of Higher Education*, September 21, 1988, pp. A17–A23, quotes p. A18. History majors have begun to grow again since then.

and slaves (or about the values and belief systems of
...s), accounts of the past would be fuller. Social historians did not oppose the standards of objectivity or the codes of
professional discipline; they used those very standards to challenge the traditional interpretations which had excluded marginal or nonconforming historical groups.

Social historians hoped to fill out the record by offering a
more complex picture of the past, but one of the main effects of
their work has been to reveal how limited the previous histories
were. In effect, they underlined the fact that history writing had
always been intensely ideological. The story of "one nation
under God," for example, served the interests of some, not all,
of the people. American history—and the history of Western
civilization more generally—could be construed as political
propaganda for ruling elites. Thus, the new social history can
be used (and sometimes abused) by those who insist that history can no longer offer one national narrative, that it is always
partial, always political, always propagandistic, indeed, mythical. Ironically, then, the work of social historians fostered the
argument that history could never be objective. It is as if the
social historians with their passion for breaking apart the historical record had dug a potentially fatal hole into which history
as a discipline might disappear altogether.

This opening has been seized upon by a new group of critics
called postmodernists who question the objectivity of the social
sciences more generally. Their critique has gone beyond specific
denunciations of the ideological character of American history
or Western science to attack the very foundations of historical
and scientific knowledge. Although "postmodernism" has become a ubiquitous term in the latest cultural wars between
traditionalists and their opponents, it is a notoriously slippery
label.[3] At times, it seems as if everyone is a postmodernist; at
others, that everyone avoids a category that can be synonymous
with nihilism and ridiculous self-posturing. (If you think of

3. For a convenient and sensible overview, see Pauline Marie Rosenau, *Post-modernism
and the Social Sciences: Insights, Inroads, and Intrusions* (Princeton, 1992).

both Jacques Derrida and Madonna as postmodernists you get some sense of the definitional problem.) Defining postmodernism involves three related terms: "modernity," "modernism," and "poststructuralism." Briefly put, modernity is the modern, industrial, and urban way of life; modernism is the movement in art and literature that aims to capture the essence of that new way of life (the skyscraper, for example); and poststructuralism is the theoretical critique of the assumptions of modernity found in philosophy, art, and criticism since the seventeenth and eighteenth centuries.

The term "postmodernism" first gained currency in the arts and especially architecture as a way of designating antimodernist forms of art. Postmodernist architects rejected the pragmatic, efficient, rationalist functionalism of modernist architecture in favor of more whimsical, historical, and unpredictable shapes and lines. As the use of the term spread outward from the arts, it came to mean more generally the critique of modernity as a set of assumptions about industrial and technological forms of life. As we have defined it, modernity stands for a specifically Western set of notions that took root in the eighteenth century; it entails a new periodization of history (ancient, medieval, modern) in which the modern denotes the period when reason and science triumphed over Scripture, tradition, and custom. At the heart of modernity is the notion of the freely acting, freely knowing individual whose experiments can penetrate the secrets of nature and whose work with other individuals can make a new and better world.

Postmodernists' primary goal has been to challenge convictions about the objectivity of knowledge and the stability of language. This is not the place for a history of theories of language, or for an account of the transformation of poststructuralism into a more general form of postmodernist cultural criticism.[4] We focus instead on the questions raised by post-

---

4. We are grateful to Gabrielle Spiegel for pushing us to refine our sense of the difference between poststructuralism and postmodernism. Many commentators, it should be noted, consider them synonymous; others see them as radically different. See, for example, Rosenau, *Post-modernism*, p. 3.

modernism about the meaning and writing of history. Our goal is to navigate a course between the traditionalist critics and the postmodernists, by defending the role of an objective and inclusive history while recognizing the need for exploring its conceptual fault lines.

Postmodernism renders problematic the belief in progress, the modern periodization of history, and the individual as knower and doer. The very notion of the individual self, so central both to the Enlightenment's philosophy of human rights and to historians' accounts of American destiny, is threatened when postmodernists stress the inevitable fragmentation of personal identity. In one of the most striking formulations of the so-called death of the subject, Michel Foucault proclaimed that the concept of man "is an invention of recent date" and would soon disappear, "like a face drawn in sand at the edge of the sea."[5] Postmodernists assert that the individual self is an ideological construct, a myth perpetuated by liberal societies whose legal systems depend upon the concept of individual responsibility. By making this argument against the unified self—postmodernists call it "the subject" to underline its lack of autonomy—they also, perhaps inadvertently, undermine the premises of multiculturalism. Without an identifiable self, there would be no need to worry about differing cultures, ethnic pride, and battered identities. Without a subject, there could be no identity politics, no politics of cultural self-affirmation.

Postmodernist critics of history and science operate in the attack mode. They take on all that the modern has come to represent. They insist that the experiences of genocide, world wars, depressions, pollution, and famine have cast doubt on the inevitability of progress, enlightenment, and reason, even while they implicitly deny human access to certain knowledge of these same disasters. Indeed, they argue against the possibility of any certain knowledge. Postmodernists question the superiority of

5. Michel Foucault, *The Order of Things: An Archaeology of the Human Sciences* (New York, 1970), p. 387.

the present and the usefulness of general worldviews, whether Christian, Marxist, or liberal. For them, as Foucault has claimed, "each society has its regime of truth, its 'general politics' of truth."[6] With them, there is no truth outside of ideology.

Since science has supplied the foundation of Western knowledge from the eighteenth century onward, it has predictably drawn the attention of postmodernists. One postmodernist explains, "Science was the alpha and omega of the modernists and the structuralists; they saw science as . . . the ultimate given of modernity."[7] According to Foucault, "in societies like ours, the 'political economy' of truth . . . is centered on the form of scientific discourse and the institutions which produce it; it is subject to constant economic and political incitement."[8] Science and technology, in this view, are seen as constantly propelled by hegemony-seeking interests. The claims scientists make for objectivity and truth are part of an intellectual economy in which paucity and manipulation characterize truth-seeking, a tortured enterprise trapped within discourses, themselves the products of biased institutions.

Other postmodernists ask if the cognitive methods of science can be neutral when the larger aims of scientists figure in gendered, ideological, and political agendas. They argue that the emphasis on the objectivity of scientific facts is itself an ideological construction put forward by scientists to mask the active role that they play in selecting and shaping the facts. Seeing the laboratory as primarily the nexus for power relations

6. Michel Foucault, *Power/Knowledge: Selected Interviews and Other Writings, 1972–1977*, ed. Colin Gordon, trans. Colin Gordon, Leo Marshall, John Mepham, and Kate Soper (New York, 1980), p. 131.

7. F. R. Ankersmit, "Historiography and Postmodernism," *History and Theory*, 28 (1989): 140.

8. Foucault, *Power/Knowledge*, p. 131. For a more nuanced, yet similar, view, see Steven Shapin and Simon Schaffer, *Leviathan and the Air-Pump: Hobbes, Boyle and the Experimental Life* (Princeton, 1985), pp. 333–43: "There are three senses in which we want to say that the history of science occupies the same terrain as the history of politics. . . . The politics that regulated transactions within the philosophical community was equally important, for it laid down the rules by which authentic knowledge was to be produced."

and political gestures, postmodernists believe that they have been successful in "dissipating previous beliefs surrounding science." "Nothing special," they maintain, "nothing extraordinary, in fact nothing of any cognitive quality" occurs in the laboratory. In this view, scientific laboratories are entirely shaped by political agendas. Paradoxically, they assign historians and sociologists the task of figuring out how the laboratories got to have so much political power in the first place.[9]

Postmodernists often put the word "reality" in quotation marks to problematize the "there" out there. To them, no reality can possibly transcend the discourse in which it is expressed.[10] Scientists may think that the disciplined practices employed in laboratories—the seeing in the microscope or telescope—brings them closer to reality, but they are simply privileging the language that they speak, the technologies of their own self-fashioning.[11] And, needless to say, such privileging has led to the horrors of our century. In this line of argument, Westerners are particularly prone to the conceit that reality is fixed and knowable.

As this brief review shows, postmodernists have not yet developed a unified critique of science. Some consider it to be simply another form of discourse, and hence no more privileged than any other; others relegate it to the status of information and separate it from society and the disputes about social knowledge. In general, postmodernist critics devote more

9. Bruno Latour, "Give Me a Laboratory and I Will Raise the World," in Karin D. Knorr-Cetina and Michael Mulkay, eds., *Science Observed: Perspectives on the Social Study of Science* (London, 1983), p. 161. Latour calls himself an "a-modernist," but his position seems indistinguishable from postmodernism.

10. Mari Sorri and Jerry H. Gill, *A Post-Modern Epistemology: Language, Truth and Body* (Lewiston, N.Y., 1989), p. 198.

11. Some postmodernists are completely indifferent to the relationship between science and society. In one view, science simply supplies information and any attention that is paid to it should come not from philosophers or historians but from politicians. In this view, the postmodernist maintains "the same aloofness with respect to science as . . . towards information . . . science and information are independent objects of study which obey their own laws." Ankersmit, "Historiography and Postmodernism," pp. 140–41.

of their energy to the realm of history, especially narrative, and even to the modern idea of time itself. Appropriately Delphic, one postmodernist critic called attention to the coming time when "the tellable time of realism and its consensus become the untellable time of postmodern writing." This entails nothing less than "the disappearance of history," a prediction accompanied by the promise that "the postmodern subversion of historical time" will in turn threaten the idea of human rights, the definition of disciplines, the possibility of representation in politics and art, and the informational functions of language.[12] These are not small stakes!

The nature of historical truth, objectivity, and the narrative form of history have all been targeted by postmodernists. The mastery of time becomes merely the willful imposition on subordinate peoples of a Western, imperialistic historical consciousness; it provides no access to true explanation, knowledge, or understanding. The mastery of facts disguises the wily ruse of the aggrandizing master historian who—like the idea of the author or the scientist—is simply a figment of the Western, capitalist imagination. Moreover, these are figments that do damage. They reinforce the hegemony of white Western men over women, other races, and other peoples. In the postmodern account of Western history, totalitarianism refers not to specific regimes or governments but to every possible form of domination: "The historical names for this Mr. Nice Guy totalitarianism are no longer Stalingrad or Normandy (much less Auschwitz), but Wall Street's Dow Jones Average and Tokyo's Nikkei Index." By this account, the very idea of development is a form of terror, and democracy is simply more "discreet" than Nazism.[13]

Where does this fury of negation come from? And can it be taken seriously? It is not hard to understand why events since

12. Elizabeth Deeds Ermarth, *Sequel to History: Postmodernism and the Crisis of Representational Time* (Princeton, 1992), pp. 6, 7, 9.

13. Jean-François Lyotard, *Toward the Postmodern*, ed. Robert Harvey and Mark S. Roberts (Atlantic Highlands, N.J., 1993), pp. 159–62.

the 1930s have cast doubt on the eighteenth- and nineteenth-century idea of ineluctable progress. The experience of the twentieth century shows that science and technology can be used to build death camps and atom bombs as easily as they can be used to light streets, increase crop yields, and prolong life. History professors went to work for Nazis, communist regimes, and right-wing dictators as often as for democratic governments. The discipline of history does not disengage its practitioners from the demands of politics, nor does the objectivity of science guarantee benign applications. Progress can be a double-edged sword.

Although the general sources of discontent with modernity are easy enough to identify, it is much harder to follow the logic of postmodernist arguments or determine their political agenda. The aims of postmodernists have been the subject of intense debate. Although they tend to believe that all knowledge is deeply political, their own politics are only obliquely expressed, and usually as criticism rather than as prescription. Their notions about power have been questioned because two of their most important intellectual forebears, the German philosophers Friedrich Nietzsche and Martin Heidegger, made notoriously antidemocratic, anti-Western, and antihumanist pronouncements and were associated, sometimes fairly, sometimes not, with anti-Semitism. Hitler cited Nietzsche's writings in support of his racial ideology, and Heidegger himself joined the Nazi Party. Although most theorists of postmodernity have clearly rejected the proto-fascist and anti-Semitic implications of the work of Nietzsche and Heidegger, doubts remain about the ease with which one can separate the strands in their thought.

In our view, postmodernists are deeply disillusioned intellectuals who denounce en masse Marxism and liberal humanism, communism and capitalism, and all expectations of liberation. They insist that all of the regnant ideologies are fundamentally the same because these ideologies are driven by the desire to discipline and control the population in the name of science and truth. No form of liberation can escape from these parameters of control. In many ways, then, postmodernism is an ironic, perhaps even despairing view of the world, one which, in its most extreme forms, offers little role for history as previously known. On the other hand, postmodernism raises arresting questions about truth, objectivity, and history that cannot simply be dismissed. Moreover, these questions hit the nerve exposed by the widespread realization that the nineteenth-century models of science and history are in urgent need of refashioning.

## The Historical Lineage of Postmodernism

The foremost contemporary apostles of postmodernism are two French philosophers, Michel Foucault (1926–84) and Jacques Derrida (1930– ). Much of postmodernist criticism can be traced to their influence and through them back to Nietzsche and Heidegger. This is not to say that Foucault and Derrida endorsed the claims made by all those calling themselves postmodernists. Many other (mostly French) names might be cited in an honor roll of poststructuralist and postmodernist critics—Jacques Lacan in psychoanalysis, Roland Barthes in literary criticism, and Jean-François Lyotard in philosophy. But Foucault and Derrida provided the crucial arguments for postmodernism, particularly for postmodernism as it has taken shape in America.

Both philosophers grew to adulthood in the difficult postwar years of the late 1940s and early 1950s. They were not personal friends, but they helped shape a common intellectual agenda with a wide international resonance. In their work, they made poststructuralism, if not exactly a household word, at least a label to conjure with—even if both of them rejected most exercises in labeling. Moving beyond French intellectual circles, Foucault worked in Sweden, Germany, Tunisia, and California, and Derrida, born in Algeria, has taught extensively in the United States.

Despite their considerable differences in approach—and their polemics against each other—both Foucault and Derrida sought to challenge the most fundamental assumptions of Western social science.[14] Put most schematically, they deny our ability to represent reality in any objectively true fashion and offer to "deconstruct" (a word made famous by Derrida and his followers) the notion of the individual as an autonomous, self-conscious agent. With writings that are part literary criticism and part philosophy (and in Foucault's case, part historical commentary), they leveled their sights on Western Man, defined as rational, capable of objectivity, and in possession of knowledge that corresponds to the truth of nature and society. In short, they attacked the entire Enlightenment project.

Taking Nietzsche as their inspiration, Foucault and Derrida made Western Man into a modern-day Gulliver, tied down with ideological ropes and incapable of transcendence because he can never get beyond the veil of language to the reality "out there." The Nietzschean vision, conveyed through irony and satire, permits varying interpretations, and postmodernists offer a multiplicity of responses to his iconoclastic writings. Foucault described reading Nietzsche as a "philosophical shock" and a "revelation," but that hardly distinguishes him from most American undergraduates.[15] Thus the Nietzschean influence could be partly stylistic and literary, partly philosophical. Foucault and Derrida often tried to emulate aspects of Nietzsche's difficult, aphoristic, and allusive writing style because they saw it as consonant with his central intellectual argument that all concepts are in the end illusory creatures of the moment. Knowledge, Nietzsche taught, is an invention that masks a will to power.

Nietzsche fashioned himself into the ultimate philosophical ironist and amoralist. He insisted that the West's "infinitely complex cathedral of concepts" was built "on a movable foun-

14. For a similar approach to these thinkers, see Richard Wolin, *The Terms of Cultural Criticism: The Frankfurt School, Existentialism, Poststructuralism* (New York, 1992), part 3.

15. As quoted in James Miller, *The Passion of Michel Foucault* (New York, 1993), p. 67.

dation and as it were on running water." [16] Human beings do not discover a truth in concordance with nature; they invent it, so that truth is always changing just as the water in a river is always changing. Claims for truth can therefore only be dissimulations, invariably advanced by those who have power. The noble, true, and good in Western values is only what the ancient nobility claimed them to be; then came the transgressive revolution of Christianity that led the underclasses to effect a fateful reversal of values. In Christianity, according to Nietzsche, the meek, weak, and lowly got their revenge. Democracy furthered the reversal of values because the "herd" of humanity made itself the arbiter of truth and reinforced the Christian "slave" morality.

Nietzsche's argument often approached the morally repugnant. In *The Genealogy of Morals,* for example, he exclaimed, "Let us face facts: the people have triumphed—or the slaves, the mob, the herd, whatever you wish to call them—and if the Jews brought it about, then no nation ever had a more universal mission on this earth. . . . I don't deny that this triumph might be looked upon as a kind of blood poisoning, since it has resulted in a mingling of the races. . . ." [17] Perhaps unaware of the proven historical dangers of such statements, some postmodernists have wandered recklessly into commenting upon Nietzschean perspectives. Alice Jardine confidently asserts that "the shock of recognition that Western Truth, and the Western desire for Truth, have been a terrible error is what Nietzsche leaves for the twentieth century to gain the hard way." [18] In a more extreme rendition, Jean-François Lyotard advanced the hypothesis that "the characteristic features of the Judaic religion, and of the West to the extent that it is a product of that religion,

16. From "On Truth and Falsity in an Extra-Moral Sense," as quoted in Alan Megill, *Prophets of Extremity: Nietzsche, Heidegger, Foucault, Derrida* (Berkeley, 1985), p. 52.

17. From *The Birth of Tragedy and the Genealogy of Morals,* tr. Francis Golffing (New York, 1956), p. 169.

18. Alice Jardine, *Gynesis: Configurations of Woman and Modernity* (Ithaca, N.Y., 1985), p. 148.

are not to be sought in obsessional neurosis but in psychosis." Lyotard has devoted much of his work to criticism of the "defaillancy [in French *défaillance* means extinction or decay] of modernity," the collapse of all emancipatory narratives.[19]

Like Nietzsche, the postmodernists want to use history against itself, to attack the certainties and absolutes that provided the foundation for positivism and for the human sciences that emerged in the course of the nineteenth century. Foucault, for example, described his version of history in Nietzschean language: it "disturbs what was previously considered immobile; . . . fragments what was thought unified; . . . shows the heterogeneity of what was imagined consistent with itself." Foucault proclaimed grandly that "I am well aware that I have never written anything but fictions." He nevertheless insisted, in typically Nietzschean ironic terms, "I do not mean to go so far as to say that fictions are beyond truth (*hors vérité*). It seems to me that it is possible to make fiction work inside of truth. . . ."[20] Yet Foucault never specified how he could determine this "truth" or even what its epistemological status might be.

Assistance in the enterprise of going "beyond truth" came also from Martin Heidegger. This debt to Heidegger has further embroiled postmodernism in political controversy, for his unrepentant membership in the Nazi Party has long raised questions about the political meaning of his work. Like Nietzsche before him, Heidegger depicted Western philosophy and culture in dire crisis. We are "latecomers in a history now racing toward its end," he insisted in 1946. Heidegger rejected Enlightenment values of reason and objectivity even more extremely than Nietzsche. In an essay titled "The Word of Nietzsche: 'God is Dead,' " Heidegger insisted that "thinking

19. Jean-François Lyotard, *The Lyotard Reader*, ed. Andrew Benjamin (Cambridge, Mass., 1989), quote p. 102. In the same source see also "Universal History and Cultural Differences," pp. 314–23.

20. As quoted in Megill, *Prophets of Extremity*, pp. 235, 234.

begins only when we have come to know that reason, glorified for centuries, is the most stiff-necked adversary of thought."

Unlike Nietzsche, who could identify with aspects of scientific method, at least in the study of language, Heidegger explicitly attacked science for assaulting nature. The "technological frenzy" of modern man treats nature—and human beings—only in terms of pure manipulation and thus manifests a "spiritual decline" in the West.[21] For Heidegger, "agriculture is today a motorized food industry, in essence the same as the manufacture of corpses in gas chambers and extermination camps, the same as the blockage and starvation of countries, the same as the manufacture of atomic bombs."[22] Faced with this moral sensibility—or lack thereof—many have denounced Heidegger for advocating an attitude of *Gelassenheit*, of "letting beings be." His conflation of mechanized agriculture and death camps seems to be all too much in line with his own political self-interest as a former Nazi who never expressed any regret for his actions in the 1930s.[23] His attack on modernity concealed an insensitivity with deeply disturbing moral implications.

Although writing in different eras, both Nietzsche and Heidegger attacked historicism and its central concern, man. History, they argued, did not unfold in linear fashion, revealing truth in the process of development over time, but rather moved through an arbitrary set of crises, disjunctures, and disruptions. Nothing necessarily followed from what came before, so causation should be pitched out along with human agency and social structuring. The historians who invented the myths of modernity could no more hope to be objective than any other social scientists. Human beings do not achieve a separation from the objects they study; they simply invest them with their own values. Thus along with modern history, the idea of the human

21. As quoted in ibid., pp. 145, 106, 140.

22. As cited in Wolin, *Terms of Cultural Criticism*, p. 239, quoting Wolfgang Schirmacher, *Technik und Gelassenheit* (Freiburg and Munich, 1983), p. 25.

23. For a useful survey of Heidegger's thought, see George Steiner, *Martin Heidegger* (New York, 1979).

being as an autonomous, subjectively willing, rational agent was brought into question. As Foucault said, Nietzsche killed man *and* God "in the interior of his language." [24] Heidegger, like Nietzsche before him, insisted that thinking always generates further complexity, further murkiness.

Foucault and Derrida endorsed many of these perspectives on history, but they cannot be described as disciples of Nietzsche and Heidegger in any usual sense. Nor did they do philosophy in the expected manner, even in the style of Nietzsche or Heidegger. Foucault composed a series of historical works on madness, medicine, prisons, and sexuality (among other topics) that aimed to show how the modern individual or self was produced by the disciplines and discourses of institutions. Derrida wrote essays that criticized thinkers from Plato to Foucault, arguing that all of them were trapped in the binary categories of Western metaphysics: good vs. evil, being vs. nothingness, truth vs. error, nature vs. culture, speech vs. writing. In order to draw attention to the straitjacket of Western literary and philosophical expectations, Derrida deliberately upset the conventions of writing with his unusual typography, constant flow of neologisms, and strange titles (*The Postcard: From Socrates to Freud and Beyond;* "wriTing, encAsIng, screeNing"). What the two authors shared was an emphasis on the effects of language, or what Foucault called discourse. Discourse produced knowledge, not the other way around. Thus Foucault and Derrida opened up the possibility that the search for truth itself might be seen as the prime Western illusion.

Some might argue that neither Foucault nor Derrida should be read as relativist because neither posited a subject who might hold a subjective position (you cannot be a relativist unless you occupy a position that is relative to others). Both aimed to decenter the subject, that is, question her or his primacy as a location for making judgments and seeking truth. They challenged the entire Enlightenment project that rested on a con-

---

24. As quoted in Megill, *Prophets of Extremity,* p. 101.

cept of autonomous subjectivity. Foucault in particular, although at moments respectful of the eighteenth century's search for a new foundation for knowledge, urged rebellion from it in the form of a practical critique of reason that "takes the form of a possible transgression." [25] In many ways, then, their critiques of the subject and of language fostered a deeper skepticism about the (disappearing) self and truth.

Foucault made truth nothing more than the will to power within discourse, whereas Derrida questioned the enterprise of seeking something called "truth" in the face of the endless play of signifiers. Although their approaches were radically different and in some respects opposite, both aimed to deconstruct truth as a value in the West. [26] The influence of such views can be seen in many places. In criticizing a biography of Foucault, which dealt explicitly with his homosexuality, one disciple argued, " 'Truth,' then, is not the opposite of error; 'truth' is a discursive strategy that (among other things) blocks inquiry into the conditions—dynamic and erotic—of its own production." [27]

Language thus stands as an insuperable barrier to truth. Foucault and Derrida depict human beings as caught in a prison of language, a prison even more confining than the economic determinism attributed to Marx or the psychological determinism of Freud. Marx and Freud, after all, believed themselves to be scientists capable of establishing an objective relationship to historical or psychological reality, which was open to further

25. See Michel Foucault, "What Is Enlightenment?" in Paul Rabinow, ed., *The Foucault Reader* (New York, 1984), p. 45.

26. We recognize that postmodernists, including Foucault and Derrida, have held a variety of (not always consistent) positions about truth. We have elided some of those differences here, no doubt to the consternation of some readers, in the interest of moving forward with our own account about history. We thank Joseph Rouse for bringing to our attention the complexities of the postmodernist response to the question of truth. He bears no responsibility for our rendition of this question, with which he most likely disagrees. For an attempt to sort out the postmodernist positions on these issues, see Christopher Norris, *What's Wrong with Postmodernism: Critical Theory and the Ends of Philosophy* (Baltimore, 1990). For an example of the ambiguity surrounding truth found among postmodernists, see Lyotard, *Toward the Postmodern*.

27. David M. Halperin, "Bringing out Michel Foucault," *Salmagundi*, 97 (Winter 1993): 69–93, quote p. 88.

elaboration. They believed that their theories gave them a vantage point on reality—and a means for transforming it. Foucault and Derrida reject this kind of fix on reality and with it the possibility of an objectivity predicated upon the separation of the self and the object of knowledge. They deny any direct, personal relation to the reality of the world out there because reality is the creature of language.

Foucault and Derrida built upon the fundamental work of Ferdinand de Saussure on the nature of language.[28] At the beginning of the twentieth century, Saussure's work suggested that language provides no direct access to reality because it itself is based on difference and distance, beginning with the essential difference between the *signifier* (the sound or appearance of the word) and the mental *signified* (the meaning or concept of the word). Signifier and signified are not the same; the word "s-n-o-w" is *not* snow itself but rather a representation or signifier of the tiny white frozen crystals we call snow. The signifier *represents* the signified, but is not identical to it, and in the process of representation lies the possibility for veiling, distortion, obfuscation. Language is constructed on the basis of difference, on the relationship of signifier to signified and of words to each other, not on the basis of a direct correspondence to reality. This can be seen if the usual contexts for snow are reversed. "The snow melted as the temperature dropped" is technically a sentence which nevertheless throws the reader into consternation about the meaning of snow.

Thus, it could be argued, reality, or what metaphysics called "presence" (*logos,* whether in the form of reality, presence, reason, or the Word of God), is never directly available to us. Reality is always shrouded by language, and the workings of

---

28. The essential text derived from Saussure is based upon notes taken by his students. Ferdinand de Saussure, *Course in General Linguistics,* ed. Charles Bally and Albert Sechehaye, tr. Roy Harris (La Salle, Ill., 1983). For Foucault on Saussure, see *The Order of Things,* pp. 294–300. For Derrida on Saussure, see *Of Grammatology,* tr. Gayatri Spivak (Baltimore, 1976). Note that Saussure was himself a believer in science; see *Course,* p. 16.

language are in turn veiled by the operation of cultural codes.[29] Derrida summed up his position in one of his typically elliptical pronouncements:

> Whose discourse tells you: the column *is* this or that, *is there* . . . the column *has* no Being, nor any being-there, whether here or elsewhere. It belongs to no one. . . . And from this column's not being (a being), from its not falling under the power of the *is*, all of Western metaphysics, which lives in the certainty of that *is*, has revolved around the column.[30]

In Derrida's view, it can no longer be assumed that the truth of the signifier (the word, the column) is guaranteed by some transcendental meaning or prior truth (God, the mind, or the necessary correspondence between nature and language).

Derrida advocated a method of reading called deconstruction that aimed to show how all texts repressed as much as they expressed in order to maintain the fundamental Western conceit of "logocentrism," the (erroneous) idea that words expressed the truth of reality. Deconstruction demonstrated that texts could be interpreted in multiple, if not infinite, ways because signifiers had no essential connection to what they signified. It is perhaps not surprising that French intellectuals who grew up during the Nazi occupation would find the metaphor of entrapment—or its antonym, total freedom—compelling; in Derrida's terms, Westerners are wrong to believe that the column has Being, but they can't give it up. And given the difficulties postwar French intellectuals faced in trying to find an exit from what they saw as the competing and hegemonic demands of American capitalism and Eastern-bloc communism—or liberal humanism and Marxism—it might be expected that they would be suspicious of easy proclamations of liberation or truth.

29. A useful presentation of Derrida's views can be found in Barbara Johnson's introduction to Jacques Derrida, *Dissemination*, tr. Barbara Johnson (Chicago, 1981), pp. vii–xxxiii.

30. Derrida, *Dissemination*, p. 352.

Once revealed as the creation of language and ideology, the self either stands exposed like a caged animal (Foucault) or disappears like smoke dissipating in the sky (Derrida). The single, individual identity is, in the postmodernists' view, a historical creation whose days are limited. The self does not speak language; language speaks through the self, just as Heidegger had maintained. The very idea of the author, Foucault concluded, was the creation of the same discourses of the seventeenth and eighteenth century that insisted more generally on personal responsibility. The reading of a text, according to Derrida, has "nothing to do with the author as a real person."[31] The author, along with the idea of "man," would disappear with the passing of time because it was a cultural artifact.

The influence of postmodernism among late-twentieth-century historians would have remained entirely marginal—the stuff of philosophical disputation—if the discipline of history had not been changing. Crucial to the change was the entering wedge of relativism and skepticism. As early as the 1930s, the American Progressive historians Carl Becker and Charles Beard raised the clarion call of historical relativism by insisting that every man (their term) would write his own history. They seemed to imply that since every man had his own version of history, history functioned as a cultural myth rather than as an objective account of the past (a position not far from Nietzsche's). They argued that the ideal of a definitive, objective reconstruction of the past was chimerical. Facts did not present themselves directly to the historian; the historian picked and chose among them, guided by his ideological presuppositions. In Beard's words, the historian performed "an act of faith," based on "subjective decision, not a purely objective discovery."[32] Thus, not long after historians had established their discipline as an autonomous field of study emulating scientific methods of research,

---

31. As quoted in Rosenau, *Post-modernism,* p. 30.

32. For a review of Becker and Beard's positions and the controversy aroused by them, see Peter Novick, *That Noble Dream: The "Objectivity Question" and the American Historical Profession* (Cambridge, 1988), pp. 250–64; quote from Beard on p. 257.

belief in its scientific status and capacity for objectivity began to waver.

But these were faint murmurs compared to the muscular expansion of Marxism, the Annales school, and modernization theory, which after World War II became competing paradigms in the organization of ever-larger chunks of global research. Criticism of these enterprises remained dormant until the 1970s and 1980s, when it began to explode, detonated in part by the democratization of the university. Groups only recently admitted to the university proved especially receptive to skeptical postmodernist claims, having seen that leading representatives of all three major schools of history had left women and minorities out of their accounts or had treated them in stereotypical ways. Even though individual social historians held tenaciously to a model of objective scholarship, the results of their research also reinforced the postmodernist disaggregation of all unitary interpretive schemes. The history of what postmodernists called "subaltern" groups—workers, immigrants, women, slaves, and gays—in fact proved difficult to integrate into the story of one American nation. How could the tragic stories of the lives of slaves, for example, be incorporated into a single narrative governed by optimism and progress? Social history, once the great hope of an increasingly inclusive and yet scientifically minded profession, seemed inadequate to the task of offering a new, gendered, and inclusive narrative.

## The Rise of Cultural History

Within the context of universities more democratized than anything Beard or Becker could have imagined, cultural warfare erupted along a front running from history and literature to law and education. Indeed, among the human sciences, history fared better than most because until very recently, the methods and goals of social history rather than the philosophical dilemmas raised by postmodernism remained at the center of controversy. While debates about social history still dominated the headlines of historical controversy, some historians turned away from social history, now criticized as having failed to live up to its promise, and toward the history of culture. The mind as a repository of society's prescriptions, as the site where identity is formed and reality linguistically negotiated, focused the new historical inquiry. There resided culture, defined as society's repertoire of interpretive mechanisms and value systems.

The historian of culture sought to dig beneath the formal productions of law, literature, science, and art to the codes, clues, hints, signs, gestures, and artifacts through which people communicate their values and their truths. Most important, scholars began to see that culture particularizes meaning because cultural symbols are endlessly reshaped in everyday social encounters. Only insiders get access to the message; being inside the social loop of signals makes one a member of the group, be it a community, a class, a congregation, or a nation. This cultural point of view can, but need not, deny the universality of a conceptual language along with the uniformity of human reasoning. From a postmodernist perspective, however, cultural history could be used to further the attack on reason and universal human values.

In the cultural perspective, a different view of rationality comes into play, one which stresses that human reason operates within a specific cultural context. People think within the parameters of their mental universe; they cannot catapult out of that universe in order to form independent judgments about it. Within a mental universe they can, however, arrive at scientific or moral truths that are accessible to people in different mental universes. Nothing in the cultural perspective necessarily supports the notion that languages are incommensurable, having no common meaning to people who did not initially partake in their formulation. The new cultural history still reflected developing interest in uncovering the social or contextual sources of motive and action discussed in our earlier chapters on American history and the history of science. But whereas historians, modernization theorists, and Annalistes alike pressed economics and sociology into service, cultural historians turned to anthropology and literary theory.

"Culture" is a notoriously loose term, and anthropologists have long debated its meaning. During the 1970s and 1980s, the anthropologist most often cited by historians was Clifford Geertz. In his wonderfully provocative essay "Thick Description," Geertz insisted that "culture is not a power, something to which social events, behaviors, institutions, or processes can be causally attributed; it is a context, something within which they can be intelligibly—that is, thickly—described."[33] Anthropology, with this emphasis on an intelligibility derived from extensive contextualization, came to be an interpretive science in search of meaning rather than an experimental one in search of laws. Geertz thus explicitly rejected the positivist scientific model in favor of an increasingly literary model of cultural criticism. His position had obvious affinities to those advanced by postmodernists such as Foucault and Derrida.

Many cultural historians soon jumped on the interpretive bandwagon. Historians proclaimed the advantages of "history in the ethnographic grain," for it seemed to offer a way of interpreting the meaning people in the past ascribed to their experiences. A recent study has shown that between 1976 and 1990, studies of French history shifted decisively away from political and social history toward intellectual and cultural history, no doubt reflecting a general trend.[34] The emphasis on decoding meaning, rather than inferring causal laws of expla-

33. Clifford Geertz, "Thick Description: Toward an Interpretive Theory of Culture," in *The Interpretation of Cultures* (New York, 1973), p. 14.

34. Between 1976 and 1990, the percentage of English-language publications in French history that were devoted to political and diplomatic history decreased by half and publications in economic and social history declined by one-fourth, while those in intellectual and cultural history doubled. The trend toward decline in social history was even more pronounced in France, the home of the Annales school. The percentage of French-language publications in French history devoted to political and diplomatic history declined by about one-fourth and those in social and economic history declined by half, whereas those in intellectual and cultural history doubled. Based on Tables 1 and 2 in Thomas J. Schaeper, "French History as Written on Both Sides of the Atlantic: A Comparative Analysis," *French Historical Studies*, 17 (1991): 242–43.

nation, was taken to be the central task of cultural history, just as Geertz had named it the central task of cultural anthropology.[35]

The increasing interest in culture and cultural theory came originally from theoretical sources and historical trends other than postmodernism. Primary among them was disenchantment with explaining everything in economic and social terms—what is often called economic and social reductionism. The emphasis on culture implied that people's beliefs and ritual activities interacted with their economic and social expectations and did not simply mirror their socioeconomic situations. In the United States, the growing awareness that American culture included many different and sometimes competing subcultures also fostered an interest in the history of culture. In response to these trends, the very models of explanation that most contributed to the rise of social history in the first place went through a major shift of emphasis in the 1970s and 1980s. Turning first to theorists of culture within their own ranks, Marxists and Annalistes alike became increasingly captivated by the history of culture. Even diehard modernization theorists placed increasing emphasis on cultural factors.

Marxist attention to cultural forms was inspired by the work of Antonio Gramsci, a founder of the Italian Communist Party who wrote down his thoughts in a series of prison notebooks in the 1920s and 1930s. Gramsci's most influential concept was that of "hegemony," the idea that an elite can establish its power only if it exerts a cultural domination over other social classes. Material strength alone cannot give a group power; it must also develop the means to exercise cultural and intellectual leadership. Thus the working class could come to power only if it could set up its own independent culture, "its own original conception of the world."[36] Gramsci's emphasis on culture,

---

35. See, for example, Robert Darnton, *The Great Cat Massacre and Other Episodes in French Cultural History* (New York, 1984), for an explicit affiliation with Geertz.

36. As quoted in A. Pozzolini, *Antonio Gramsci: An Introduction to His Thought,* tr. Anne F. Showstack (London, 1970), p. 109.

which only gradually spread in Marxist circles after World War II, was evident in E. P. Thompson's pioneering and influential history of the English working class. Thompson explicitly devoted himself to the study of what he called "cultural and moral mediations" and "the way these material experiences are handled . . . in cultural ways."[37]

Other influences also pushed Marxists toward an interest in culture, from the work of the literary critic Raymond Williams in Great Britain to the studies of the Frankfurt school of critical theory in Germany. In France, Louis Althusser explicitly tried to reorient Marxism in a poststructuralist direction by arguing that Marx's own work showed that the notion of an actively willing, freely acting human subject was only the product of bourgeois ideology. Many historians in the British Marxist tradition, including Thompson, drew back from the more extreme postmodernist positions associated with the cultural turn, viewing them as a threat to historical materialism. Thompson explicitly attacked Althusser for denying human beings a role in the shaping of their own historical destiny.[38] He and his many followers worried that postmodernism, especially with its emphasis on discourse, stood aloof from real history by wrenching language loose from social reality. One especially vociferous Marxist critic denounced "writing that appears under the designer label of poststructuralism / postmodernism" as trivializing, academic wordplaying that promotes a kind of solipsistic navel-gazing rather than serious intellectual work.[39]

An alternative Marxist approach to culture has been proposed by the French sociologist and anthropologist Pierre Bourdieu. Bourdieu recast the Marxist model by giving more

37. As quoted in Ellen Kay Trimberger, "E. P. Thompson: Understanding the Process of History," in Theda Skocpol, ed., *Vision and Method in Historical Sociology* (Cambridge, 1984), p. 219. Thompson's *The Making of the English Working Class* was first published in 1963.

38. E. P. Thompson, *The Poverty of Theory and Other Essays* (New York, 1978).

39. Bryan D. Palmer, *Descent into Discourse: The Reification of Language and the Writing of Social History* (Philadelphia, 1990), pp. 198–99.

attention to culture as a set of practices used differently by different social groups. Though he insisted that "the mode of expression characteristic of a cultural production always depends on the laws of the market in which it is offered," he directed his own work to uncovering the "specific logic" of "cultural goods."[40] Central to this logic are the ways and means of appropriating cultural objects. In contrast to Foucault, who underlined the effects of a general discursive field, Bourdieu drew attention to the importance of social distinctions in the uses of culture, and reaffirmed the vitality of social history.

The turn toward cultural history has been even more enthusiastic in the Annales school, whose younger members have grown increasingly disenchanted with Braudel's original paradigm of levels of historical experience. First evident in a preoccupation with what the French rather enigmatically called *mentalités,* the Annalistes' embrace of culture focused on the collectively shared mental practices or structures of a society.[41] As a label, *mentalité* served to set off cultural and mental life from the economic, social, or demographic processes that had previously occupied Annales historians.

For the new generation of the Annales school, *mentalités* or culture could no longer be characterized as part of the "third level" of historical experience. In their view, the third level is not a level at all but a primary determinant of historical reality, because mental structures cannot be reduced to material elements. Economic and social relations are not prior to or determining of cultural ones; they are themselves fields of cultural practice and cultural production. In this view, cultural practices cannot be explained deductively by reference to an extracultural dimension of experience. All practices, whether economic or cultural, depend on the cultural or mental representations or

40. Pierre Bourdieu, *Distinction: A Social Critique of the Judgment of Taste,* tr. Richard Nice (Cambridge, Mass., 1984), pp. xiii, 1. For a critical overview, see Richard Jenkins, *Pierre Bourdieu* (London and New York, 1992).

41. Volker Sellin traces the history of the word and of the concept in "Mentalität und Mentalitätsgeschichte," *Historische Zeitschrift,* 241 (1985): 555–98.

codes that individuals use to make sense of their world.[42]

The new generation of Annalistes and their counterparts elsewhere did not simply propose a new set of topics for investigation; rather their approach to culture raised questions about the methods and goals of history generally. Although the concept of culture need not preclude an interest in social and economic explanations, a belief in reality, or a practice grounded on empiricism, the concept does pose fundamental problems about historical explanation when elevated to the status of the prime force in historical change. If ready assumptions about the social and economic causes of events are thrown out, what will take their place? If all practices are culturally and linguistically inscribed, if all meaning, even the meaning of scientific laws, depends on cultural context, then how can any causal explanation be derived? (Geertz seemed to suggest that it could not and should not.) As often happens with sudden enthusiasms, culture as a category ran the risk of encompassing everything and thus, in a sense, explaining nothing; what can it mean to say that everything is due to culture? Should historians concentrate on offering thick descriptions and forget about causal analysis? In this way, the challenge to materialist reductionism (explaining action by reference to economic and social factors or causes) turned into a challenge to causal explanation itself. When swimming in culture, neither causes nor effects could be distinguished. As a consequence, cultural history and the philosophical issues of relativism and skepticism began to intersect and reinforce each other.

## Postmodernism and Historians

At first glance, it might seem unlikely that either Foucault or Derrida would have much influence on the practice of his-

42. For an influential statement of the recent Annales view, see Roger Chartier, "Intellectual History or Sociocultural History? The French Trajectories," in Dominick LaCapra and Steven L. Kaplan, eds., *Modern European Intellectual History: Reappraisals and New Perspectives* (Ithaca, N.Y., 1982).

tory. Both of them argued vehemently against any research into origins (perhaps the classic historical approach to any problem), and both advanced methods of discourse analysis that required none of the usual forms of grounding in economics, society, or politics. Both consequently have been accused of fostering nihilism. While Derrida seemed to offer no motive at all for the play of language, the only consistent "cause" cited by Foucault for the formation of discourses was the Nietzschean will to power, usually expressed through institutions, rather than by individuals.[43] Foucault's definition of his work as a history of the conditions for the "production of truth" thus risked reducing all truth, and all his historical explanations of it, to an all-encompassing will to power—in many ways, the opposite of Derrida's motiveless play of language. In either rendering, women and men are stripped of the meaningful choices whose reality had once served to distinguish human beings from animals. Change comes about through unexpected and unpredictable slips in the fault lines of broad discursive configurations, through lucky breaks in the war of all against all, not through self-determined human action.

Despite much resistance to postmodernism, it has gained ground through the rising influence of literary theory in all forms of cultural studies in the last two decades. In the 1980s, Geertz pointed anthropologists in this direction by linking his "interpretive theory" to what he called "the Text analogy . . . the broadest of the recent refigurations of social theory."[44] In the "text analogy," culture is likened to a text or language. Like a text, it has to be studied as something in itself rather than as a transparent representation of some more basic set of codes such as economic or social trends. If culture is like a text or language, then it is presumably susceptible to all the criticisms leveled by Foucault and Derrida.

43. We are grateful to Ruth Bloch for her comments on this question. See also Wolin, *Terms of Cultural Criticism*, pp. 185–86.

44. Clifford Geertz, "Blurred Genres: The Refiguration of Social Thought," in *Local Knowledge: Further Essays in Interpretive Anthropology* (New York, 1983), p. 30.

All historians of culture must grapple with how to relate the cultural artifact—text, painting, or steam engine—with the other beliefs, knowledge systems, interests, and structures affecting the human agents who gave rise to it. But postmodern theories of interpretation invariably go further than simply insisting on the integrity of the cultural artifact. They challenge all endeavors to relate culture (or discourse or text) to something outside or beneath it, either to nature or material circumstances, and in so doing they undermine the traditional foundations of knowledge claims in both the natural and the human sciences. If postmodern theories are taken seriously, there is no transhistorical or transcendent grounds for interpretation, and human beings have no unmediated access to the world of things or events.[45] Taken at its word, postmodernism means that there can be no straightforward passageway to the world outside the text, nor, by implication perhaps, any access to the text by peoples or cultures foreign to it. "Beauty" like "truth" like "reality" would lie in the "eye," as it were, of language. Neither reality nor the individual knower stands outside of the cultural construction. The world, the knower, and knowledge are all profoundly relativized and cut off from the social processes that grind or swirl wordlessly around the bearer of culture. In this rendering, scientific knowledge becomes simply another linguistic convention, a form of discourse related to the excessively rationalist form of life in the West.

Reactions to postmodernist theories within history have varied widely. Traditionalists reject the new forms of theory just as they rejected all previous forms of theory as unnecessary, even unhealthy, intrusions into the domain of history. Social historians have resisted cultural theory as too removed from concrete social conditions, though in some instances social historians have themselves moved to embrace the new theories. As is so often the case with an academic discipline, the introduc-

---

45. John E. Toews, "Intellectual History After the Linguistic Turn," *American Historical Review*, 92 (1987): 879–908, especially pp. 901–2.

tion of new theories has served to divide scholars into opposing camps. Our view is that the new cultural theories, including postmodernist ones, have helped, like their predecessors, to revitalize discussion about methods, goals, and even the foundations of knowledge. Provocative and unsettling, they raise questions that demand some new answers.

Some academic feminists have found postmodernist theories congenial because such theories underline the contingency, the human-madeness, and hence the changeability of cultural norms and practices. In the United States, in particular (and perhaps uniquely), women's history and gender studies have been at the forefront of the new cultural history. Feminist historians pioneered the use of anthropological insights, and now some of them are in the vanguard of those who utilize postmodern theories. The very notion of gender shows the influence of the cultural and linguistic term in the humanities. From its origins as a term of grammar, gender has come to refer in English increasingly to the cultural and social construction of sexual identity. In her influential collection of essays *Gender and the Politics of History,* Joan Wallach Scott insisted that "a more radical feminist politics" required "a more radical epistemology," which she found in postmodernist theory. Citing the approaches of Foucault and Derrida as models, she praised postmodernist theory for relativizing the status of all knowledge.[46]

The issues raised by the feminist use of postmodernist theory are characteristic of the debate about the text analogy and postmodernist theory more generally. Central to the debate has been the blurring of the distinction between text and context (or between language and the social world). Classic social

---

46. Joan Wallach Scott, *Gender and the Politics of History* (New York, 1988), quote p. 4. Scott has been the target of much criticism directed against historians' use of such theories. Traditional historians, Marxists, and other feminists have all criticized her for an excessive allegiance to postmodernism, for a stance of extreme relativism, and for a tendency to reduce history to the perception of meaning. See, for example, Palmer, *Descent into Discourse,* pp. 172–86. For a philosophical response to deconstruction, see Hilary Putnam, *Renewing Philosophy* (Cambridge, Mass., 1992), ch. 6.

theory rested on a heuristic separation of text and context. Something was taken as the thing to be explained (the text, the effect, or the dependent variable), such as the rise of capitalism, the workings of bureaucratic rationalization, or the increasing impersonality in modern society; something else was posited as the means of explanation (the context, the cause, or the independent variable), e.g., the Protestant work ethic, the spread of markets, or the increasing differentiation of functions in modern society. Denying the possibility of any separation of text and context (or cause and effect), postmodernist theory jeopardizes all social theorizing.

If postmodernist cultural anthropology is any guide, the concern with developing causal explanations and social theories would be replaced in a postmodernist history with a focus on self-reflexivity and on problems of literary construction: how does the historian as author construct his or her text, how is the illusion of authenticity produced, what creates a sense of truthfulness to the facts and a warranty of closeness to past reality (or the "truth-effect" as it is sometimes called)?[47] The implication is that the historian does not in fact capture the past in faithful fashion but rather, like the novelist, gives the appearance of doing so. Were this version of postmodernism applied to history, the search for truths about the past would be displaced by the self-reflexive analysis of historians' ways of fictively producing convincing "truth-effects." Similarly, people in the past who believed themselves to be engaged in the search for truth would have to be either indulged or disabused by the historian, their futile struggle seen to be analogous to the odyssey to which any superstition or self-delusion consigns its believers.[48] Relativism, possibly tinged with cynicism or arrogance, would characterize the historian's aesthetic stance toward

47. For a critical review of this tendency in cultural anthropology, see Frances E. Mascia-Lees, Patricia Sharpe, and Colleen Ballerino Cohen, "The Postmodernist Turn in Anthropology: Cautions from a Feminist Perspective," *Signs*, 15 (1989): 7–33.

48. For this point, see Phyllis Mack, *Visionary Women: Ecstatic Prophecy in Seventeenth-Century England* (Berkeley, Calif., 1992), pp. 6–7.

such people, becoming the alternative to and replacement for respect. In the face of their myopia or futile discursive strategies, the ironic voice would overshadow the historian's wonder, presenting the passion to linger among human beings struggling to find truths as a quest for their "truth-effects."

Under the impact of postmodernist literary approaches, historians are now becoming more aware that their supposedly matter-of-fact choices of narrative techniques and analytical forms also have implications with social and political ramifications. Essays on the state of the discipline often have a canonical form all their own: first a narrative of the rise of new kinds of history, then a long moment for exploring the problems posed by new kinds of history, followed by either a jeremiad on the evils of new practices or a celebration of the potential overcoming of all obstacles. The literary form that the argument takes has a very strong influence on the way that evidence and arguments are presented.

Authors of essays about the "new history" in the early twentieth century or about social history in the 1950s and 1960s often wrote in heroic and romantic terms of the advance of social and economic history, with the brave historian marching hand in hand with the forces of progress and democracy to do battle with backwardness and tradition. More recently, the ironic mode has become dominant among those historians, who, like other cultural critics, have wondered whether their work could ever be other than fragmentary and partial, with little relevance to the grander narratives of the past. Despairing of the validity of what they describe as macrohistories, they embrace irony and claim only to be writing microhistories.

Questions of form or technique justifiably extend to the chapters in this volume. In our emphasis on the need for narrative coherence, causal analysis, and social contextualization, as exemplified in our own narratives, we are attempting to go beyond the current negative or ironic judgments about history's role. We as historians are nonetheless making our own aesthetic choices, just as others have chosen comedy, romance, or irony for their writings. We are emphasizing the human need for self-understanding through a coherent narrative of the past and the need for admittedly partial, objective explanations of how the past has worked. In this sense, we have renounced an ironic stance.[49] Rather than try to prove our superiority to past historians by focusing on their failures, we are trying to learn from their efforts to make sense of the social world. Rather than underlining the impossibility of total objectivity or completely satisfying causal explanation, we are highlighting the need for the most objective possible explanations as the only way to move forward, perhaps not on a straight line of progress into the future, but forward toward a more intellectually alive, democratic community, toward the kind of society in which we would like to live.

These are aesthetic or literary choices because they involve ways of organizing a narrative, but history is more than a branch of letters to be judged only in terms of its literary merit. Our choices are political, social, and epistemological. They are political and social because they reflect beliefs in a certain kind of community of historians and society of Americans. They are epistemological because they reflect positions on what can be known and how it can be known. With diligence and good faith they may also be at moments reasonably, if partially, true accounts of the distant and recent past.

The assumption of a clear hierarchy of explanation running from economy and society up to politics and culture was present in the Annales school, Marxism, and modernization theory, and it can still be seen in the table of contents of many social history monographs. We agree that the focus on culture and language undermines this hierarchical view by showing that all social reality is culturally constructed and discursively construed in the first instance. Culture can no longer be considered a phenomenon of "the third level" in Annales terms, if

49. On irony as a trope in historical writing, see Hayden White, *Metahistory: The Historical Imagination in Nineteenth-Century Europe* (Baltimore, 1973).

the "basics" of life (demography, economy) are themselves constructed in and through culture. In that sense, discursive or linguistic models throw into doubt the once absolutist forms of conventional historical explanation, and they thereby open up the way to new forms of historical investigation. Foucault's own work is perhaps the best-known example of such a new form with direct historical relevance.

We are not, therefore, rejecting out of hand everything put forward by the postmodernists. The text analogy and aspects of postmodernist theories have some real political and epistemological attractions. The interest in culture was a way of disengaging from Marxism, or at least from the most unsatisfactory versions of economic and social reductionism. Cultural and linguistic approaches also helped in the ongoing task of puncturing the shield of science behind which reductionism often hid. By focusing on culture, one could challenge the virtually commonsensical assumption that there is a clear hierarchy of explanation in history (that is, in all social reality), running from biology and topography through demography and economics up to social structure and finally to politics and its poor cousins, cultural and intellectual life.

Yet postmodernism has also raised its own set of concerns, just as every previous theoretical intervention did. Chief among them has been the problem of linguistic determinism or conflation, the reduction of the social and natural world to language and context to text. If historians give up the analogies of levels (the Annales school) or base-superstructure (Marxism), must they also give up social theory and causal language altogether? Paradoxically, as theory has developed from the days of Hegel and Marx, one trajectory that went from Nietzsche and Heidegger and on to the postmodernists has progressively shed any ambition to explain. As the exponents of that trajectory take aim at history, its original theoretical and empirical project, the explanation of long-term social and political development, then comes under attack. In other words, postmodernism throws into question the modern narrative form, proving once again that the philosophy of history does matter.

## The Problem of Narrative

Philosophical questions about epistemological foundations inevitably touch upon the narrative form that gives cohesion to history as a discipline. Narrative continues to be fundamental, albeit in different ways, to history as a form of knowledge about human life, even though few professional historians now write what was classically known as narrative history—grand panoramic stories about the emergence of a new nation or major crises that threatened national identity. Despite the decline of grand narratives, history has retained a strong narrative cast, even in the most specialized monographs of social and cultural history. Like memory itself, every work of history has the structure of a plot with a beginning, middle, and end, whether the subject is social mobility in a nineteenth-century American city, the uses of art as propaganda in the Russian Revolution, or the analysis of the rise of postmodernist theory in historical writing. Thus, to argue for a return to narrative, as some traditionalists have done, is to miss the cardinal point that historians have never entirely departed from it.[50]

Not surprisingly, "narrative" has become one of the charged code words of the current struggles over history. Those who resist the changes in the discipline, including the rise of social history, tend to defend narrative as the form of writing specific to history, while those who champion disciplinary innovation tend to demean narrative as an unsophisticated form of writing about the past or as simply another version of fiction camouflaged as history. More important than this essentially superfi-

---

50. For a discussion of some of these issues, see especially Hayden White, "The Question of Narrative in Contemporary Historical Theory," in *The Content of the Form: Narrative Discourse and Historical Representation* (Baltimore, 1987), pp. 26–57. For an account of the attempt to revive narrative, see Novick, *That Noble Dream*, pp. 622–25.

cial debate about the place of narrative within the profession (superficial because it focuses on the most immediately evident form of writing rather than on its deeper significance) is the question of what have been called meta-narratives or master narratives.

A meta-narrative or master narrative is a grand schema for organizing the interpretation and writing of history. In earlier chapters we described three of the most important meta-narratives of modern history: the heroic model of progress through science, the epic of an unfolding American nation, and the idea of the "modern." Marxism, liberalism, even postmodernism itself are all examples of meta-narratives, for they all offer sweeping stories about the origins of American and Western problems and the direction that lives may take in the present, as well as remedies for the future. Of these philosophies of history, only postmodernism attacks meta-narrative along with the narrative form itself as inherently ideological and hence obfuscating. In the postmodernist view, present in the works of Foucault and Derrida, among others, history in general and narrative in particular are denounced as "representational practices" by which Western societies produced individuals especially well suited to life in a postindustrial state.[51] (It isn't entirely clear why this is a bad thing.)

At best, in this line of postmodernist argument, narrative and meta-narrative are useful fictions for modern industrial society, nothing more. At worst, they are insidious ways of hiding the partiality and propaganda aims of the author of the narrative and the normalizing tendencies of modern states and societies. For some postmodernists, all meta-narratives are inherently totalitarian. They cannot, by this overarching analysis, be in any sense true. One postmodernist proclaimed, "History is the Western myth."[52] In place of plot and character, history and individuality, perhaps even meaning itself, the most thorough-

51. See the account in White, *Content of the Form*, p. 35.
52. Descombes as quoted in Rosenau, *Post-modernism*, p. 62.

going postmodernists would offer an "interminable pattern without meaning," a form of writing closer to modern music and certain modern novels.[53]

In the most extreme form of the postmodernist critique of narrative, special scorn is reserved for those who write for an "ordinary educated public," since they turn the contradictions, political forces, and ideological tensions of history into "dis-thought,"[54] that is, a form of propaganda for the status quo. This is the ultimate *reductio ad absurdum* of postmodernist criticisms of history-writing. Such critics take to heart the post-modernist notion that history is irrelevant to identity (a position not shared, by the way, by Foucault, who attributed all identity to historical processes). They deny that story or narrative is one of the major ways in which human intelligence ascribes meaning to life. For them, the entire historiographical tradition simply fosters "a consciousness that is never able to arrive at criticism."[55] Narrative and critical thinking are incompatible.

Several different levels of argument are involved in these condemnations of meta-narratives: historiography as the tra-dition of history writing over time; narrative as a form of his-torical writing; and storytelling as a form of ascribing meaning to social life. The most extreme postmodernist position denies the validity of all of them at once. Meta-narrative is denounced as myth, historiography dismissed as "a mode of bureaucratic-ideological organization," narrative as a form of propaganda, and story or plot (beginning-middle-end as an essential way of viewing action in the world) as part of the "myth that history is a condition of knowledge." It is less clear, however, what such critics would have historians do instead, except, perhaps, that they ought not to write history at all or admit that in the end history is another form of fiction.[56] As one contemporary phi-

53. Ermarth, *Sequel to History*, p. 212.

54. Sande Cohen, *Historical Culture: On the Recoding of an Academic Discipline* (Berke-ley, 1986), p. 326.

55. Ibid., p. 77.

56. Ibid., quotes pp. 8, 12, 21.

losopher puts the objection to this kind of nihilistic criticism, "deconstruction without reconstruction is irresponsibility."[57]

No one argues any longer, as Ranke seemed to do, that historical narrative in any way exactly mirrors past reality, "as it actually was." Historians cannot capture the fullness of past experience, any more than individual memories can; they only have the traces or residues of the past, and their accounts are necessarily partial. Even those who argue that narrative structure inheres in the events themselves and that narration actually constitutes action and experience grant that historical narratives do not simply mirror or reproduce the firsthand experience of reality.[58]

Although most historians continue to believe that narrative is a universal mode of organizing human knowledge, others have questioned this position. One previous defender of narrative recently concluded that master narratives and narrative itself might be tainted with "the guilt of culture and history." He speculated that the death of history, politics, and narrative might all be aspects of another great transformation, similar in scope and effect to that which marked the initial emergence of Greek thought.[59] Similarly, it has been argued that postmodern narrative will no longer rely on the time of Newton, "the time of history . . . the time of clocks and capital." Instead, it will collapse the subject and object of knowledge and with it the distinction between "invention and reality."[60]

It is probably impossible to develop an airtight defense of narrative and meta-narrative (in Newtonian time). One commentator recently acknowledged, "There is no global defense of the narrative form that will insulate it, once and for all, from

57. Putnam, *Renewing Philosophy*, p. 133.

58. David Carr, "Narrative and the Real World: An Argument for Continuity," *History and Theory*, 25 (1986): especially pp. 117–31.

59. White, *Content of the Form*, pp. 1, 168.

60. Ermarth, *Sequel to History*, p. 22.

skeptical doubts."[61] Similarly, philosophical efforts to define precisely the workings of causal analysis in historical explanation have become hopelessly entangled in debates about general laws of explanation and history's relationship to the natural sciences. If the nature of the particles that make up physical reality is up for grabs in contemporary philosophical and scientific thought, then the concept of a once-lived reality in the past and its relation to historical representations is even more vexed. Yet the mere existence of questions and doubts does not prove the inherent falseness of the narrative form with its incorporation of causal language.

We see no reason to conclude that because there is a gap between reality and its narration (its representation), the narration in some fundamental sense is inherently invalid. Just because narratives are human creations does not make them all equally fictitious or mythical. In our last two chapters, we will examine the ways in which historians determine the truth or falseness of their narrative creations. Suffice it to say for now that in our view, narrative is essential both to individual and social identity. It is consequently a defining element in history-writing, and the historiographical tradition, as we have reviewed it briefly here, is an important element in identity, both for historians in a profession and for citizens in modern societies. We believe that historians must try to develop new and better social theories or new and better meta-narratives, even while making problematic their old ones. Just as the meta-narrative of progress replaced that of Christianity in the West, so too it is possible to believe that people will want to develop new meta-narratives in order to prepare for the future. New experiences will always require new interpretations and new explanations.

Postmodernism is in fact one such meta-narrative, and many

61. Andrew P. Norman, "Telling It Like It Was: Historical Narratives on Their Own Terms," *History and Theory*, 30 (1991): 119–35, quote p. 128.

commentators have pointed to its unstated reliance on a narrative of modernism to make its point. As one historian reminds us, to proclaim the end of historical meta-narratives is itself "a (quite totalizing) piece of historical narrative."[62] Rejecting all meta-narratives cannot make sense, because narratives and meta-narratives are the kinds of stories that make action in the world possible. They make action possible because they make it meaningful. Postmodernism offers another interpretation of meaning, including historical meaning, even as it claims to contest the foundations of all meanings. There is no action without a story about how the world works, and action is all the more deliberative if the stories are all the more theorized. The stories will always be changing (they are in fact stories about how change works), but historians will always have to tell them in order to make sense of the past, and it matters whether they tell them well—as truthfully and fully as possible—or not.

The move toward the most radically skeptical and relativist postmodern position inevitably leads into a cul-de-sac. Dismissals of history, politics, and narrative as hopelessly modern ideas, now outmoded in the postmodern world, might seem up-to-date, but history, politics, and narrative are still the best tools available for dealing with the world and preparing for the future. A similar kind of crisis that foreshadows a turning away from the postmodern view can be seen in almost every field of knowledge or learning today. Postmodern art often consists of critiques of the function of art and especially past art (the mounds of shopping carts piled around the statue of Mozart in downtown Salzburg, for instance, in the year of the Mozart bicentenary) rather than new art. Similarly, postmodern history too often seems to consist of denunciations of history as it has been known rather than of new histories for present and hence future time. Periodic exercises in theory have an undeniably useful function as criticism of unself-conscious assumptions about art

---

62. William Reddy, "Postmodernism and the Public Sphere: Implications for an Historical Ethnography," *Cultural Anthropology*, 7 (1992): 135–68, quote p. 137.

or history or science, but postmodernism cannot provide models for the future when it claims to refuse the entire idea of offering models for the future. In the final analysis, then, there can be no postmodern history. We turn now to the task of elaborating models for the future of history, models for understanding the search for historical truths within the framework of a revitalized and transformed practice of objectivity.

# A New Republic of Learning

PART THREE

A New Republic
of Learning

°7°

# Truth and Objectivity

IN THE PRECEDING CHAPTERS we have traced the development of three kinds of intellectual absolutism and looked at their consequences for historians. The first, the Enlightenment faith in the heroic model of science, prompted historians to become like scientists and turn themselves into neutral and passionless investigators in order to reconstruct the past exactly as it happened. The second, the idea of progress, encouraged them to look to history to discover the laws of human development as those laws worked themselves out in sequential stages. This search for enduring principles of social action, of course, carried with it the assumption that beneath the flow of the daily actions of men and women there was an undertow of forces pulling those actions into orderly processes of change.

The last intellectual absolutism arose from the powerful national sentiments that nineteenth-century men and women drew upon for a sense of identity. Powered by the revolutionary forces unleashed at the end of the eighteenth century, the engine of nationalism drove historians to place their countries—and by extension their fellow citizens—into the larger design of world history. Building the nation became an absolute value, and history's contribution to that effort was assumed unreflectively. Behind all of these absolutisms was the radiant concept of nature—not the lush and untamable nature of the primitive world or the nature that pushed Adam and Eve to sin, but the nature of science, of progressive improvement and spontaneous order that human inquirers now perceived beneath the flotsam and jetsam that floated to the surface of daily life.

This highly volatile mix of aspirations for history coexisted with surprising ease for over a hundred years. All these ideas could harmoniously occupy the same intellectual space because they were freshly minted theories unscarred by rough encounters with verification. The notion that random events actually composed themselves into invisible processes of change compelled belief in part because Newtonian laws of gravity had made people familiar with the paradoxical contrast between appearances and reality: what was seen deluded the senses and belied the invisible, real structuring of the physical world. Throughout the nineteenth century, science—its methods, projects, expectations, and heroes—put into circulation new coins for cultural negotiation as Western societies moved at different paces toward modernity. Science gradually replaced religion as the provider of models and metaphors for comprehending social experience.

Every carefully researched work of national history shared in the warm approbation accorded science because it revealed how each country figured in the overall framework of social progress. This twinned respect for science and nationalism deflected attention from the possibility of their divergence, from the real prospect, for instance, that histories about national grandeur might conflict with those that used scientific methods to investigate how nations have persecuted their minorities. The tension between patriotic presentations of one's country and accurate reconstructions of national failures remained to be probed in the future, leaving nineteenth-century scholars free and undisturbed to gather records and perfect research methods, taking in their industry hostages for future skeptics to liberate.

Since the scientific enterprise involved drawing a fixed boundary between the objective reality of things-as-they-are and the subjective realm of things-as-we-would-like-to-them-to-be, historians were loath to explore the subjective component of history-writing. Fact had to be distinguished from opinion, documentary evidence from interpretation. In this intellectual milieu of the nineteenth and early twentieth centuries, the historian's practice of merging the two remained in a conceptual limbo, undiscussed and unacknowledged. A Carl Becker might wryly comment that the historian "does not stick to the facts; the facts stick to him," but this belle-lettristic needling was easily shrugged off. American historians chose to think of themselves as empiricists seeking to discover and document objective facts.[1] Even to entertain the proposition that knowledge was an intellectual production rather than a disinterested reading of physical and textual evidence induced a dizzying uncertainty that one scholar aptly termed the "vertigo of relativism."[2] Quite naturally wishing to avoid the seasickness of shifting personal perspectives, historians generally sought to avoid philosophical issues, which they dismissively categorized as "theory." Many wrote as though analyzing the course of human progress was as straightforward a task as isolating disease-causing germs. Others recognized changes in standard interpretations of events, but ascribed them to a kind of Oedipal tendency for successive scholarly generations to revise the findings of their fatherly predecessors.

## The Relativist Attack on Truth and Objectivity

Since the 1960s, all the regnant absolutisms of the nineteenth century have been dethroned. A many-pronged attack coming from a variety of perspectives has zeroed in on the goals of objectivity and truth-seeking. A fluid skepticism now covers the intellectual landscape, encroaching upon one body of thought after another. The study of history has been questioned and its

---

1. Peter Novick, *That Noble Dream: The "Objectivity Question" and the American Historical Profession* (Cambridge, 1988). The Becker quote appeared in Carl Becker, "Detachment and the Writing of History," *Atlantic Monthly,* CVI (October 1910): 528.

2. Clifford Geertz, "The Impact of the Concept of Culture on the Concept of Man," in *The Interpretation of Cultures* (New York, 1973), p. 44.

potential for truth-finding categorically denied. "Who said that history is about truth?" asks the skeptic. Having been made "scientific" in the nineteenth century, history now shares in the pervasive disillusionment with science which has marked the postwar era.

Some skeptics are social constructionists, once called strong programmers, who see both science and history as intellectual contrivances or discourses, spun out of words, which only incidentally touch things that exist outside the separate, seamlessly interwoven linguistic tapestry. In the Anglo-American academy, social constructionism surfaced in the history and philosophy of science in the late 1970s. Postmodernists, many with debts to French theorists, have since then joined the ranks of skeptics. In their deconstructive enterprise, they have fastened onto the irreducible element of arbitrariness in the production of all knowledge, going on from this observation to question the capacity for human beings to understand anything outside of their own closed systems of communication.[3]

All of these contemporary thinkers have attacked the scientific influence of their forebears with a passion equal to the rage once reserved for the infamies of the old regime. Raising a banner more appealing than that of the esoteric philosophers of science, postmodernists have captured the public attention as the quintessential relativists of the day. In their view, since all historical inquiries grow out of the inquirer's linguistic frame, the results follow all too predictably from the hegemonic power of the Western white males initially responsible for the linguistic structure. The writing of history, these critics maintain, is not about truth-seeking; it's about the politics of the historians. One man's truth is another woman's falsity, and they point to the historiographical wars of the last twenty years as proof. Dorothy's dog Toto exposes the Wizard of Oz as an ordinary middle-aged man; similarly, the skeptics believe, they have re-

---

3. There are differences and disagreements between postmodernists and strong programmers. See Andrew Pickering, ed., *Science as Practice and Culture* (Chicago, 1992).

vealed historians to be no more than specialized storytellers whose claims to recover the past as it actually happened belong to the smoke screen of scientific pretentions. Historians, as Hayden White has maintained, "do not build up knowledge that others might use, they generate a discourse about the past."[4]

Moving beyond the undeniable subjectivity of history-writing, contemporary critics have also weighed and found wanting the rhetorical strategies and narrative form of historical scholarship. As hermeneutically astute analyzers of how words can promote illusions, these commentators rightly point out that historians have minimized the limitations of their perspective by speaking from an omniscient point of view: "Napoleon marched his armies across the continent of Europe," "Americans believed that a manifest destiny carried them across the North American continent." With such verbal derring-do, historians, they charge, give the impression that they have levitated themselves off the ground to a superior observational position.

The language of scholarship, moreover, makes it sound as if history, not historians, were doing the talking, the authoritative voice of the all-seeing author lulling readers into believing that the information comes from a transcendent place. These conventions for presenting historical knowledge, moreover, create the appearance of a dispassionate approach, uncontaminated by partiality or interest, unconstrained by the limitations of a single vantage point. Flawed too, in the critics' opinion, are the words employed to describe the past, because words lack the fixing precision of a photograph and hence can change their meaning, chameleonlike, with every reading. Evicting history from the category of knowledge, these doubters prefer to lodge it along with poetry and novels in the expansive domain of literary constructions, thus turning a grand pillar of objective knowledge into a literary genre.

4. As quoted in Sande Cohen, "Structuralism and the Writing of Intellectual History," *History and Theory* 17 (1978): 184–85.

Much must be given up to the discerning skeptics who have done battle against the nineteenth-century scientific claims that objective truth can be definitively captured. In dragging out from the shadowy world of unexamined assumptions the discrete propositions undergirding the objectivity of science, these Davids of dissent have taken on the mighty Goliath of Western metaphysics. Refusing to become worshipers at the altar of progress, successive groups—inspired first by Nietzsche—confronted the celebratory self-defining ideas of the West and showed that they owed more to the hubris of power than to any rigorous examination of how knowledge was constructed. Their efforts to liberate the thinking of historians from the tyranny of positivism have continued to generate intellectual excitement, because these critics forced into the open the centrality of interpretation in all historical scholarship. Moving beyond the reconstruction of the past to the whole domain of written histories where research designs and rhetorical strategies are worked out, they have alerted an unwary public, as well as their peers, to how the different perspectives of historians enter into their books. Focusing fresh attention on the range of interpretive and linguistic choices at play, all this detective work has led critics to the scene of the primal crime—the individual consciousness where choices are negotiated. The understanding of the processes through which human beings create information has been greatly extended by examinations of historians as the carriers of culturally encoded ideas. Similarly, hermeneutics has shown scholars and their readers how words shape consciousness.

These sophisticated insights into how knowledge is produced have been greeted more as clever exposés than as advances in human understanding. We attribute this perverse reaction to the fact that despite this generation's well-broadcast scorn for positivism, positivism has left as its principal legacy an enduring dichotomy between absolute objectivity and totally arbitrary interpretations of the world of objects. When postmodernists mock the idea that the human mind mirrors nature or that historians write the past as it actually happened, they are knocking over the straw men of heroic science and its history clone. Similarly, when readers, confronted with various interpretations of the causes of the First World War, conclude that subjectivity taints all history, it is heroic science's disdain of any element of subjectivity that prompts this resort to the lexicon of impurities. Nineteenth-century philosophers so overdichotomized the difference between objectivity and subjectivity that it is difficult, when using their terms, to modify the absolute doubt that springs from the recognition that human minds are not mirrors and recorders.[5] Denying the absolutism of one age, the doubters, however, seem oblivious to the danger of inventing a new absolutism based upon subjectivity and relativism.

## Practical Realism

In the post-heroic situation, the world described by science is separate from language and yet inextricably tied to it.[6] Contemporary understanding of how knowledge is created now prompts calls for a different, more nuanced, less absolutist kind of realism than that championed by an older—we would say naive—realism. The newer version—what is called practical realism—presumes that the meanings of words are never simply "in our head," nor do they lock on to objects of the external world and fix reality for all time. Linguistic conventions arise because human beings possessed of imagination and understanding use language in response to things outside of their minds. The structure of grammar is a linguistic artifice, but significantly one that has been developed through an interaction with the objective world, through a struggle to name things that human beings would encounter, even if unnamed. In con-

5. Lorraine Daston and Peter Galison, "The Image of Objectivity," *Representations,* 40 (Fall 1992): 81–128.

6. We are indebted here to Hilary Putnam in James Conant, ed., *Realism with a Human Face* (Cambridge, Mass., 1990), pp. 274–75.

trast to poststructuralists, practical realists emphasize the function of words in articulating the multifarious contacts with objects. Communicative and responsive, words serve the goal of truth-seeking exactly because they are not the arbitrary tools of solipsists. Grammar may be deeply embedded in the human mind, but words result from contact with the world.

Contemporary philosophers have reminded historians, as well as readers of histories, that there cannot be an exact correspondence between words and what is out there, between the conventions employed when speaking about the world itself and its contents. Their admonitions point to the fact that the myth of correspondence inherited from the philosophical realists owed much too much to heroic science and not enough to the intuitive wisdom of the practitioners of history.

Let us try now to conceptualize the relationship of the world and human investigators shorn of a belief in correspondence, i.e., in the precise fit between what is in the human head and what is out there. Put in terms useful to the historian, there are the records of the past and there is the interpretation of those records. The gap between them is the source of concern. At best, the past only dimly corresponds to what the historians say about it, but practical realists accept the tentativeness and imperfections of the historians' accounts. This does not, however, cause them to give up the effort to aim for accuracy and completeness and to judge historical accounts on the basis of those criteria. By contrast, relativists (who are antirealists) say that such confidence in historical narrative is self-serving and untenable, because any kind of correspondence is impossible.

Making modified, practical realism an ally in the campaign against relativism does require some explaining of motives. The aesthetic appeal should not be overlooked. Some historians, like old-fashioned artists, find realism attractive.[7] They are attracted by the challenge of reconstructing what appears in the

---

7. For such artists, see Michael Fried, *Courbet's Realism* (Chicago, 1990); and Svetlana Alpers, *The Art of Describing: Dutch Art in the Seventeenth Century* (Chicago, 1983). For another perspective on realism, see Christopher Braider, *Refiguring the Real: Picture and Modernity in Word and Image, 1400–1700* (Princeton, 1993).

mind when it contemplates the past, much as Vermeer might have been attracted to the challenge of representing the city of Delft. However, historians must deal with a vanished past that has left most of its traces in written documents. The translation of these words from the documents into a story that seeks to be faithful to the past constitutes the historians' particular struggle with truth. It requires a rigorous attention to the details of the archival records as well as imaginative casting of narrative and interpretation. The realist never denies that the very act of representing the past makes the historian (values, warts, and all) an agent who actively molds how the past is to be seen. Most even delight in the task.

The experience—as distinct from the writing—of history can help to make practical realism more concrete. The very effect of historical change, the ending of wars, for example, and the influence that such external changes have upon thinking give the lie to the notion that words are arbitrarily connected to things. Events can irretrievably alter the way words are arranged in our minds. Yet, as the phrase "better dead than red" illustrates, words can also be arbitrarily affixed. Once the phrase described a bellicose mind-set and, for those who possessed it, a conviction. Yet the time may soon come when children will need an explanation for the statement lest they think it to have been the rallying cry of an especially violent school of expressionist painters. Descriptions of "reality" can on occasion lose their meaning, and then the words become unstuck from the reality which their believers once so ardently endorsed.

People who think or write about the past should take consolation from knowing that no philosopher (whether from Paris or Vienna) has ever succeeded in proving that meanings are simply "in our head" or, the reverse, that human language can be fixed on objects and describe for all time the way the external world is. In other words, the "facts" need the "conventions" and vice versa. Put another way, the historian does not say that an interpretation can exist separate from the practices and discourses employed by the author. The historian is not the alchemist who invented the reality of the past by happily mixing the black facts of the past with white verbal descriptions nor the scientific observer who claims to produce a gray narrative that transparently corresponds to what went on back there, then. The historian is someone who reconstructs a past pieced together from records left by the past, which should not be dismissed as a mere discourse on other discourses.

Practical realists are stuck in a contingent world, using language to point to objects outside themselves about which they can be knowledgeable because they use language. This slightly circular situation in which the practical-minded find themselves may not make for heroes, but it does help locate truths about the past. More important, practical realism thwarts the relativists by reminding them that some words and conventions, however socially constructed, reach out to the world and give a reasonably true description of its contents. The practical realist is pleased to have science as an ally, because the study of nature suggests that having knowledge of a thing in the mind does not negate its being outside of the mind behaving there as predicted.

Well over a century ago, the American pragmatist Charles S. Peirce said that the realist makes "a distinction between the true conception of a thing and the thing itself . . . only to regard one and the same thing from two different points of view; for the immediate object of thought in a true judgment *is* the reality."[8] That something exists as an image of something's being in the mind does not in the least diminish its external existence or its knowability through the medium of language. That it could be in both places, out there and in here where words reside, seems only to verify the objective nature of everything from buildings to time. They are knowable, usable things separate from the linguistic expressions used to describe them, yet capable of being "captured" in the mind by words that point back out toward the thing itself.

8. Charles S. Peirce, "Critical Review of Berkeley's Idealism," in Philip P. Wiener, ed., *Values in a Universe of Chance: Selected Writings of Charles S. Peirce* (New York, 1958), p. 84. (Originally published in 1871.)

The modified, or practical, realism endorsed here connects words to things by using words, but it does more than that. Practical realism serves another goal: it fuels, rather than debunks, the passion to know the past. Practical realism endorses knowability experienced by human agents able to use language, whether alphabetical or numerical. This is not, however, to presume that there can be any "algorithm" or single path to truth. At the philosophical level, realism permits historians to aim language at things outside themselves. Being practical realists means valuing repositories of records as laboratories. The archives in Lyon, France, are housed in an old convent on a hill overlooking the city. It is reached by walking up some three hundred stone steps. For the practical realist—even one equipped with a laptop computer—the climb is worth the effort; the relativist might not bother. Historians find more than dust in archives and libraries; the records there offer a glimpse of a world that has disappeared. Assuming a tolerance for a degree of indeterminacy, scholars in the practical realist camp are encouraged to get out of bed in the morning and head for the archives, because there they can uncover evidence, touch lives long passed, and "see" patterns in events that otherwise might remain inexplicable.

From the seventeenth century onward, science made such spectacular progress that almost everyone fell under its sway. Historians once called their methods scientific and strove for detachment because they thought science provided the only road to truth. Having become less awestruck, less convinced that all truth must be packaged in an equation, historians now look back on the yearning to behave like scientists as part of their own past. It is time to move on, but not without retrospective gratitude.

## The Link Between Natural and Human Sciences

Leaving behind heroic science and heroic models of knowledge, historians must still participate in the ongoing discussion between the natural and human sciences. The debt of the social and human disciplines to science is so great—they share so much history and so many common epistemological problems—that divorce is simply not an option. Many of the same theoretical issues, as well as moments of cultural optimism or pessimism, affect all the available forms of human inquiry. Notice that just like historians, scientists confront relativism, if only in the form of anti-science movements, from creationism to New Age cults, or simply as promoted by the information disseminated by the Tobacco Institute. These may not seem like very formidable challenges in comparison to those faced by the social sciences, but science's relative insulation from skepticism has more to do with the public's old habits of deference than with any natural protection. The privileged position of postwar American science may also require—as our final chapter suggests—some new and serious rethinking.

Despite their relationship to the natural sciences, the human sciences, such as history, have a distinct set of problems. Any analogy to natural science falters because the historian or sociologist, even the economist, cannot effectively isolate the objects of inquiry. Even when they study living creatures, the scientists' and historians' attentions diverge. Humanists study action which is responsive to intentions, whereas naturalists investigate the bounded world of behavior.

Because they are most often found in texts, the remnants of the past usually present themselves in words. Unlike atoms, however, words cannot be disentangled from one another or their referential framework. There are no supercolliders into which historians can funnel the words from old records and manuscripts to be bounced around in a sealed environment and examined for traces of meaning. Indeed why would historians want to? The point of any scrutiny of texts for evidence of the past is not to isolate the language, however delightful and liberating the play of words disconnected from "reality" can seem. The task is to connect one text to another, to retrieve word by word, a forgotten, but never wholly lost moment in time. If by deconstructing a text the critic means to show its inability to represent a fixed past, this can only be done as a result of a prior reconstruction.

Historians cannot comprehend all the variables bombarding a single event. Human beings participate in a dense circuitry of interacting systems, from those that regulate their bodily functions to the ones that undergird their intellectual curiosity and emotional responses. A full explanation of an event would have to take into consideration the full range of systematic reactions. Not ever doing that, history-writing implicitly begins by concentrating on those aspects of an event deemed most relevant to the inquiry. The historians' laboratories, which are seminar rooms and archives, are also constantly being invaded by robust words—those used in the past as well as those currently in use. Historians cannot quarantine their texts, even though such attempts at isolation occur every time a text gets classified, e.g., "Those records are about shipping," "That book is about religion." In fact, these classificatory systems are always porous and frequently misleading. Historians think categories like science, magic, gender, and sexuality are value-free, but then their divisions turn out to reveal more about present-day categories than about what people in the past thought or did. Even the academic disciplines around which university departments are organized represent rough-and-ready classifications which can't stop historians from drawing upon anthropologists, philosophers, biologists, or literary theorists.

The most distinctive of historians' problems is that posed by temporality itself. For the historian, truth is wrapped up with trying to figure out what went on in time past. The records are left by people who lived in the past, but—and this is the tricky part—the records are extant in the present. The past, insofar as it exists at all, exists in the present; the historian too is stuck in time present, trying to make meaningful and accurate statements about time past. Any account of historical objectivity must provide for this crucial temporal dimension.

## A New Theory of Objectivity

A theory of objectivity for the twenty-first century will owe as much to science's critics as to its champions. Most of all it will be indebted to this generation's collective capacity to hold on to what can be known while letting go of much of the territory staked out for mastery during the heyday of positivism. We think that a case can be made for a qualified objectivity after this refurbished objectivity has been disentangled from the scientific model of objectivity. What we will offer is a late-twentieth-century understanding of historical truth. We start with the object that first engages historians—the past—and build our case by retrofitting the house of history that we've inherited, stripping away the plaster of grand expectations so that we can see once more the beams and joints of modest inquiries about what actually happened and what it meant to those who experienced it.

No longer able to ignore the subjectivity of the author, scholars must construct standards of objectivity that recognize at the outset that all histories start with the curiosity of a particular individual and take shape under the guidance of her or his personal and cultural attributes. Since all knowledge originates inside human minds and is conveyed through representations of reality, all knowledge is subject-centered and artificial, the very qualities brought into disrespect by an earlier exaltation of that which was objective and natural. Our version of objectivity concedes the impossibility of any research being neutral (that goes for scientists as well) and accepts the fact that knowledge-seeking involves a lively, contentious struggle among diverse groups of truth-seekers. Neither admission undermines the viability of stable bodies of knowledge that can be communicated, built upon, and subjected to testing. These admissions do require a new understanding of objectivity.

At the popular level where deconstruction still refers to razing buildings, there is a pervasive opinion that somehow the past lingers on to force the hand of those who study it. In reality, the past as a series of events is utterly gone. Its consequences, which are very real, remain to impinge on the present, but only a retrospective analysis can make their influence apparent. What stays on visibly in the present are the physical traces from past living—the materials or objects that historians turn into evidence when they begin asking questions. These traces, alas, never speak for themselves (even oral histories occur after the event). Neither do they totally disappear. Usually they remain where people left them in discarded trunks in attics, in inscrutable notations in ledgers, in the footings of abandoned buildings; sometimes they are collected in repositories and archives. Some of this physical residue lies forgotten, but close enough to the surface of life to be unexpectedly happened upon. Then like hastily buried treasure or poorly planted land mines they deliver great surprises. History is never independent of the potsherds and written edicts that remain from a past reality, for their very existence demands explanation. The past cannot impose its truths upon the historian, but because the past is constantly generating its own material remains, it can and does constrain those who seek to find out what once took place.

Two questions go to the heart of the issue about historical objectivity. Just how much and in what ways does the inert past exercise an influence upon active historians? The extreme, literal answers would be "not at all" and "in no way," since the past has no power to impose itself, whereas the historian is a human agent capable of initiating almost anything. But the question becomes more meaningful when a specific social context is posited. Thus a philosophical question leads to a different answer when posed sociologically. How much and in what ways do the material remains of the past affect the historian who works in a scholarly community whose principal task is to reconstruct, interpret, and preserve artifacts from the past? In this cultural milieu the practitioners of history are constrained by a complex set of rules. Within a society committed to accuracy in representations of the past, the preservation of evidence imposes definite limits to the factual assertions that can be made;

it even sets up boundaries around the range of interpretations that can be offered about an event or development.

There are limits, however, even to the efficacy of rules; they cannot discriminate among interpretations that rest on different assumptions. Let's take the examples of a historian who concludes that the American Revolution happened because colonial leaders construed the new British tax measures as efforts to curtail their colonies' self-governing traditions and another scholar who is convinced that colonial merchants and farmers resisted British authority in order to protect the profitability of their firms and farms. Material remains from the past cannot resolve the disparity between these two interpretations because they start from different assessments of the interests, values, and motivations of the principal actors. Indeed, the two historians would use a different scale for weighing the influential actions of the participants themselves—be they legislators, pamphleteers, or entrepreneurs.

For some of history's critics, the presence of different interpretations suggests the impossibility of validating historical knowledge. The very existence of a variety of witnesses and partisans in past events is evoked in arguments to make the skeptic's point. Differences of perspective, however, should be distinguished from different interpretations. The two explanations given for the causes of the American Revolution reflect different assessments of human motives and social action and could only be reconciled, if at all, by extensive debate. Historians' interpretations can be mutually exclusive, but their differing perspectives are not. If one sees an event from a slave's point of view, that rendering does not obliterate the perspective of the slaveholder; it only complicates the task of interpretation.

Taking the metaphor of perception literally helps make the point. Perspective does not mean opinion; it refers to point of view—literally, point from which something, an object outside the mind, is viewed. Let's imagine witnesses to a violent argument arrayed around the room where it took place. The sum of their vantage points would give a fuller picture, but the action they were witnessing would not be changed because there were many people watching it. Unless they were standing in each other's way, the perspectives would not be mutually exclusive; nor could the multiplication of perspectives affect the viewers. The validity of each reconstruction would depend upon the accuracy and completeness of the observations, not on the perspective itself. Objectivity remains with the object. As one contemporary philosopher trenchantly put it, "Objectivity does not require taking God's perspective, which is impossible."[9]

Genealogists, antiquarians, and chroniclers share the historian's concern with the past, but the differences among them help clarify the role of interpretation in the historians' work. Genealogists, as the word suggests, search the past for the carriers of a specific genetic endowment. They follow human beings backward as they exponentially collect forebears—two parents, four grandparents, etc. They labor to gather the vital statistics of a specific family. Chroniclers take each day at a time, recording events from the immediate perspective of the moment past. Antiquarians range more widely, but their abiding passion is for things that are old. They love the past in the raw, as it were, unmediated by analysis or interpretation. Curiosity stays fixed to the something that is old whether it is a battlefield or a set of china. With all of them, the historical imagination never sails beyond the object to the larger social universe that produced it. Antiquarians preserve, chroniclers record, and genealogists trace. Historians aim at more. They share with all these others an orientation toward the past as an object of curiosity, yet also seek significance, explanation, and meaning, a triumvirate of intellectual entailments that has exposed their work to the radiating skepticism of the age.

Postmodernists have collapsed the tension between the conviction that objects have an integrity that can sustain itself through external investigation and the awareness of the snares

9. Mark Johnson, *Body in the Mind: The Bodily Basis of Meaning, Imagination, and Reason* (Chicago, 1987), p. 212.

and delusions that accompany efforts to make sense of objective reality. As Carlo Ginzburg has put it, they have turned evidence into a "wall which by definition precludes any access to reality." The postmodernist critics of historical objectivity have made "knowing the past completely" so fixed a concept that they have had to rely on a "sort of inverted positivism" to press their case against historians.[10] The full unknowability of a past event becomes the only real thing in contrast to which the imaginative effort to reassemble a picture of past reality from the remaining fragments appears pathetic. It is a rhetorical exaggeration that calls to mind William James's retort to an insistent disputant at one of his lectures: "Madam, I cannot allow your ignorance however great to take precedence over my knowledge however small."

Knowledge of the past, however small, begins with memory. Because people have a memory, they know from experience that there was a past, although it should be noted that an important philosophical tradition associated with David Hume denies the knowability of things outside ourselves, even of memory as an indicator of past experiences. Taking the more commonsensical view of the reality of objects, we credit memory with the verification of there having been a past.[11] History fulfills a fundamental human need by reconstituting memory. Memory sustains consciousness of living in the stream of time, and the *amour propre* of human beings cries out for the knowledge of their place in that stream. Westerners have learned how to externalize this curiosity about the past. They even distance themselves from its impertinent subjectivity by directing questions to such objects as the rise of the nation-state or the impact of the printing press, but the renewable source of energy behind these inquiries comes from the intense craving for insight into

10. As quoted in Cushing Strout, "Border Crossings: History, Fiction, and *Dead Certainties*," *History and Theory*, 31 (1992), p. 153.

11. An extreme form of skepticism would argue that people have no way of disconfirming the assertion that the world was created yesterday complete with fossils, a geological record, and our memories of the past.

what it is to be human. Thus memory that has been trained to seek an objective verification of the past is nevertheless inextricably tied up with the powerful personal longings of all who write or tell histories.

A convincing case for the qualified objectivity we advocate must come to terms with the undeniable elements of subjectivity, artificiality, and language dependence in historical writing. We have redefined historical objectivity as an interactive relationship between an inquiring subject and an external object. Physical scientists validate their work through the external process of experimentation. Many social scientists attempt to imitate them by reducing their questions to phenomena explicable by survey data, experimentation with laboratory animals, or other external tests. Historians cannot similarly rely on external validation because they seek to understand the internal dispositions of historical actors: what motivated them, how they responded to events, which ideas shaped their social world. Such understandings depend upon convincing, well-documented and coherently argued interpretations that link internally generated meanings to external behavior.

Having talked about remembering and believing in the transactions between the historian and the past, we want also to consider the role of curiosity. Knowledge is above all the accumulation of answers to questions that curious men and women have asked about the physical and social worlds they encounter. History is crucially distinguished from fiction by curiosity about what actually happened in the past. Beyond the self—outside the realm of the imagination—lies a landscape cluttered with the detritus of past living, a melange of clues and codes informative of a moment as real as this present one. When curiosity is stirred about an aspect of this past, a relationship with an object has begun.

Objects can be tough to abandon, for they exist. The very objectiveness of objects—their failure to accommodate all interpretations—helps explain why scholars quarrel among themselves. The skeptic says that the quarreling is proof of subjective perspectives. We're inclined to think it attributable to the commanding and often unyielding presence of those objects which people seek to incorporate into their world of understanding. In the West, natural philosophers were the first to grapple in disciplined ways with the otherness of objects around them— think of Newton in his alchemical moments, sitting in his Cambridge laboratory trying to turn an ordinary metal into gold. Like science, objectivity in history began with curiosity about the otherness of the past.

As long as people assumed that those in the past were essentially like them, there was little curiosity about the past itself and little sense that past societies were as different from their own as a foreign country. The fact that curiosity about objects is a deeply personal response produces the conundrum that objective investigations begin with the subjective curiosity of an inquirer. Having made subjectivity itself an object of investigation, theorists in recent years now claim to have revealed the fallacy of objective knowledge. Because positivists ignored the undeniable subjectivity of the sentient beings who alone initiate all scientific inquiries, they had set up a straw man just waiting to be pushed over once the cultural cloak of awe draped over science had been lifted. Realists now must think more deeply about the nature of the relationship between a curious, imaginative, culturally shaped investigator and the passive objects under investigation. Objects arouse curiosity, resist implausible manipulation, and collect layers of information about them. Objectivity can only refer to a relationship between persons and these fascinating things; it cannot reside outside of persons. Any standards of objectivity we erect must focus on that relationship.

Heroic science went wrong by grounding objectivity upon value-free, neutral experimentation. The notion of objectivity inherited from the scientific revolution made it sound as if the researcher went into a trance, cleared his mind, polished the mind's mirror, and trained it on the object of investigation. Of course, there were methods to be followed, but the beliefs, values, and interests that defined the researcher as a person were simply brushed aside in this depiction to allow the mirror to capture the reflection of nature's storehouse of wonders. The positivists simply developed too restricted a definition of objectivity. We have redefined historical objectivity as an interactive relationship between an inquiring subject and an external object. Validation in this definition comes from persuasion more than proof, but without proof there is no historical writing of any worth.

## Psychological Dynamics of Knowing

In exploring how memory affects the writing of history, we have drawn attention to the psychological need for comprehending experience which calls for accuracy, as well as the human drive for personal recognition that encourages myth-making. Either can come into play, whether the product is a study of constitutional law or a biography. What this book insists upon is the human capacity to discriminate between false and faithful representations of past reality and, beyond that, to articulate standards which help both practitioners and readers to make such discriminations. Here the crucial relationship between the creators of knowledge and their critics enters in. When we say that the memory of the past or the objects left over from past living restrain historians, we are not saying that all people submit themselves to the discipline of studying evidence. The contemporary example of the bogus scholars who say there was no Holocaust painfully demonstrates the contrary. Rather we are pointing to the fact that history-writing and history-reading are a shared enterprise in which the community of practitioners acts as a check on the historian just as Newton's experiments on moving objects and Darwin's observations of fossils constrained what they could say.

Historians' questions turn the material remains from the past into evidence, for evidence is only evidence in relation to a particular account. (Think of the detective who notices a telltale streak of shoe polish on a doorjamb; a perfectly ordinary trace of passage becomes a clue.) But once a story is told, an argument made, or an interpretation advanced, the objects that compose the supporting evidence come under scrutiny. Evidence adduced to an explanation can never be kept secret in a society that prizes historical knowledge, and it is the accessibility of evidence in publicly supported archives, libraries, and museums that sustains the historical consciousness of this culture. An audience of peers derives its power from equal access to the evidence and to publication, a reminder that democratic practices have an impact far beyond the strictly political. They permit replicability and testing, honest and often stormy controversy.

The bits and pieces of records left from the past can be arranged into different and contending pictures. To be more direct, since human society is composed of relationships, many of them carrying implications of power and elements of concealment, one's point of entry into a past moment will always affect one's findings. No workable definition of objectivity can hide the likelihood that students of the human past will always have to deal with more than one version of what has happened. The fact that there can be a multiplicity of accurate histories does not turn accuracy into a fugitive from a more confident age; it only points to the expanded necessity of men and women to read the many messages packed into a past event and to follow their different trajectories as that event's consequences concatenate through time.

## Narratives and Language

The human intellect demands accuracy while the soul craves meaning. History ministers to both with stories. Postmodernist critics delight in pointing out that historical narratives are actually a literary form without any logical connection to the seamless flow of happenings that constitute living. Again, summoning memory, we can concur. The routines and occasions we experience follow one another without interruption. It is only when we begin to tell another about them that a story emerges. Indeed, the very idea of an event or development depends upon already having such concepts to describe the passage of time. Western histories are embedded in a matrix of cultural properties like those of progressive development or cycles of degeneration, to speak of the regnant ideas of the eighteenth and nineteenth centuries. The storytelling voice and arrangement of incidents into a narrative are but the most familiar of these. Personal interpretive assumptions guide historians as they compose their stories, but it is only in contrast to an image of historians' mirroring the past that this fact raises doubts about the enterprise. To deny the writing of history objective validity because of the historian's essential creative effort is to remain attached to a nineteenth-century understanding of the production of knowledge.

While philosophers and literary critics in recent years have exposed the artificial status of narrative, they have also given narrative form an attention which has enhanced appreciation for it. The flow of time does not have a beginning, middle, and end; only stories about it do. Yet lives share the structure of narratives, and perhaps a familiarity with their beginnings, middles, and ends predisposes people to cast their histories into narrative form. Historians should attend to the pervasive appeal of stories. Just think of the awakening of interest that comes with the start of a tale; even the body relaxes at the sound of "In the beginning, Omaha was run by cattle men," or "Let me tell you how Joan came to buy that house."

The fascinating thing about telling stories is that they start with the end. It is a conclusion that arouses our curiosity and prompts us to ask a question, which then leads back to the beginning from which the eventual outcome unwound. A happy relationship goes on the rocks. The unhappy finale becomes the starting point for searching questions. To explain the breakup of what once was whole, a story is told, and every element in the ensuing narrative will carry with it a clue about its conclusion. It is the perception of a closure or outcome to a string of occurrences that first starts people asking questions, which then guide them toward relevant facts. The Cold War's half century of frozen immobility ended in a thaw. In China, the Statue of Liberty briefly graced Beijing's Tiananmen Square. Germany recomposed itself into its earlier national entity. Yugoslavia has disaggregated into warring ethnic factions. All these recent and unexpected happenings provoked new questions, and from them will come new histories of this century.

This impulse to tell new stories points up that time itself is a perspective. Nineteenth-century men and women posed different questions about the settling of the trans-Mississippi plains than are currently brought to the subject. They called it the westward movement, kept their eyes glued to the white "pioneers," and sought out those incidents that explained the fulfillment of America's continental destiny. Contemporaries now have located the Plains Indians on the landscape along with those Mexicans whose homes had been rudely denationalized by war. The presence of these groups powerfully shapes the imaginative recreation of the territory between the Mississippi and the Pacific, prompting consideration of the multiple encounters with others involved in the westward trek of black and white Americans.

Distance and changes of sensibility regularly open up novel lines of inquiry as boredom and irrelevance close others. Through most periods of our national existence, slavery was too acutely embarrassing a subject to permit historians to probe its origins in colonial Virginia. Nor was much research done on the work routines, the housing, and the family lives of slaves until the atrocities of World War II shocked scholars into exploring the origins of American race prejudice. Soon African-Americans entered the academic profession, changing forever the limited perspective of their Euro-American colleagues. With different time periods as with the diverse vantage points, the past as an object of curiosity changes, and so do the stories told about it.

The written word preserves the histories told; time makes

those words obsolete. Because historical accounts always explain the meaning of events in terms relevant to the immediate audience, curiosity about the past is inextricably bound up in the preoccupations of the present. The past as an object will be read differently from one generation to another. Nineteenth-century Southern defenders of slavery when writing about the causes of secession placed their facts in an altogether different context from that of twentieth-century historians who connect the Civil War with the momentous accomplishment of abolishing slavery. Or, to take another example, historians, no longer believing that women are incapacitated for public life, now read older prescriptions of their natural domesticity with a degree of skepticism, if not anger. The very plausibility of a historical account, dependent as it is upon the interpretive interlarding of values, will always be subject to change.

Skeptics count this constant reassessing of the past against history's claim to objectivity, whereas it can better be considered testimony to the urgency each generation feels to possess the past in terms meaningful to it. The incontrovertible existence of various interpretations of past events by no means proves the relativist's case, but it certainly demands that everyone shed the positivist's notion of historical truth. If the past was simply composed of material objects or recordable actions, one good "snapshot" of it could capture the essential contours for all eternity. Happily, it is the human experience both in the past and the present which compels attention.

Successive generations of scholars do not so much revise historical knowledge as they reinvest it with contemporary interest. Each generation's inquiries about the past actually carry forward the implications of its predecessors' learning. New versions of old narratives are not arbitrary exercises of historical imagination, but the consequence of the changing interest from cumulative social experience. If history did not involve a relationship with an object outside the self, it would have no capacity to extend the range of human understanding; its disclosures would only be reflections of ideas already known. The Dutch historian Peter Geyl commented that all history is an interim report, but he would not have denied that within those interim reports were residues of research that would be studied long after the interim of the report had passed.

## The Textuality of Texts

The difference between oral and written traditions is critical to the consideration of objectivity. When storytellers narrate in person, they can change the details or modify their meaning every time they give a rendition of their story. An oral tradition is almost always the work of successive retellings of a past event, each narrator transmitting and refashioning the tales that form the collective memory. In written history, the text itself becomes an object with properties of its own. Preserved in an unvarying form, it freezes in time one rendition that can disclose over time just how meaning and the words that convey meaning have changed. Written histories permit—even compel—readers in one age to take stock of the distance they've moved from their forebears. These confrontations, more than anything else, have deepened an understanding of the interpretive element in historical writing, reinforcing the strength of the link between present and past.

When written history takes over from memory, as we have noted, it creates an object—a text—which itself invites external examination. Unlike the stories told by balladeers or the oral traditions kept alive in small communities, written histories are exposed to the critical scrutiny of unknown, unseen outsiders. Since at least the seventeenth century the histories written by Europeans or Euro-Americans have been subjected to intense criticism, but it is only with the postmodernists that the probing scalpel of the expert has cut through the histories to the words that compose them.

In analyzing texts, postmodernists have made two linked assertions. First, texts—a word which ranges far beyond the meaning of a piece of writing to include any element of culture—conceal as much as they express and must not be read literally or solely with an eye to recovering the authors' intentions. Instead they must be deconstructed, which means locating the blanks, gaps, and interruptions of thought or plot which, once found, will bring to light the contradictions, inversions, and secrets embedded in the text. Writing, for the postmodernists, bristles with perversity, reflecting the bad faith and hidden agendas within a given culture. Secondly, they insist that the fact that a given text can be read so many different ways proves that there is no stability to language. Hence the authors don't exercise any control over the reader's imaginative reconstruction of their words. Decoupling these central contentions of postmodernism is profoundly important, for the benefits to be derived from their first insight must be separated from the exaggerated skepticism about the stability of language in the second.

To interrogate a text is to open up the fullness of meaning within. Everyone uses language largely unaware of the cultural specificity of words, the rules and protocols of expression, the evasions in their euphemisms, the nuances from group associations, or the verbal detours imposed by social taboos. When an astute reader points out these intriguing elements in a text, our understanding of what is being communicated, both intentionally and unintentionally, is vastly increased. The fact that authors do not intend all that they say does not render their intentions uninteresting or irrelevant; it merely highlights the subterranean quality of many of the influences that play upon word choices.

The stability of language is a different matter. Building on Ferdinand de Saussure's insight that words change their meanings in relation to other words, linguists have described languages as internal systems rather than organizations of referents to an outside world. Postmodernists have gone one step further and given a new fluidity to words by denying that there is any bonding between the word signifier and the object signified. Without this bonding, they say, it is theoretically possible to have an infinite number of meanings to any sentence. With rapturous playfulness, they have spoken of words dancing, cascading, colliding, escaping, deceiving, hiding, leaving less imaginative word users to wonder why they bother with them at all.

Once again, the true situation has been overdichotomized. Words rarely separate from their conventional referents, nor are they glued to them either. Their adhesion to a definition is more like Velcro, strong enough to stick if undisturbed, but not so strong that social usage can't peel them off for reattachment elsewhere. To lavish all one's attention on the possibility of personal inventiveness on the part of those reading a text to the neglect of the probability of shared understanding of words is to distort the reality. Worse than this distortion is the fact that this emphasis obscures the more important fact that people living at the same time construct their own lexicons. Words change meaning in response to experience; shared experience creates a shared language. Far from exercising individual idiosyncrasies in reading, a community of readers will build up a strong consensus on meaning.

Still, language presents problems for historians, particularly those unwilling to acknowledge the code-making propensities of human groups and the use of those codes to distinguish insiders from outsiders. Because words can change their meaning without changing their visual representation—the word "freedom" always looks the same even though its import has varied dramatically over the centuries—the historical text should be addressed as a puzzle. Its expressions will certainly be read differently by successive generations, but the survival of its material integrity guarantees that someone's curiosity about its original meaning will be provoked.

With this stronger, more self-reflexive and interactive sense of objectivity, historians are more likely to submit to the rules of evidence. Recognizing that everyone is situated, hence embedded in a cultural perspective, they can use that perspective as a foil against which to project the particularities of the age being studied. Standing firmly in the place that heritage and experience have put them, inquirers into the past can use their self-understanding to probe the past with imagination. They can be "finite, embodied, and fragile" and still seek and find knowledge.[12] The telescope of an inquiring mind that they train on objects may later seem concave or convex, at moments fogged, even cracked, in constant need of repair, but it remains an operational tool. Knowing that there are objects out there turns scholars into practical realists. They can admit their cultural fixity, their partial grasp of truth, and still think that in trying to know the world it's best not to divert the lens from the object—as the relativist suggests—but to leave it on and keep trying to clean it.

Americans keep telling themselves that they are a pragmatic lot, eager to judge methods by their results. This has led to an instrumental approach to life, a tendency captured in a billboard depicting a happy group with the caption "The family that prays together stays together." The profundity of sacred worship is thus reduced to the utility of staying out of divorce court. In this book, we have avoided utilitarian arguments in our defense of objectivity because we think that they trivialize the important issues skeptics have raised. If it is possible to create knowledge, then one believes it because reason compels one; no list of good consequences can redeem the falseness of a proposition. This being said, it is not amiss to point out the benefits of a shared commitment to objective knowledge. It forces people to examine rigorously the relation between what they bring to their subject and what they find; it undergirds methodological rules that facilitate debate; it encourages people to perform the arduous tasks of knowledge-seeking. Edward Leigh Mallory said that he climbed Mount Everest because it was there; historians carry their laptop computers up the three hundred stone steps in Lyon because records from the

---

12. Seyla Benhabib, *Situating the Self: Gender, Community and Postmodernism in Contemporary Ethics* (New York, 1992), p. 5.

past are there. From that conviction of their knowability, knowledge grows.

Both the promise and the problems of history spring from its linkage to memory. The promise is memory's validation of the objective reality of the past. The experience of remembering underpins the belief that the past existed and hence makes possible, even imperative, an effort to reconstruct what happened. At the same time, the personal craving for meaning which memory serves also fosters the temptation to use history to inflate reputations, deny past cruelties, dispense comfort, and rationalize actions. It is exactly the psychological potency of written history that makes it so important to nations. Just as memory in all its visible and invisible forms sustains personal identity, so national memory, kept alive through history, confers a group identity upon a people, turning association into solidarity or legitimating the coercive authority of the state. Milan Kundera has said that the struggle of people against power is the struggle of memory against forgetting. As a novelist, Kundera conceived this contest as a conflict between the independent witness and the official manipulators of evidence. For historians the struggle of memory against forgetting also involves power, but with them it requires the power to resist the debilitating doubts that the past is knowable, that the forgetting is about something real.

# The Future of History

TALK ABOUT THE FUTURE OF HISTORY pivots around the question of how best to deploy the passion to know. Focusing that passion is the investigators' belief that the past can reveal an aspect of what it is to be human. The desire to touch the past is a yearning to master time, to anchor oneself in worldliness, to occupy fully one's own historical context by studying its antecedents. Given the immediacy of human passion, the present is always implicated in the study of the past. Lived experience alters the questions historians ask, foreclosing some research agendas while inspiring new ones. This sensitivity of historians to the lived moment is particularly visible at times of deep and significant historical change such as the world is witnessing now.

The Cold War riveted international affairs to the foreign policies of the United States and the Soviet Union. For almost a half century, it determined identities, magnified anxieties, and permeated every intellectual enterprise. All that has now abruptly ended. The future of history, like the future of much else in the world, can now be imagined in markedly different ways. A new republic of learning is possible because bunkerlike positions staked out on the treacherous landscape of battle can be abandoned, because old absolutisms have fallen, taking down with them many of the absolutist elements within Western democracies. New thinking is possible, even required. A part of this new thinking will include a return to the intellectual center of the Western experience since the seventeenth century, to scientific knowledge and its philosophical foundations, revitalized and reconceptualized.

## History and Science After the Cold War

If recent controversies are any indication, there will be great reluctance to moving into the imaginative space opened by the collapse of Cold War empires and ideologies. Throughout the globe, for forty years, rigid categories of right and left have polarized all thinking about society both between nations and within those societies where free speech was tolerated. Frontiers of thought, so long patrolled by muscular ideologues, will not now be easily crossed even though the guards have been retired. Because the conflict was waged as vigorously with ideas as with guns, people will continue policing their minds long after the threat of attack has subsided.

The resistance to occupying the newly opened spaces can be seen on both the right and the left in the United States, but it has been especially forthright among those defenders of the status quo whom we will call traditionalists. Rallying with a fresh sense of urgency to a new set of threats to their America, these critics have mobilized opposition to an array of educational initiatives. Lumping postmodernism, multiculturalism, and even social history together as one large target, they have taken the offensive against these designated left-wing enthusiasms. Even though they have identified some real weaknesses in postmodernism, they have moved beyond target practice to an all-out war on multiculturalism and the democratization of the university. In the *New York Times* an advertisement by the National Association of Scholars catalogued the objectionable features of current school curriculum reform. The list included the addition to students' required reading of more works by women and minorities; the introduction of "issues of race, gender, and class" into courses; the development of women's and minority studies; and the adoption of undergraduate course requirements in women's or minority studies.[1]

In combating these innovations, the NAS has wrapped itself in the tattered mantle of scientific objectivity, criticizing the diversification of the curriculum because it is polemical, that is, strongly urged by an interested group. Any alteration of the curriculum in response to contemporary needs or pressures would presumably be polemical, by this definition. Adopting a stance of neutrality, the organization has argued that " 'multicultural education' should not take place at the expense of studies that transcend cultural differences," like mathematics, the sciences, and history, which do not, they say, vary for "people of different races, sexes or cultures."[2] Linking history with the sciences and the sciences with mathematics and all of them with the transcendence of value-free objectivity, of course, is itself a polemical tactic in that old cultural war which has engaged scholars since the eighteenth century. These claims for the eternal pertinence of certain truths cannot be taken at face value. By characterizing as political those who would revise inherited courses and canons, traditionalists are trying to protect the school curricula from contemporary scrutiny, using the dead hand of the past, in this instance, to muzzle the voices of the present.

The threat of cultural relativism has encouraged the traditionalists to find similarities among all the programs they dislike and to unify their efforts as a campaign to defend the old status quo. According to them, universities now "expel" Homer, Aristotle, and Shakespeare from their required courses, because professors no longer believe in standards. The language of politics pervades the traditionalists' rhetoric. Academic leaders, they charge, are cravenly pandering to the rising number of minority and women students when they replace the epic poems

1. *New York Times*, April 5, 1992, Op Ed page.
2. Ibid.

of Homer with stories from a Guatemalan Indian woman. These willful destroyers of a venerable Western curriculum, so the argument goes, are embracing the view that all cultural values are of equal merit. Implicit in the demands for both a broadened curriculum and a diversified faculty, according to one of the traditionalists, "is a denial of the ability of scholarship to make any meaningful distinctions between valid and invalid claims."[3] Even more exercised by the non-Western readings introduced in college courses, political scientist Thomas Pangle has described the minds of the authors of the newly assigned texts as "enserfed to the self-hating intellectual frameworks concocted by European leftists of the postwar period."[4]

Traditionalists maintain that cultural relativism and its logical entailment, moral nihilism, now dominate the university, thanks to the combined influence of postmodernism, affirmative action, and curricular reforms. The universities have been seized by "arrogant and often philistine critics who treat the works of the past as a pathologist treats the corpses of the carriers of a plague."[5] These "philistine critics," traditionalists allege, are filled with venomous hatred of Western civilization. Worse, they want to legislate equality rather than gain it through their own hard work. The "tenured radicals" who are reshaping the nation's schools, according to this critique, have imperiled merit itself.

By deliberately stuffing affirmative action, curricular reform, and various strands of philosophical skepticism into one kit bag, traditionalists have adopted an offensive strategy that bears striking resemblances to the ideological marching orders of the Cold War. They have exaggerated the influence of postmodernists within American universities and created a new national bogey in the form of political correctness. When they

3. Dinesh D'Souza, *Illiberal Education: The Politics of Race and Sex on Campus* (New York, 1991), p. 85.
4. Thomas L. Pangle, *The Ennobling of Democracy: The Challenge of the Postmodern Era* (Baltimore, 1992), p. 79.
5. Ibid., pp. 75–76.

write, as Pangle has, about "the debilitating relativism that now seeps its poison through the mass consciousness of the Western democracies" and link it with a recommendation of the teachings of Pope John Paul II "and everything he stands for," the fear arises that "debilitating relativism" may take the place of communism as the necessary enemy in a resurgence of Cold War bellicosity.[6]

The workings of Cold War logic can be seen most clearly in Dinesh D'Souza's *Illiberal Education*, which explicitly links the decision by an American university to recruit postmodernist faculty members to affirmative action policies because both undermine "the notion of standards of merit."[7] Searching for scholars with a particular expertise is thus linked to a decline in the commitment to excellence, which in turn is characterized as the inevitable consequence of reforming the traditional curriculum and seeking an ethnically diverse faculty. In his rendering, postmodernism is attached, like a clanking tin can, to the tail of multiculturalism, a term now standing in for a variety of changes in American education. If postmodernists are red, the multiculturalists are pink, the cultural relativists mauve, and all seek to color our perceptions of the achievements of Western culture.

Like a long line of postwar ideologues of both right and left, the traditionalists are themselves guilty of faulty logic. They use the most extreme views of some postmodernists to disparage all critics of the status quo. They take the most ill-advised pronouncements of curricular reformers to represent the entire effort to democratize the university. They claim to support freedom, but in fact preach an updated form of absolutism where scientific neutrality transcends human agency. They appear to stand for greater openness, yet actually they are demanding a return to the old days when truth was absolute and dissent adjudicated by those like themselves.

In time of war, one attacks; in time of peace, one tries to

6. Ibid. p. 84.
7. D'Souza, *Illiberal Education*, p. 158.

find a common ground. Marxism, liberalism, and even post-modernism, which initially offered a third way, became weapons of thought control rather than tools of analysis because the Cold War politicized all social thought. Of course, the categories of left and right are far older than the Cold War, so battle lines can easily be reestablished along new borders, if public commentators are more intent on fighting than thinking. Their heirs will enjoy the promise of peace only if the habits of war can be abandoned.

Although this book has argued against the contention that history, science, and all efforts at generalizing truth have ended in failure, as the postmodernists assert and the traditionalists fear, it did begin with the premise that a great transformation has recently occurred in Western thinking about knowledge. This transformation—accelerated by the end of the Cold War—affects Americans' understanding of national history, of standards of truth and objectivity, of the practice of history and the human sciences in general. As the twentieth century closes, it becomes obvious that new definitions of truth and objectivity are needed in every field of knowledge. People today are rightly questioning those values of nineteenth-century science that accompanied the institutionalization of history along with the facile equating of modernity with progress.

Where relativists and traditionalists have both gone wrong is in their analysis of the nature of the crisis. The chief cause of the present crisis of knowledge is the collapse on all fronts of intellectual and political absolutism. Just as totalitarian governments continue to crumble everywhere on the globe in favor of democratic polities, so too are absolute claims to knowledge giving way to the recognition of the multiplicity of points of view and their importance in generating knowledge. In a profound sense, burying the belief that definitions of knowledge about humankind can be fixed unconditionally is as important to democracy as the removal of autocratic rulers.

Having the opportunity to examine the enterprise of truth-seeking in history without the straitjacket imposed by the Cold

War lowers the stakes for ideologues on both right and left. It does not, however, render the search any less compelling. In the past, most truths in the intellectual traditions of the modern West, whether about nature or society, were couched in scientific language. Until well into this century science conjured up in the public imagination truths that were both immensely comforting and morally reassuring. Although few today doubt that science embodies ever greater power as it continues to demonstrate mastery over nature, most Westerners question its automatic contribution to progress. Rightly they fear the military uses to which Western science has been put, and they recoil from the ease with which scientists have served odious regimes. Late in the twentieth century the word "scientific" conveys power without the assurance of benevolence.

In the 1940s, as a result of the struggle to defeat Nazism, science became one of the mainstays of the militarized state. On an unprecedented scale, science entered war service. Despite the postwar warnings of scientists and statesmen like James Conant and Dwight D. Eisenhower, whose presidential farewell address in 1961 spoke ominously of the emergent power of the "military-industrial complex," the scientific establishment retained its ties to the defense establishment. University after university, laboratory after laboratory, coveted federal funds. With the defense buildup of the 1980s, military research and development spending exceeded (in constant dollars) the levels of the mid-1960s.[8] Even the discipline of physics, once regarded as the most theoretical, abstract, and hence value-free of all the scientific disciplines, became useful in unprecedented ways, with the bulk of its practitioners working on military technologies in the service of national security.[9]

8. One place to start, with regard to industrial development, is Ann Markusen, Peter Hill, Scott Campbell, and Sabina Deitrick, *The Rise of the Gun Belt: The Military Remapping of Industrial America* (New York, 1991).

9. We are grateful here to the discussion in Stuart W. Leslie, "Science and Politics in Cold War America," in Margaret C. Jacob, ed., *The Politics of Western Science, 1640–1990* (Atlantic Highlands, N.J., 1993).

With this linkage of science and war-making, a precious piece of the past that had been forgotten now needs to be remembered. The Enlightenment campaign to replace clerical learning with scientific knowledge bequeathed the legacy that all intellectual inquiry be open, free, and secular. These became the preconditions for truth-seeking. In the eighteenth century, reformers carved out a public arena in which the arts and sciences could flourish, a space between the domain of official authority and the privacy of the family. Speaking for the first time through voluntary associations that included scientific societies, reading clubs, salons, reform associations, and masonic lodges, members of a newly constituted, yet restricted, literate public eagerly addressed the issues of the day. They read, conversed, learned, and applied their new critical faculties through pamphlets, tracts, and novels to problems as pressing as the power of oligarchies and the corruption of courts. Novelists, journalists, publishers, clandestine writers— money-hungry as well as idealistic—created a new realm physically situated in drawing rooms as well as coffee houses. Their ideals of openness might sometimes have been more honored in the breach, but they promoted advances from the original application of mechanics to the environmental reform movements of the present. Because of these humane underpinnings, the practice of science—indeed, of all intellectual life—could be imagined as a form of virtuous living. Freedom to read and think prepared the ground for other freedoms—for constitutions, charters, declarations of rights—without which no one amid the repressions and injustices of their world could ever have imagined freedom or endorsed equality.

Nothing could be further from the contemporary image of science, shaped as it has been by national sites shrouded in secrecy and screened by security clearances. Cold War censors, tyrants, and spies have systematically whittled away the Enlightenment legacy when they have not actually tried to destroy it. Beating back their efforts has required a constant struggle. All from Andrei Sakharov to underfunded teachers in urban schools are victims of that struggle, and all have a stake in ensuring the expansion of knowledge open to public scrutiny. Critics of contemporary science have also exposed the appalling neglect of women's scientific training and the gender bias of Western science's rhetoric and research agendas. Still other, principally non-Western, critics have pointed out the disinclination of Western scientists to learn from other systems of knowledge.[10] These aspects of contemporary reality make it harder to reinvent a new republic of learning in the aftermath of the Cold War. The legacy of Cold War science also helps to explain the cynicism, even nihilism, and certainly the intellectual relativism, that greet even the mention of truth and objectivity.

Yet while no one would wish, or indeed be able, to go back to the nineteenth-century absolutist understanding of what it is to be scientific, most scholars in the human and natural sciences still wish to recognize some distinctive benefits derived from the Scientific Revolution. Most scientists and philosophers of science continue to be realists of a sort—that is, they think that experimental methods and theoretical statements, while often in tension with each other, capture enough about nature to be close to what is there.[11] The investigations of social scientists still have a lot to do with those of the natural scientist. All are bound in time and done within a particular social context: all select evidence for examination, and all are in need of constant reform because their practitioners can impose biases of gender, class, and culture. All can produce workable truths and in the case of science those truths can also be lawlike in

10. For some of these critics, see Ziauddin Sardar, ed., *The Revenge of Athena: Science, Exploration and the Third World* (New York, 1988).

11. For the mainstream philosophy of science in which its participants routinely say, "I have nothing to say to 'the Skeptic,' " see Paul M. Churchland and Clifford A. Hooker, eds., *Images of Science: Essays on Realism and Empiricism with a Reply from Bas C. van Fraassen* (Chicago, 1985); the quotation, of Richard N. Boyd is on p. 4. For philosophers of science who deny realism and assign relativism the status of "the Big Bang" in their discipline of science studies, see the essays in Andrew Pickering, ed., *Science as Practice and Culture* (Chicago, 1992).

their replicability and predictability. Despite these original similarities, during the past fifty years science has come to be seen as radically different from humanistic inquiry. If funding and prestige were the sole determinants of truth-seeking, 'tis little wonder.

Scholars who work in archives, libraries, and oral history laboratories far from material nature need to resist the temptation to accept a radical divorce from scientific methods. Doing so will be easier if historians, philosophers, and scientists recognize that the problem of truth—finding any, getting agreement that you have it, and then someday having to revise it—has been immensely complicated by the Cold War and more precisely by the role that what is called Big Science played in the service of the military-industrial complex from 1945 onward. To say that physics is just too sophisticated and complicated does not adequately explain the distance, even hostility, that has now developed between scientific knowledge and learning about humanity and society. In identifying and examining these postwar developments, historical knowledge can be helpful.

Hope for the future republic of learning derives from the capacity of the human sciences to offer criticism, both of natural science and of themselves. Historians and sociologists of science and technology are increasingly documenting the impact that the Cold War has had on the natural sciences. Just as physicians are never good at examining themselves, so historians may have difficulty assessing how the practice of history has also been affected by the ideological warfare of the past forty years. Indeed despairing of objectivity as an ideal may have a great deal to do with the fact that most historians now writing have spent all of their professional lives in the shadow of the Cold War. It is time to come out of the trenches.

The scholarship of the postwar generation has led to a thoroughly argued and historically grounded appreciation for the social construction of knowledge. Cynics have claimed that this approach to knowledge proves the omnipresence of ideologies, not truth, in all human learning. They fail to grasp the actual message that the social approach to knowledge formation offers—that all scientific work has an essentially social character. The system of peer review, open refereeing, public disputation, replicated experiments, and documented research—all aided by international communication and the extended freedom from censorship—makes objective knowledge possible. Research programs must be established and findings constantly tested. These involve social processes which leave traces to be encoded within the resulting knowledge, necessitating even more decoding of inherited knowledge.[12] The official secrecy and mimetic authoritarian styles of big-money science further disfigure the state of the sciences just as surely as the retreat into relativism undermines the will to know in the human sciences. By declaring knowledge a by-product of each speaker's situation, relativism turns every consensual group into a universe unto itself, while propagating the idea that truths just emerge from the place where one is coming from or the language one happens to use. It permits a mental segregation among researchers and a privileging of ironic discourse, an effect not so different from scientific publications that may only be read by people with security clearances.

If knowledge and the discourses it generates offer power, then the issue of access to it becomes vitally important. Just as the barriers to free access within science must now, urgently, be dismantled, so too the accessibility of history to the peoples of this nation must change. Far from diluting or distorting knowledge, democratic practices have toughened and seasoned the truths that have been generated since the eighteenth century. Demanding that all research be open recalls a part of Western history, the importance of the Enlightenment's principal legacy, the freedom to communicate and the forum of civil society that makes truth possible.

---

12. For part of this argument we are indebted to Helen Longino, *Science as Social Knowledge* (Princeton, N.J., 1991).

History will flourish in a revitalized public arena. It will do so, we would suggest, because relativism and the intellectual postures that feed into it will recede, departing in the company of the alienation engendered by the rigidities of the Cold War. So too the traditionalist critics of the democratizing of the academy will increasingly sound like a background chorus singing old Cold War tunes.

Since the eighteenth century all Western reform movements have depended upon the existence of a relatively unfettered, uncensored domain of public discourse. In the seventeenth century every inch of that space had to be fought for, and only gradually was it wrested from the hands of clerical and governmental officials whose censorship silenced voices and stifled curiosity and wonder about nature and society. Scientific and technological knowledge prospered because of the struggle for freedom of press and association, but during the protracted Cold War, significant segments of scientific knowledge became the property of security agencies. Large areas of scientific learning were, and still are, configured by the need for defense and domination rather than humanitarian needs. This sequestering ironically has eased the move away from science as humanists have made the "linguistic turn." The wonder that science once evoked in students has been replaced by boredom, suggesting that the authoritarian style of much science teaching may be traceable to Big Science and its postwar alliance with military needs.[13]

Mystifying, ignoring, decrying, or relativizing scientific knowledge makes trivial that which is central to Western cultures. Perhaps because of the development of the history of science as a separate field, general history teaching largely ignores the scientific realm of social life, that arena where people might still display their wonder about nature and their efforts to satisfy an aroused scientific curiosity. The size of the gap

13. On the problems in science education, see Sheila Tobias's essay in W. Stevenson Bacon, ed., *Revitalizing Undergraduate Science* (Tucson, 1992).

between science and the humanities operates as an obstacle to the renewal of both. Leaving the history of specialized bodies of knowledge to a variety of subdisciplines may work for the history of music or art—although there too, general historical knowledge loses a vital piece of the human spirit—but consigning science and technology to that status in this particular culture severs a tap root. Teaching science to examine its biases as well as its truths, its arrogance as well as its elegance, would enrich the public as well as scientists and humanists because both participate in similar systems of knowledge construction and both are utterly dependent upon the vitality of civil society for the rigor, originality, and competitiveness of their theories and practices. Similarly, where democratic ideals and practices have faltered in either the community of the arts or that of the sciences, their critics rightly sound the alarm and proclaim the need for renewal within the republic of learning.

### *Pragmatism, Practical Reason, and the Public Realm*

The democratic practice of history here advocated needs a philosophical grounding compatible with its affirmations. We find that grounding in a combination of practical realism and pragmatism, that is, in an epistemological position that claims that people's perceptions of the world have some correspondence with that world and that standards, even though they are historical products, can be made to discriminate between valid and invalid assertions.[14] The intellectual spirit of democratic scholarship celebrates a multiplicity of actors, diversely situated and skeptical of authority. They are seekers of a workable truth communicable within an improvable society. Sometimes the public might even venerate its scientists and savants, considering their accomplishments the work of sheer genius, but this

14. For a general discussion of these issues as they apply to Charles Peirce, Hilary Putnam, and Richard Rorty, see Richard J. Bernstein, "The Resurgence of Pragmatism," *Social Research*, 59 (1992): 825–26.

would not put them off-limits to searching examination or historical analysis.

Within Western philosophical traditions sympathetic to democracy only pragmatism promotes the criticism and debate, dissent and irreverence vital to the kind of history we are advocating, yet pragmatism makes a distinction we consider crucial: all knowledge can be provisional, in theory, without eliminating the possibility of some truths prevailing for centuries, perhaps forever. And one of the responsibilities of history is to record both the survival and reformulation of old truths.

Pragmatism has been available as an approach to learning since the 1860s when Charles Peirce published a now classic set of papers. As discussed in the preceding chapter, Peirce laid out a philosophy of mind that emphasized the empirical as the very foundation for rationality. Here empiricism stands for systematic investigation and rigorous experimentation, confident of the objectivity of the objects of analysis. The past easily qualifies as one such object insofar as it resides in the artifacts that survive from it. The no-holds-barred approach of the pragmatist permits any claim about any object to be questioned, but rejects the relativism inherent in questioning all claims on principle. Its measured relativism springs from the knowledge of facts and theories that have failed to survive extended examination; it is not a philosophical position premised on categorical doubt. In addition, the pragmatist asks about the purpose of a knowledge claim. What goal will be achieved when modernity is debunked? If combined with dedication to the moral ends of action and a prophetic sense of the necessity for improvement, pragmatic empiricism can well serve a democratic agenda.

Pragmatism appealed to the great philosopher John Dewey, who embarked in the 1920s on a critical inspection of American education. In Dewey's mind, pragmatism's reliance upon the outcome of experiments to determine the truth of philosophical propositions supported the highest aspirations of democracy. Pragmatism's passion for constantly reforming the aims and methods of scientific inquiry supported a liberal society's moral obligation to develop and redevelop the fullest capacity of each member of society.

Practical realism works well with pragmatism, for both of these theories require a commitment to a knowable world outside, one which people experience as they check and alter what they say about it. Realists accept the objectivity of objects and consider the objects' frequent resistance to accurate representations as an invitation to further investigation. Because pragmatism endorses the democratic practice of truth-seeking, it accepts the babel of tongues in the day-to-day practice of knowing, learning, and teaching. In this arena, objects and the inquiring subjects they attract help keep the playing field level because, while the struggle to establish a truth is being waged, no privileged perspectives are recognized. Rather than grounding truth on first principles, pragmatists make truth's attainment a matter of self-correcting endeavors where any factual claim can be called into question, although not in the manner of the relativist who calls all propositions into question, all at once.

Because their notion of truth arises from a consensus of practitioners, pragmatists are exposed to tyranny from that group. What if the vast majority of investigators in a relevant field were to decide that all women are inferior or that one ethnic group failed to measure up to the standards of others? Pragmatism does not offer within its system of verification a formal set of criteria for determining that science directed to invidious distinctions is ultimately evil and frequently bunk. Indeed, pragmatism only works if democratic institutions are strong and functioning daily. Nor can the purpose to which knowledge is put be left to the decisions of any single group of knowledge seekers. Here the problem of exclusion bears directly on the fostering of relativism which occurs when any natural or social science is conducted in secrecy. If the playing field is restricted, leaving those excluded by virtue of race or class or gender to gape from the sidelines, then the pragmatic game devolves into entertainment for intellectuals, not the site for testing knowledge appropriate to the needs of a working democracy. With an absence of first principles, pragmatists can easily become relativists when the relevance of truth to the needs of society becomes more and more remote and anti-intellectual governments sponsor that remoteness.

For these reasons, pragmatism is only a provisional philosophy, but one that can be immensely useful for its endorsement of practice, verifiability, rationality, and progress achievable by reasonably well educated people. Pragmatism leaves unquestioned the consequences of the convergence of the popular will with the scientist's drive for knowledge. Assuming a commonality of interests without demonstrating their existence, pragmatism depends on democracy. Hence pragmatism is implicated in democracy's flaws, the principal one being exposure to the unchecked power of a majority when that majority acts capriciously.

This problem is as old as the American republic and has prompted a succession of astute observations about the nature of popular government. In his famous *Federalist No. 10,* James Madison set forth with wonderful clarity the dilemma of the majority being the greatest threat to its own political system. He began with factions, which he defined as groups acting against the rights of others or the long-term interests of the whole. Minority factions could be disruptive, but only majority factions, Madison shrewdly pointed out, could do mortal damage to republican government, for only they could seize control of the agencies of government. Two correctives to this threat presented themselves to Madison: elimination of the cause of majority faction or control of its effects. Naming freedom an essential component in the galvanizing of the passions and interests which animate majority faction, Madison rejected the idea of getting rid of the causes as a cure worse than the disease and concentrated instead upon managing its effects.[15]

Madison made the Constitution, then being considered for

15. *Federalist No. 10,* in Edward Mead Earle, ed., *The Federalist* (New York, 1937), pp. 54–59. (Originally published in 1787–88.)

ratification, his solution to majority faction because it would enlarge the scope of national governance and thereby increase the number of interests in the nation, making it unlikely that any one group could command the unchecked force of a majority.[16] Approaching politics as a predicament, the drafters of the Constitution were determined to erect barriers to the exercise of arbitrary power. Madison boldly proclaimed that "ambition must be made to check ambition." It "may be a reflection on human nature, that such devices should be necessary," he continued, but "what is government itself, but the greatest of all reflections on human nature?"[17] As weapons against abuses of power, resorts to ambition and competition have some justification, but they have also undermined Americans' faith in a public arena where collective goals can be discussed.

Alexis de Tocqueville, visiting the United States in the 1830s, saw a different majoritarian threat from the one that had preoccupied the revolutionary generation. For him the unchecked power of the majority in the United States sapped the individual's capacity to act independently by silently encouraging Americans to conform to majority taste, whether in ethics, in politics, or in philosophical views. Pervasive and invisible, Tocqueville's tyranny of the majority worked on individuals with an efficacy unknown in absolute monarchies. Without knowing it—even while extolling their freedom and autonomy—Americans, Tocqueville observed, conformed to a limited range of aspirations, preferring the psychological comfort of equal treatment over the emotional risks of genuine independence from the herd.[18]

16. Out of this rationale arose the pluralism of the political scientist as exemplified in David B. Truman, *The Governmental Process: Political Interests and Public Opinion* (New York, 1951). This pluralism is not to be confused with the cultural pluralism of Horace Kallen, who wrote in the 1920s. On this see John Higham, "Ethnic Pluralism in Modern American Thought," in *Send These to Me: Immigrants in American Life* (Baltimore, 1984). See also James A. Banks, "Multicultural Education: Characteristics and Goals," in Banks and Cherry A. McGee Banks, eds., *Multicultural Education: Issues and Perspectives* (Boston, 1989), pp. 7–11.

17. Earle, ed., *The Federalist*, p. 337. See also the discussion in Chapter 4.

18. Alexis de Tocqueville, *Democracy in America* (New York, 1835).

Both of these analyses bear on the problem of creating, testing, and spreading knowledge in a democracy. They also expose the risk present in pragmatism's reliance upon the public to scrutinize the production of knowledge. Madison worried that majority factions could crush individual rights through the exercise of majority rule, and Tocqueville feared that majority opinion would eclipse the desire to soar beyond conventions, both results especially threatening to original scholarship. The history of American race relations amply supports their fears. White Americans have repeatedly acted as a majority faction toward blacks, using both informal violence and formal statutes to curtail the free exercise of their powers. At present a lesser threat to individual freedom has surfaced in the form of political correctness. Political correctness refers to a wall of sympathy raised to ward off challenges to policies directed at minorities. In an effort to protect minority students, some would declare off-limits debates that bear on issues affecting their concerns. Critics of "p.c." have a point when they focus on the dangers of limiting public discussion, since the curtailment of spirited, open dissent threatens the very democratic practices that affirmative action was created to serve.

Political correctness patronizes people by assuming that their interests are too fragile for public scrutiny. Political pluralism sells them short by ignoring the deliberative component of democratic decision-making. Both aggravate the problems of nurturing knowledge in a democracy. By accepting the proposition that bargaining among separate interest groups determines public policy, pluralism legitimates the competition for public resources. It is relativism in action; "truth" belongs to the winners. Opposed to both is a conception of a republic where lawmakers are informed by particular needs, but attentive to the general well-being. Such a republic can only come into existence when there is a popular supportive ethic. As Madison's and Tocqueville's critiques indicate, despair at achieving a consensus about the good of the whole entered American discourse early. An even deeper skepticism about the concept of a public good, transcendent of the nation's parts, pushed Americans toward the muscular masculinity of interest-group competition, a kind of arm-wrestling approach to politics which has stifled debate and limited public access for those without sufficient clout to push their way into the bargaining arena. Pragmatism, dependent as it is upon exhaustive testing of knowledge claims, has offered a reasoned support of public debate, but its deference to practice over principle has left democracy without an adequate defense against majority factions and majority tyrannies, not to mention the silent influence of well-financed interest groups.

Democracy and history always live in a kind of tension with each other. Nations use history to build a sense of national identity, pitting the demands for stories that build solidarity against open-ended scholarly inquiry that can trample on cherished illusions. Here the pressing question is which human needs should history serve, the yearning for a self-affirming past, even if distortive, or the liberation, however painful, that comes from grappling with a more complex, accurate account? Skepticism offers a way of resolving this tension by rejecting all truths, but in doing so it flies in the face of the common experience of knowing. Consider the outrage felt when a remembered experience is misrepresented. Where does this passionate sense of violation come from if truth is such a chameleon?

In important ways historians support the long-term goals of democratic societies when they insistently and honestly reconstruct past experience. They work for greater social inclusiveness because they bear witness to the records that have been suppressed. Having a history enables groups to get power, whether they use a past reality to affirm their rights or wrest recognition from those powerful groups that monopolize public debate. History doesn't just reflect; it provides a forum for readjudicating power and interests. If historical accounts remain in some sense interim reports, it is because the meaning of human experience can never be exhausted.

A recent example of historical scholarship shaping public

perceptions of a contemporary issue occurred when the Supreme Court deliberated on the constitutionality of the Pennsylvania abortion law in 1992. Then the court had at its disposal a short history of abortion in America which gave an account of responses to unwanted pregnancies spanning more than three centuries. This historical record gave clear evidence that abortions had been well known and had been practiced without serious regulation in the United States until the late nineteenth century, when the practice met with new overt strictures. Knowing about the relevant past in this instance subtly shifted one's perspective. Historical knowledge proved satisfying because it quickened the sense of being linked to the past. Unexpectedly women and men discovered a common tie to the world of long-dead ancestors. Suddenly the burden of dealing with contemporary crises was lessened by the awareness that whatever people might do, they are not the first, nor probably the last, who will be forced to wrestle with this human problem.

This didactic function of history has long been recognized. Voltaire gave classic expression to it when he referred to history as philosophy teaching by example. Less frequently talked about is the derangement felt when the established consensus about national history breaks down, as it did in the last years of the USSR. Soviet scholars had so slavishly served the state that they had written histories with little foundation in the widely shared documentation about the Russian Revolution and its aftermath. As a consequence of *glasnost,* comparisons could be made between the official Soviet histories and competing accounts of the same events written in the West. Painfully aware of these discrepancies, Mikhail Gorbachev placed a ban on teaching the once-official history to Russian youth until scholars could catch up with the pace of reform. And then he boldly canceled the Soviet Union's national high school history exams, because, as he said with startling candor, there was no point in testing the students' knowledge of lies. Here is exposed the linkage of truth, power, and meaning. However much skeptics deride the possibility of historical truth, when it confronts absolute falsehood the potency of a provisional accuracy becomes salient.

In the West we associate "party line" history with totalitarian governments, but even where there is academic freedom there are public repercussions when the delicate balance between consensual interpretations and open inquiry is upset. This was demonstrated in France during the celebration of the bicentennial of the French Revolution in 1989, only in this case it was not political but rather academic orthodoxy that generated a crisis. Disputes about the causes and character of the revolutionary events of '89 and '93 became so heated and so well publicized that French educational authorities deleted questions about the French Revolution from the secondary school examinations that year.

The similarity between the examples from the Soviet Union and France can be traced to the critical role their revolutions played in modern nation-building. If the historical accounts of these momentous events are muddied, then the nation's collective identity is put at risk. For the United States, nation-building started with the ideals that justified independence and then gave cohesion to an aggregation of transplanted people establishing homes in a conquered land. Giving heterogeneity a good name, the nation's unifying creed endorsed the inclusiveness of an open society while falling far short of creating one in practice. Pragmatic initially without philosophers, Americans developed democratic practices which promoted experimentation, invention, and education. A century later a formal theory of pragmatism emerged which depended upon the rules and civility of an open republic and a commitment to the knowability of nature and hence to scientific truth. Today the nation's democratic creed as well as its pragmatic tradition rely upon a consensus of beliefs about reality and the possibility of arriving at common goals.

## The Future of Multiculturalism

The demographic reconfiguration of the American population and the enduring vitality of ethnic differences make it increasingly clear that the exclusive dominance of European cultural forms in the United States is now consignable to a specific time period, let us say 1676 to 1992 (a terminal date fittingly coincident with the Columbian quincentenary). It is no longer a question of whether Americans must work on a multicultural understanding of their past, but how. The very inevitability of this development raises the stakes in current discussions of national history, whether debate swirls around multiculturalism or the search for a single narrative. Disputes over the relative merits of social and political history and the need for stories that build schoolchildren's self-esteem now elicit passions normally triggered only by anticommunist campaigns and sex scandals.

The more extreme multiculturalists celebrate the virtues of fragmentation. History for them has become an adjunct to "identity politics," which seeks to realign political forces according to voters' ethnic, social, and sexual identities. Some insist that since all history has a political—often a propaganda—function, it is time for each group to rewrite history from its own perspective and thereby reaffirm its own past. National identity, in this view, is a chimera created by the elite to indoctrinate other groups in society with its self-serving conception of the country's purposes. This position has attracted the most outspoken adherents in the African-American community. The head of Temple University's African-American Studies Department, Molefi Kete Asante, is leading a nationwide crusade among educators to install an Afrocentric curriculum in schools that will stress the contributions of Africans to Western culture and of African-American people to the history of the United States.

Few would disagree with Asante when he points out, "If African-American children were taught to be fully aware of the struggles of our African forebears they would find a renewed sense of purpose and vision in their own lives."[19] Although

19. Molefi Kete Asante, "The Afrocentric Idea in Education," *Journal of Negro Education*, 60 (1991): 170–80.

Asante presents Afrocentrism as a "valid, nonhegemonic perspective" directed to a "correct, accurate history," he also argues that "the acceptance of Africa as central to African people" has to be the first article of a multicultural curriculum. At the same time, Asante's efforts are directed toward reorienting the entire Western historical record by insisting that Greek philosophy and art originated in Africa and that African civilizations predate all other civilizations.[20] Statements like these sent off alarm signals because it seemed that Asante and his followers were advocating the deliberate distortion of the past to instill pride in those children whose ancestors had been so long excluded from American textbooks.

The history taught to children in the United States has become a national issue precisely because the old bastions of American cultural leadership have been vigorously challenged. The cutting edge of the movement that has thrust class, race, and gender into the nation's classrooms has been sharpened on the left and used, most effectively, to slice through the self-congratulatory histories of America's older, self-proclaimed patriots. Traditionalists have been quick to identify the threat to their values in history books that scorn the notion of a united people and adopt a critical stance toward American individualism and, by implication, the competitive *élan* of American capitalism. These same critics have excoriated political correctness, a term they use derisively to refer to a kind of regimented sympathy shown to the nation's minorities and women.

Yet a good deal more than political correctness is at issue in the controversy over the teaching of American history. Diverse groups—many of them having been fully politicized in recent years—are now struggling, with good reason, for control of the nation's memory. The political empowerment of women and blacks along with the intensification of ethnic loyalties among descendants of immigrants from Europe, Asia, and the Americas has made more salient than ever just how many separate—

20. Ibid., pp. 177, 172, 178.

and sometimes discordant—parts of the United States there are. As diverse as the ethnic groups to be embraced in a truly inclusive curriculum are the opinions voiced about curricular reform. Indeed, the proponents of multiculturalism can be placed along a continuum ranging from Afrocentrists who demand a complete overhaul to accommodators who would mechanically tack on new teaching material without addressing its transformative content.

Elected officials play key roles in this combat over the curriculum. In having to decide the history that is taught in the schools they are necessarily setting the terms of imaginative citizenship for everyone, but a consensus about nationhood no longer exists in the government, the academy, or the educational establishment. Insiders and outsiders, school superintendents and school boards, mobilized parents and teachers contend today because they see both the possibility and the desirability of rewriting the story of American nationhood. By insisting on the teaching of divergent historical truths, the multifarious communities within the nation rightfully contest the privilege of officialdom to establish the parameters of national identity. Asian-Americans, Hispanics, homosexuals, and women have joined African-Americans in the battle over the books while Christian fundamentalists vie for the power to censor texts that challenge their religious convictions. In such a contentious setting, authoring a history text has become a hazardous occupation.

The history of the United States has become fragmented in recent years not in comparison to the actuality of an earlier simplicity, but in reference to the simplified story that was told about the nation's past. Slowly and painfully disengaging from that and the conception of nationhood imbedded in it, historians now confront the task of creating a new narrative framework. Textbooks, like abusive governments, can make people disappear, but only temporarily, for the objects from the suppressed past—the public records, private papers, and oral traditions—survive to pique the curiosity of another generation of inquirers. A comprehensive national history is not now an educational option for the country; it is a cultural imperative. Fragments—whether of research findings or of tangential groups—do not exist independent of the whole that makes them fragments. The full story of the American past can make that evident.

These generalizations will be clarified by looking at the historical treatment of African-Americans. We begin our account in the nineteenth century with the centrality of the American nation. Anthropomorphized into a being with personal traits and lofty purposes, the nation walked away with the principal part in the historical drama of the United States that was taught to successive generations of students. Slightly amended at the beginning of this century by the incorporation of the Progressives' work on class conflict and later by Perry Miller's rehabilitation of the Puritans, the typical narrative of national history followed the successful development of political freedom and economic prosperity from the Revolution to the present. Despite the arrival of blacks in England's American colonies in 1619, they formed a shadowy presence in history textbooks. Two and a half centuries later, their emancipation appeared to ennoble the Civil War slaughter, but the actual freed men and women retreated to the sidelines. This episodic attention calls to mind the wry comment of British historian George Unwin that slavery figured in English history only in connection with its abolition. *A fortiori*, this was true for the United States.

Historians are frequently exposed to the charge that they write the present back into the past, putting into the record concerns that did not earlier exist. The reverse holds true for African-American history. When scholars began researching the details of slave life in the Chesapeake and free black communities in the urban South, they were recovering stories that had always been there. For ten generations, white Americans had suppressed evidence of the black presence and excluded their experience from the national narrative. By doing so they had shaped memory to the psychological needs of a white citizenry deeply conflicted by its persistent racial hostility. A peculiarly sensitive bearer of the troubled spirit of white racism, Thomas Jefferson explained why freed slaves and their ex-masters could never live together in peace, cursed as their relation was by "deep rooted prejudices entertained by the whites; ten thousand recollections, by the blacks of the injuries they have sustained."[21]

Divided soon after the Revolution by the abolition of slavery in the states north of the Mason-Dixon line, Northern and Southern whites were paradoxically reknit by the Civil War Emancipation because both now feared the liberated African-Americans. Unable to expel African-Americans from their midst, as Jefferson had wished to do, the arbiters of the new national community made them invisible.[22] Scholars, for the most part, complied by taking a vow of silence, proving Louis Hartz's point that American historians represented "an erudite reflection of the limited social perspectives of the average American himself."[23] Here the influence of the narrative upon historical construction is particularly instructive. As long as history writers only recounted the progress of natural rights and democratic governance, there could be no place for collective shortcomings, unless they were remedied. The sooty, haggard workers of the twelve-hour factory shift found a place in history books once the New Deal successes of the union movement rectified their situation. Similarly, women could figure in history texts in connection with their long, tenacious struggle for the vote, but this tying of national identity to the achievement of equality and liberty has prevented the custodians of national history from publicly coming to terms with the import of slavery and its legacy of racial prejudices.

21. Thomas Jefferson, *Notes on the State of Virginia*, ed. William Peden (Chapel Hill, 1955), p. 138.

22. For a powerful fictional exploration of this phenomenon see Ralph Ellison, *The Invisible Man*, New York, 1947.

23. Louis Hartz, *The Liberal Tradition in America: An Interpretation of American Political Thought since the Revolution* (New York, 1955), p. 29.

Nothing embarrassed white Americans more than slavery, because they had pitched their political identity on the fulfillment of the doctrine that all men are born equal and endowed by their creator with certain inalienable rights. While slavery could figure in European histories as a barbaric enterprise, explicable in the context of the fiercely competitive Atlantic economy of the seventeenth and eighteenth centuries, it became for the United States an incubus better denied than confronted. The successful end of slavery did demonstrate the overcoming of an original injustice, but African-Americans quickly receded from the national consciousness when the segregation era overtook slavery and then Northern urban poverty replaced Southern segregation.

As Mary Douglas explained, nations keep their shape by molding their citizens' understanding of the past, causing its members to forget those events that do not accord with its righteous image while keeping alive those memories that do.[24] This effort to control the collective memory necessarily affronts those committed to recovering the fullness of the past record. Ironically, it is perhaps the excluded African-Americans who can most easily comprehend the urgency European-Americans once felt for constructing a story of national origins. Giving the United States an exceptional destiny in 1776 was a means of providing a collective identity to a detached and fragile fragment of European society, a way of sinking down ideological roots in the alien and conquered soil of the New World. Demands today for an Afrocentrist education for African-American children is an echo of the imperative that European-Americans responded to throughout the nineteenth century and well into the twentieth.

For much of their history, Americans have shown a preference for hypocrisy over cynicism. Forced to choose between giving up their allegiance to the highest ideals of the Declaration of Independence and living with the tension caused by the

---

24. Mary Douglas, *How Institutions Think* (Syracuse, 1986), p. 112.

shortfall between ideal and reality, most have elected to remain what foreigners consider naively idealistic. Rather than become the cynics of dashed hopes, they have evaded the evidence of their hypocrisy, or worse, have blamed and stigmatized the victims of their failures. In his pathbreaking study, the Swedish sociologist Gunnar Myrdal called the contradiction between the natural-rights philosophy of the national creed and the country's extravagant race consciousness an American Dilemma.[25] Highly attuned to the profound sense of otherness that white Americans projected upon their black fellow citizens, Myrdal explored the dilemma of having to let go of aspirations or to deracinate prejudice. Also measuring the full weight of Americans' affirmation of enduring moral precepts, he called it "a gross mistake" to think that the appeal of justice and tolerance could ever be easily extinguished.[26] The civil rights movement which climaxed in Southern desegregation a score of years later proved him right. Living with a post-civil-rights backlash, Americans now confront that temptation to retreat to cynicism.

With improved vision, the post–World War II generation of social historians saw and made conspicuous for all what had always been there—the fascinating and frightening drama of Africans in America, beginning with "20 and odd Negroes . . . bought at the best and easiest rate" from a Dutch man-of-war in Jamestown in 1619 through the swelling of a half million slaves at the time of the Declaration of Independence to the population of 3,838,000 on the eve of the Civil War.[27] Given an opening toward freedom in the revolutionary era, free blacks— the fastest-growing group in the United States until 1810— laid the basis for the African-American community that offered

25. Gunnar Myrdal, *An American Dilemma: The Negro Problem and Modern Democracy* (New York, 1944).

26. Ibid., p. 1028.

27. Letter of John Rolfe to Sir Edwin Sandys, January 1620, in Susan Myra Kingsbury, ed., *The Records of the Virginia Company of London* (Washington, D.C., 1933), vol. 3, pp. 241–48; U.S. Bureau of the Census, *Historical Statistics of the United States, Colonial Times to 1957* (Washington, 1960), pp. 756, 8.

a template for churches, occupations, and voluntary associations in the post-Emancipation period.[28] Incorporating these details of the African-American experience in national history, however, proved almost impossible, because they represented such an indigestible element in the tale of American democracy. If in the late twentieth century Americans can accept the less lofty truth that despite its goals, the United States was the promised land of those who were free, male, and white, it is because that era appears to be ending.

Recreating the details of African-American history has had two potent effects upon contemporary thought: it has vivified the black presence in the American past, and it has simultaneously destroyed the coherence of the Whiggish account of national progress. With African-Americans present, the story line has blurred; the unifying destiny dissolves into statistical projections of how diverse groups will fare in the United States. Critics of social history have missed the point when they complain that attending to the insignificant lives of the many trivialize the grand epic of the American nation. The problem lies closer to the spiritual link between history and national identity in the United States. Far from trivializing standard histories, experiences cruelly at odds with the narrative of American success subvert them.

The fight between the traditionalists and multiculturalists over the nation's textbooks resonates with the arguments and emotions that flared up in the 1960s when the Black Power movement challenged the goal of assimilation.[29] The territorial separatism then called for has found a spiritual echo in current demands for a separate curriculum, even separate schools for minority children in danger of intellectual oppression from Anglos (now defined as including all white Americans of non-Hispanic descent). Stirring up the staid decorum of the educa-

28. Ira Berlin, "The Revolution in Black Life," in *The American Revolution: Explorations in the History of American Radicalism,* ed. Alfred Young (Dekalb, Ill., 1976).

29. John Higham, "Multiculturalism and Universalism: A History and Critique," *American Quarterly,* 45 (June 1993).

tional establishment, Afrocentrists since the mid-1980s have vigorously assailed that assimilationist faith that provides the soul of American public schools.

To a remarkable degree, the nation's colleges and universities have become negotiating centers mediating the heightened sense of commonality and difference that the classes of the 1990s have brought to their campuses. While parents of all walks of life wonder what's happening, their college-age children are living the reality of multicultural tensions, veterans at eighteen of white flight, busing, the feminization of poverty, and the expansion of entitlements. Actually, the two generations have set the agenda in tandem, for as Erik Erikson has wisely noted, "the values of any new generation do not spring full blown from their heads; they are already there, inherent if not clearly articulated in the older generation. . . . The younger generation makes overt what is covert in the older generation; the child expresses openly what the parent represses."[30]

From the perspective of the nation's fourteen million college students, the permeability of inherited cultures stands out. Neither a genetic endowment nor an environmental stamping machine, culture stands for a fluid cluster of influences which each individual selectively responds to in fashioning an autonomous identity. For late-twentieth-century students, learning about a larger universe of meaning and significance at college perforates rather than rigidifies the boundaries set in childhood. "Appreciation is merely provincial," John Higham has noted, "if not grounded in knowledge and values that bring into judgment a range of humanity far wider than the people who are immediately at issue."[31] Whatever may have taken place in preparatory schools, colleges and universities will inexorably pry open the doors to the mind. That's why the democratization of university education will continue to transform the society at

---

30. As quoted in Robert Dallek, *The American Style of Foreign Policy: Cultural Politics and Foreign Affairs* (New York, 1983), p. 248.

31. Higham, "Multiculturalism and Universalism," p. 210.

large. Like cultural identity, personal assimilation into an American mainstream will remain an option. Meanwhile the country deserves leaders who are alert to the discrepancy in access, ambition, and hope among its disparate members.

Cacophonous or harmonic, the motifs of a multicultural history of the United States will have to incorporate themes and variations on all the identities that Americans carry with them, because only this will satisfy our awakened curiosity about what it truly means to be a part of American democracy. When people urge that the nation move beyond the politics of ethnic and sexual identity, they implicitly underestimate the power of society to make such categories the determinants of how one is viewed. Moreover, leaving unexplored the variety of ways that national institutions have perpetuated difference while celebrating universality risks reenacting the characteristically American routine of denial, e.g., ignoring present injustices by dwelling upon the future fulfillment of moral goals. Instead of rushing beyond the separations imposed in the past, the country should initiate affirmative action for the multicultural spirit and set-asides for historical honesty. Writing the multicultural history of the United States will not come naturally; it will take an act of national will. Recognizing diversity as an integral and venerable component of American life might even arouse curiosity about the contrapuntal effects of diversity and uniformity in the United States, about how the practice of differentiation played against the theme of universal values, about the collective anxiety engendered by patterned discrimination within a national self-image of tolerant acceptance.

Of course, to evoke national will is to assert the moral presence of the nation. Anathema to some multiculturalists, the nation nonetheless exists as a powerful unifying force in American public life. People who call for pride in the group often minimize the importance of engendering pride in the nation, but the two stand or fall together. It is the nation that sustains and protects the array of particular identities in the United States. Only the critical relationship between the whole, with its authority, moral force, and material wealth, and each particular group, insistent upon its share, its place, and its rights within the whole, can make the multicultural debate intelligible.

Late-twentieth-century Western consciousness contains a particular skepticism about comprehensive understanding that has been thoroughly incorporated into public thought. Everyone seems to accept the idea that truth varies with different cultures. Most people even work hard at being cultural relativists, trying to respect, without necessarily endorsing, differences in values and behavior, recognizing the venerable wisdom lodged in tolerance. It was, after all, the sixteenth-century writer Montaigne who said that "every man calls evil what he does not understand." But knowledge of the culture of others in no way obliterates the power or authenticity of one's own culture unless, as in much of Western history, cultural imperialism denies multiplicity in social values. Respect for the values of others necessarily entails an appreciative exploration of one's own group's truths; in the United States that begins with a choice of identity.

### The Invisible Force of Structure in the Past

Although a nation is an imagined community resting on intangible connections, a visit to the post office, tax auditor, or military recruiter quickly demonstrates its concreteness. One might not be self-conscious about national identity while licking a postage stamp, but news reports of American soldiers in faraway battlefields or Fourth of July parades can quicken one's awareness of the nation. Any American alive when John F. Kennedy was assassinated in 1963 knows how riveting the sense of membership in one's society can be. The visibility and invisibility of the nation mirrors the entire network of configurations of practice and belief that structure social reality.

History became a modern discipline when its major theorists began to seek knowledge of the broad, unseen structures that channel processes of change. Curiosity about great men and women or precedent-shattering events yielded early in the nineteenth century to a more compelling interest in the regularities that structured social action. With Marx, Weber, and Durkheim, the search for structure became part and parcel of the modernity of the discipline of history. They and their followers believed that time had a direction and that society, like nature, was composed of a network of systems that scientific investigation could locate. These students of structure extended the reach of historical knowledge by articulating theories and pursuing research that created comprehensive frameworks for the myriad of discrete facts building up about the past. Maintaining these structures, in their view, were causal laws of universal validity.

As interim reports, their findings were impressive, but, not being prescient, much of their work was overtaken by history itself. Disenchanted by the shortfall in the analytical grasp of the great sociological theorists, contemporary historians have retreated to smaller questions—not why capitalism triumphed in the West, but what happened to displaced weavers when mechanization came to Gloucestershire. Late-twentieth-century historians find a uniqueness in the complexity of events which mocks the earlier mimicry of the scientific model of uniform truths. In recent years, historians of culture have resisted the reduction of events to material causes, avoiding the language of explanation so completely that they sometimes appear to deny any validity at all to hypotheses about causation. Postmodernists efface the distinction between text and context, insisting on a seamless web that is violated with statements like "She wrote this because . . ." With language and culture all-determining in these circles, the distinctions between independent and dependent variables, between discourse and actions, between culture and society, has become blurred, if not totally neglected.

Causal analysis inevitably comes under fire because by its very nature it relies on distinctions of significance that are difficult to make. How can causes be assigned to an event if the number of factors involved is huge, perhaps infinite? E. H. Carr once told the story of Mr. Jones, who, returning from a party where he had had several drinks and driving a car with defective brakes, knocked down and killed Mr. Robinson at a blind corner. Mr. Robinson was on his way to buy cigarettes. What was the cause of the accident? Mr. Jones's state of semi-intoxication, the defects in his brakes, the poor visibility at the corner, or Mr. Robinson's addiction to cigarettes?[32] And doesn't any analysis of this case depend on whether Mr. Robinson and Mr. Jones were white or black, homosexual or heterosexual (perhaps one of them was on his way to a gay bar and was preoccupied), or even accident-prone or rock-steady? Would an explanation—a causal analysis—of Mr. Robinson's accident apply to anyone else? Can historians ever hope to make sense of events like the Cold War or the French Revolution if the simplest everyday event is so fraught with perplexities?

Inferential evidence of invisible structures and patterns abounds, nonetheless. The nation is one of the most important structures in present-day lives, but others, ranging from natural ones like patterns of climate to social ones like the world economy, need only be named to be recognized. And if their existence is readily conceded, can questions about their causes be stifled? Whether natural or social, these transcendent forces are rarely palpable. The falling rain is visible, but it takes meteorologists to explain the structure of climatic change. Social forces like the market organization of private bargains and the influence of images on women's behavior are more elusive. Everyone can see the paycheck or watch actresses in television commercials, but it is very hard to detect the system that welds these discrete actions into an economy or a code of gender norms. Social structures refer to consistent relationships between people, and because they are sustained by patterns of

---

32. Edward Hallett Carr, *What Is History?* (New York, 1961), p. 137.

beliefs, they cannot be located without well-articulated theories.

The nineteenth-century social scientists' invention of structure, with its corollaries of patterning, process, and interacting systems of causation, represents a powerful intellectual tool for understanding social action. Modern Westerners cannot live without causal language and generalizations about human behavior because these organize their reality. Without heuristic concepts of such things as the nation, culture, class, ethnicity, education, and the global economy, the complexity of life would break down into a welter of isolated facts. People want to make sense of their world, even if explanations are proved to be necessarily partial. Mr. Robinson's family and friends would ask why the accident happened. If accidents like his happened frequently enough, local authorities would begin asking the same question. Answers would always depend on generalizations about patterns of human behavior. Similarly, people can't help wondering why the French Revolution or the Cold War happened. Causal explanations can never be wholly satisfying, if only because new facets of human experience are always being discovered. Nonetheless, attempts to make sense of car accidents or the French Revolution or the Cold War will continue, and having a conceptual vocabulary about structure and causation greatly enhances these efforts.

Scientists from Newton on have encouraged people to think that they could master nature, and on this model, establish their own autonomy as social actors. The result was the collapse of old-regime intellectual and political absolutisms and a new search for secular explanations of nature and society. Paradoxically, that very same science also showed human beings that they were themselves the product of various causal processes. Science therefore threatened the possibility of free will and self-conscious autonomy even as it extended the intellectual grasp of those deprived of freedom of action. In one of modernity's greatest ironies, the success of science undermined the confidence that promoted its cultural dominance in the West.[33]

An enduring legacy of the nineteenth century has been the lesson that human action always occurs within institutional and cultural structures—powerful, pervasive, and invisible. The human craving for meaning expresses itself within conventions, codes, and shared understandings just as procreating and producing for survival unfold in paths cut by habit, custom, and prescription. These organize every single act of daily life from brushing one's teeth in front of a mirror each morning to reading a novel in bed at night. Historians must recreate social structures in order to interpret the human activity described in the records. To ignore the channeling and shaping done by structures because they have to be made "visible" through description and analysis or because they are so numerous as to clog the historical narrative would be to abandon the effort to reconstruct reality.

From ancient times, observers of the human scene have been divided in their weighing of free will and determinism. We think that the two exist in tension; structures confining and directing what is thought and done, and imagination in the service of personal desire breaking free from the social molds and rechanneling human effort. Structures do not determine how human beings act, but they do constrain the options for action at any given moment, even as the structures themselves are battered by the forces of change.

## A Summing Up

History springs from the human fascination with self-discovery, from the persistent concern about the nature of existence and people's engagement with it. Men and women have learned to externalize this curiosity—even to distance themselves from its impertinent subjectivity—by directing their

33. F. M. Barnard, "Accounting for Actions: Causality and Teleology," *History and Theory*, 20 (1981): 291–312.

questions to concepts and abstractions like the growth of democracy or the ascendancy of modernity, but the renewable source of energy behind these inquiries comes from an intense craving for information about what it is to be human.

Human beings are born into a group which provides answers to the first and most basic questions they pose about life. Few outlive the impress of that first organization of consciousness. Hence, ethnocentrism is common to all folk. Nonetheless, it presents special problems to a pluralistic democracy like that of the United States. Similarly, the desire to rewrite the past to accommodate group pride is too human to be viewed as a part of a conspiracy. Nor is there anything particularly sinister about the impulse to manipulate national history, even though its effects are far from neutral. Professional historians are most acutely aware of this temptation to sacrifice accuracy to the goals of glorification or lesson-teaching, but all people are the historians of their own lives and know something of the urge to point their past toward a useful moral precept. Even when people have no motive to bend history in a particular direction, they have difficulty getting it straight. There is an additional perceptual problem: once the outcome of an action is known, it is almost impossible not to project back into the past the knowledge of what happened subsequently. Or to be more psychological, it is hard to take in the fact that those living in the past were ignorant about the future. Similarly, when people reflect upon their previous actions, they tend to ascribe to stupidity what more justly should be charged to lack of foreknowledge.

Despite the naturalness of distorting or fudging the past, the cost of suppressing information comes high. Nothing could be less true than the old bromide that what you don't know doesn't hurt you. The very opposite seems more the case. What you don't know is especially hurtful, for it denies you the opportunity to deal with reality. It restricts choices by decreasing information. The health of the nation may require a careful winnowing of memory, but a democratic, and hence American, creed argues otherwise. It endorses the individual's right to liberty—and implicitly freedom of inquiry—without reference to the goal of political solidarity. The instrumental logic of keeping the nation's shape by causing people to forget those experiences incompatible with the nation's righteous image is doubly ironic for Americans because the righteous image of the United States places ideals above utility. Moreover, the freedom to explore the full record of the nation's past unimpeded by "off-limits" signs can easily be deduced from those rights to life, liberty, and the pursuit of happiness which initially endowed the nation with a moral personality.

The commitment to truth and to those intellectual traditions that underpin this resonating affirmation needs defending today from two broad attacks. The one stems from the discovery of social structuring and its restrictive impact upon the individuals whose freedom to pursue truth is being affirmed. The other comes from skepticism about the validity of the representations of reality made by freedom-seeking inquirers. To meet these provocative challenges we have summoned history, particularly the history of the idea of objectivity. Far from banishing relativism, postmodernism, nihilism, and various forms of solipsistic thinking, we authors have pooled our learning in order to locate the relationship of these critiques to the long dialogue about knowledge that began in the seventeenth century, gained momentum in succeeding centuries under the rubric of modern science, and today has yielded to a variety of noisy conversations.

Fundamental to our own engagement with reality has been a conception of women and men as creatures driven to know and to chart their lives by what they believe to be true. History can help here, for it offers a variety of tools for effecting liberation from intrusive authority, outworn creeds, and counsels of despair. Historical analysis teaches that members of society raise structures that confine people's actions and then build systems of thought that deny those structures. It also suggests that all bodies of knowledge acquire ideological overtones, because their meaning is too potent to be ignored. What is to be concluded from myth-dispelling disclosures like the ones offered here? We think they point to the power of a revitalized public, when operating in a pluralistic democracy with protected dissent, to mediate intelligently between society and the individual, knowledge and passion, clarity and obfuscation, hope and doubt. Telling the truth takes a collective effort.

# Index